Writing Realism

Writing Realism

REPRESENTATIONS IN FRENCH FICTION

ARMINE KOTIN MORTIMER

The Johns Hopkins University Press

BALTIMORE AND LONDON

© 2000 THE JOHNS HOPKINS UNIVERSITY PRESS

All rights reserved. Published 2000

Printed in the United States of America on acid-free paper

2 4 6 8 9 7 5 3 1

The Johns Hopkins University Press

2715 North Charles Street

Baltimore, Maryland 21218-4363

www.press.jhu.edu

Library of Congress Cataloging-in-Publication Data

will be found at the end of this book.

A catalog record for this book is available

from the British Library.

ISBN 0-8018-6478-x

For Irina, John, Nicolle, and Therese

Contents

Preface

Written over the course of many years, a book is often read in less than a day. The long writing time is a reality of scholarship, part of the nature of thinking, but it can put both reader and writer in a false position. The reader's experience differs so markedly from the writer's that it is a wonder they find a common ground at all. While developing a thesis in the space of many readings—pondering, simmering, rereading, rewriting, often struggling for just the right word—the writer must keep in mind the breakneck pace at which the final product of these efforts will pass before the eyes of the imaginary personage who will take up the book and hope to find it of interest. But the writer has something to say, or she would not have gone to all that trouble. Hence the need to assume that the years of work will have value for others: it suffices to persuade them of the truth of this assumption. It is then the reader's task to answer the question, Why do we need this book?

In the detail of the writing itself, I hope the reader will discover why this book serves a purpose. And it is perhaps appropriate to urge the reader toward the writing itself, because this book focuses on writing in works of representative fiction. In the analyses, I link writing events in novels to these novels' representations of reality. There are too many ways to grasp the concept of reality to list them here, and scarcely fewer concepts of writing. Perhaps before reaching the end the reader will have connected my writing to a reality I cannot even imagine.

I have just mentioned what could be considered the two parts of an argumentation: the details of its description and the conclusions to which they lead. Some guidance into the meaty matter of a book's analyses helps the reader toward the points they make. Yet, although introductions, in books like this one, first claim the reader's attention, they are almost always written last. What would happen if, instead, the book presented itself in the order in which it was written—the order in which its discoveries follow upon themselves? Our study and reading lead us to formulate ideas and positions; why do we feel the need to defend them even before they have been presented? Why not offer a true record of the process of patient discovery?

There would be an appealing sincerity in such a strategy, but at the same time it would present greater difficulties for the reader. It makes sense instead to lead a reader from a given science into new domains of knowledge conquered under the writer's guidance, after having described the territory from which we set out. In our analyses of literature, this means defining terms, delimiting the genre, language, and much more. Often our guidance also takes the form of preemptive strikes: claiming to do just so much, and not more, so that readers set their expectations no higher. All these are the functions of chapter 1, "Introduction," which is presented in two sections. The first section, "Theory," in its way a technical exercise, is the necessary extended definition of terms; they include statements of position, with credit given to those whose work has led me to them. The second section, "Texts," may strike other readers as unnecessary. Its function is to rehearse the material facts about the chosen novels and short narratives on which all my analysis is based; it is background and orientation to my readings.

The dual design in chapter 1 prepares the reader for the five chapters that follow; I claim no more for this chapter. Although I discuss the texts in chronological order, I am not tracing a historical development. In the conclusion, I gather together the themes and ideas that have separately emerged from the analyses found in the central chapters.

A NOTE ON TRANSLATIONS from the French and the use of ellipses: In quotations from "primary" works and other texts by the same authors, I give the French in the text, followed by English translations enclosed in brackets. For all "secondary" works, I give only my own translation, omitting the original. Where ellipses occur in the original text, I use three nonspaced periods. My own ellipses are given as spaced periods or, in the case of quotations from Sollers's works, three spaced periods between brackets.

Acknowledgments

We plunge into our "work" and often lose sight of the reasons we do it, but all around are people who remind us why. If it were possible to measure the enrichment we gain from this intellectual sustenance, we would realize the success of community.

For this reason I wish to thank those who brought their knowledge and intelligence to me, and helped me feel I could bring better understanding to others: The several graduate students in my seminar on "L'Écriture du réalisme," who listened so well, with all the richness of Barthes's "third reading," that their puzzlement turned to enjoyment and enthusiasm; Robert J. Nelson, whose faith in me has never wavered, for seeing and helping me see the finished book, and for awesome help with translations of Doubrovsky; Mireille Rosello, for inspiring the idea of dialogues of the deaf in chapter 3, for her rich responses to my study of *L'Heptaméron* 24, and for being the ideal reader of my early draft on *Le Livre brisé;* Laurence Mall, for help with a rhetorical figure and observations about the notion of consolation in the *siècle des lumières;* Virginie E. Greene, for helpful comments on my analysis of *La Religieuse;* Serge Doubrovsky, for his praise and approbation of both my analysis and my translations of *Le Livre brisé;* Ross Chambers, lucid analyst of the complex matrix of reading and writing, for his eye-opening work on narrative literature in a rich variety of studies; Susan R. Suleiman, for her interest and strong support; Gerald Prince, for his long-standing encouragement of my work on narrative; and Priscilla Parkhurst Ferguson for her enthusiastic backing, and her insistence that I find out what Oscar Wilde really said about Balzac.

Besides these individuals, my research for this book was supported in part by these units of the University of Illinois at Urbana–Champaign, to which I am grateful: the Center for Advanced Study, for a semester of research leave; and the Research Board, for an equipment grant and for Humanities Released Time.

I would also like to thank the editors of several journals for permitting me to publish in this book material that appeared in less complete form in the following articles: "Writing Modeste Mignon," *L'Esprit Créateur* 31, no. 3 (1991): 26–37; "The Death of Autobiography in Doubrovsky's Broken Novel," *Genre* 26 (1993): 85–108; "Dialogues of the Deaf: The Failure of Consolation in *Les Liaisons dangereuses*," *MLN* 111 (1996): 671–87; "Naive and Devious: *La Religieuse*," *Romanic Review* 88 (1997): 241–50; "Balzac's *Ursule Mirouët*: Genealogy and Inheritance," *Modern Language Review* 92 (1997): 851–63. Thanks also to the editors of two collective volumes for permission to use material from the following contributions: "Fiction and the Supplement in the *Heptaméron*," in *Les Visages et les voix de Marguerite de Navarre*, Marcel Tetel, ed. (Paris: Klincksieck, 1995), 135–48; "La Sexualité dans *La Religieuse:* Dialogues de sourds," in *Sexualité, mariage et famille au XVIIIe siècle,* Olga B. Cragg, ed. (Québec: Presses de l'Université Laval, 1998), 125–33.

Writing Realism

One

Introduction

Theory

[L'ÉMIR:] La fée le soupçonna d'ajouter à son récit quelques circonstances qui lui manquaient pour être tout à fait plaisant, et d'en retrancher d'autres qui l'auraient déparé; mais comme elle avait de l'indulgence pour ces faussetés innocentes... LA SULTANE: Innocentes! Emir, cela vous plaît à dire. C'est à l'aide de cet art funeste que d'une bagatelle on en fait une aventure malhonnête, indécente, déshonorante...[1]

[[THE EMIR:] the fairy suspected him of adding to his tale some circumstances the lack of which kept it from being entirely amusing, and of cutting out others that would have spoiled it; but since she was indulgent for these innocent falsities... THE SULTANA: Innocent! Emir, that's easy for you to say. It is with the help of this dangerous art that you make a dishonest, indecent, dishonorable adventure out of a mere bagatelle...]

This is Denis Diderot speaking through the voices of his Oriental characters in "L'Oiseau blanc, conte bleu," probably written in 1749. In lively speech animated by witty characters, Diderot articulates the ethical questions involved in the act of tale-telling. The fairy, a character speaking in the emir's story, suspects a narrator of adding circumstances to compensate for the tale's deficits, and of taking away others that spoiled it, thus apparently improving on the "reality" of the story. The fairy's indulgence for these falsities may be taken as characteristic of the normal reader of narrative fiction, who forgives—indeed, has forgiven in advance, and will for all future time forgive—the creator of the fiction for using art to improve on reality, and to make a better tale, one that is "*entirely* amusing." Even so, there is a falseness, and what the sultana's impolite expostulation reiterates is the lesson that Diderot would never have us forget, and that all his fictions repeat: *art is not innocent.*

That is one of the conclusions to which an examination of realistic writing inevitably leads, when one follows it far enough. We must eventually fill the sultana's shoes, casting off the blindfold fiction ties across our eyes, becoming critical of the very process by which it has first drawn our interest. But before we may reach that point, we first bide our time in the position of the fairy, indulgent for the innocent falsities that entertain us and improve on the narrative as it really was (if we follow Diderot). If the narrative has been falsified, so goes the implication, then there must be a reality or a truth that we can know well enough to know what circumstances have been altered in it. Both the fairy and the sultana act on this premise. The emir, a kind of metanarrator who recounts not only the story of the narration but also the fairy's reaction, and certainly a figure for Diderot himself, represents the position of the writer, the one ultimately responsible for the existence and transmission of the narrative. It is he who poses the aesthetic and moral conundrum that is the essence of fiction. Responsibility for this sinister art is laid at his feet. The writer's art, defined broadly to include, in addition to style, every effect it creates, produces the entire bundle of "reality," narration, transmission, and reception that constitutes realistic writing. It is the writer's art that I wish to examine here.

The methodological premise of this book is really quite simple. Writing produces the illusion of reality in novels and short stories, and we can best see writing at work "making reality" where acts of writing occur within the story and thus make us particularly attentive to it. To study this writing of realism, I have chosen texts from many periods (not just those included in the canons of a historically defined realism) in which the novelists have woven writing into the fabric of the story. Writing events in the story demonstrate how a novel achieves its goal of creating the illusion of reality, people like real people whom one would recognize, events that are not only plausible but well motivated, well rooted in probability and yet sufficiently different to merit narrating. The central theme of this study is thus how writing produces realism.

The remainder of this part of the chapter will present concepts that will be useful to discuss before plunging into analyses of given cases. The terms in play here—*realism, fiction, writing, illusion, reality, representation,* and so forth—have acquired so many layers of meaning and application that definition (in the sense of clarity) is lost. One almost feels the need to add explanatory footnotes to each usage, or surround the terms with protective quotation marks. The definitions given in this section are intended to orient and delimit. The second part of this chapter introduces the novels and short narratives analyzed in the following chapters.

Realism

The mimetic illusion persists and has an immense and paradoxical power to produce a sense of realism. It makes us take part in a manifestly nonexistent world as if it were real; allows us to dream about the characters; impels us to know desire, or fear, or loathing—potentially any emotion; persuades us to listen to the telling of events that never happened, with as much (if not more) interest as ones that have happened to us; convinces us to give as much credence to a narrative we recognize as fictional as to a story we are told as real. This persistence of the mimetic illusion, in our sophisticated times, is astonishing enough to demand explanation.

Realism is a historical term. It became a widespread critical concept in France only in the late 1840s and 1850s and was sanctioned in 1856 when a journal of that name appeared, Duranty's *Le Réalisme,* or in 1857 when Champfleury's essays in defense of the concept were published, with the same title. Nevertheless, most historians of French literature date realism from 1830, a year after Balzac's *Les Chouans,* and mark its end with the end of the Second Empire, or with the publication of Zola's *Thérèse Raquin.*[2] One should note, however, that the features of fiction that led to the narrowly defined critical concept of realism in the nineteenth century are not necessarily the ones we would now include in a definition, which might consist rather of features mentioned in the preceding paragraph. In the nineteenth century, fiction may have been called realistic because it contained lowborn characters or criminals (examples include Sue's *Les Mystères de Paris* and several of Balzac's novels), battle scenes (*La Chartreuse de Parme,* by Stendhal), or sex. But it is also fair to disconnect realism from any particular historical period. Long traditions of narrative literature (not only in French, of course) depend on realism or the imitation of reality, the better to involve the reader, manipulating words in such a way that the reader is led into thinking of created characters as real people and invented incidents as real events. The realistic illusion fosters the belief that fictive events can actually happen. Such are our habits of mind that we let the conditions and the qualities of human interaction mold our understanding of characters made of words: we assess psychological motivations, probe moralities, and retrace life histories. We appraise the likelihood of occurrences and confidently diagnose the skills of plotters. We visualize locations.

Typically, we know a spectrum of emotions. In short, in spite of modern self-reflective efforts to demystify realism and representation, in both fiction and criticism, the mimetic illusion persists. How does this happen?

Wolfgang Iser wrote that "to imagine what has been simulated by aesthetic semblance entails placing our thoughts and feelings at the disposal of an unreality, bestowing on it a semblance of reality in proportion to a reducing of our own reality. For the duration of the performance we are both ourselves and someone else."[3] This is a fair description of the reader's stance and the phenomenon of the mimetic illusion. If the reader can be simultaneously aware of a "semblance of reality" and something that is not a semblance, the implication is that "our own reality" plays a part in defining or understanding that semblance of reality. Our reality is put to contribution by a parallel activity of understanding.[4] Thus, a key element of realism is the reader's mental composition of a certain reality.

But reality as it is expressed by writing is not an external, unmoving, circumscribed entity that can be copied or portrayed by pictures or words. Iser rejects a common notion of mimesis that "presupposes a given reality that is to be portrayed" ("Representation," 226). Any expression of reality, like "our own reality," is defined by our participation in it. When we say that textual realism is an imitation of reality, we are really saying that it is a *creation* of reality, a reality that we recognize because it resembles our own, without being the same, and without existing in any other external space. This is an important point. Sandy Petrey, commenting on an article written in 1921 by Roman Jakobson, "On Realism in Art," provides these useful distinctions:

For Jakobson, realism and reality are irreconcilable with one another. What we call realist art is not a representation of reality but a refusal of previous representations that have become too obviously artificial. Whenever a given arrangement of semiotic material appears referential, we can be sure that the appearance depends solely on a deviation from previous arrangements of semiotic material. If realism actually depicted the extraliterary universe, its form would be stable and unvarying. In fact, its form varies dramatically and incessantly.[5]

Jakobson, as summarized by Petrey, goes so far as to reject the possibility of representing actual reality (the reality found outside the work of literature). Instead, the referentiality of the writing (not some real referent but the "arrangement of semiotic material") is all the more successful when it differs from any other representation of reality—in other words, when it is in fact a creation rather than a depiction of reality. In a classic statement about mimetic realism,

Albert Béguin wrote about Balzac's *La Comédie humaine*: "The novelistic world of the *Comédie humaine* is no longer 'another' world . . . ; it is our world, but seen 'differently.' Not a copy of reality, or of what we ordinarily consider to be reality, but a reality exalted and enlarged in such a way that by its very deformation it *expresses* the reality that an exact copy would not express."[6] The notion of mimesis as a copy or image of a reality external to the book cannot sustain critical inquiry. Instead, mimesis *expresses* reality, involving the reader's participation in this *creation*. Realism is not a relation to the real, but to the writing of the real, a composition of reality.

Representation

Like realism, representation must be considered in its modernity. I assume here what Todorov, Riffaterre, and others have persuasively argued: that representation should not be thought of as simple portrait painting of a reality that exists independently of its representation. Representation is rather, as Riffaterre has demonstrated, a construction and a performance. Similarly, Alexis Tadié observes: "Fiction is a construction, in the same way that truth can sometimes be considered a construction."[7] Mimetic fiction produces a representation of a world other than existing worlds, but that other world does not exist independently of its representation. The other world is entirely a construction of the writing in the fiction. In a sense, this is a closed system. Representation is the process by which semiosis produces mimesis, and it is also the result of that process.

In "Representation: A Performative Act," Iser writes:

> Representation is therefore both performance and semblance. It conjures up an image of the unseeable, but being a semblance, it also denies it the status of a copy of reality. The aesthetic semblance can only take on its form by way of the recipient's ideational, performative activity, and so representation can only come to full fruition in the recipient's imagination; it is the recipient's performance that endows the semblance with its sense of reality. And so representation causes the recipient to repeat the very same performance out of which it arose, and it is the repeat of this performance that initiates and ensures the transfer from text to reader of that which is to be represented. (226)

Iser prefers the term *performative* to *mimesis*. Rejecting the idea of mimesis as copying, Iser defines representation in terms of its activity in the mind or imagination of the reader, the mental re-creation of the performance of the text. The stress on the reader's imagination gives primary importance to the construction of the represented reality.

Barthes considered representation the second force of literature (after Mathesis, its ability to express a knowledge), a force he called Mimesis; it is part of the argument against an ideology of the text in the 1977 inaugural lecture at the Collège de France published as *Leçon*. Barthes obviously redefines Mimesis, adding one of those layers of meaning that make definition problematic. He would have been happy with Iser's proposal to use the word *performative* instead, because his Mimesis subtly puts into play the representing activity of people, both writers and readers:

From ancient times to the experiments of the avant-garde, literature's business has been to represent something. What? I will say bluntly: the real. The real is not representable, and it is because men are always trying to represent it with words that there is a history of literature. . . . That there is no parallelism between the real and language is unacceptable to men, and it is this refusal, perhaps as old as language itself, that, by a constant busy-ness, produces literature.[8]

The existence of literature depends, paradoxically, on the inability of language to correspond to a real. Literature exploits this failure of language to adapt to a given reality and incessantly produces realities out of its writing, and that is representation.

It is necessary, therefore, to disconnect the notion of representation from the idea of the reflecting mirror, the one that stupidly shows everything in its path. The famous passage in Stendhal's *Le Rouge et le noir* blaming the mud pit for the moral turpitude represented in the novel maintains a theory of representation almost without agency—a mirror that moves by its own motion: "A novel is a mirror moving along a highway. Sometimes it reflects to your eyes the blue of the heavens, sometimes the filth in the mud pits of the road."[9] Riffaterre calls this the referential illusion. There is no natural relation of the words to the referent; it is an illusion that words signify in a direct relation to reality. The reader interprets the writing as if it referred directly to reality and ignores or pretends to ignore the fact that mimesis refers to words. Krzysztof Jarosz cites Riffaterre to explain why "since time immemorial innumerable generations of readers have treated literature as a reflection of the real world, thus emphasizing its ability to represent what is extra-literary and not verbal."[10] Riffaterre's answer:

Words, in their physical form, have no natural relation with referents: they are the conventions adopted by a group, which are arbitrarily linked to sets of concepts about referents, to a mythology of the real. This mythology of the signified is interposed between words and their referents. Nevertheless, users of the language cling to their illusion that words signify in a direct relation to reality, for practical reasons, all the more so in that they have an idea about things partly fashioned by the very concepts of the signified.[11]

Clearly our "practical" habits of mind are implicated in the creation of representation.

It scarcely needs to be said that the original Platonic and Aristotelian ideas of mimesis have been expanded, revised, reinterpreted beyond the limited meanings found in their texts. Mimesis for Plato referred to passages of direct discourse or dialogue—direct imitation of speech, in opposition to summarizing narration. The broader Platonic idea of mimesis as a "bad copy" of a revealed, original truth—object of a keen Derridean reading—refers us back to a founding reality. Not only Derrida's critique of the notion of origin but also critical practice in general is suspicious of the idea of writing as mere copy of a nonwritten reality. The problem, I believe, is with the word *mimesis* itself. For Aristotle, imitation included showing as well as telling, so that actions in a play, for instance, are instances of mimesis. While imitative discourse was thus linked generally with drama and opposed to narration, since about 1950 critical usage has dramatically extended the idea of mimesis to embrace any sort of imitation of reality. Or, as Gérard Genette found himself concluding, "mimesis is diegesis."[12] In such a view, when mimesis includes diegesis (represented story), the represented story would resemble a known extralinguistic reality. This risks raising again the specter of the mirror fallacy, which, since long before Stendhal, characterized the naïve reader's relation to representation. In short, the term *mimesis*, for many readers, remains connected with a naïve view of representation, with the illusion of a reality, or with the notion of a real referent, and this is why, as I describe the writing of realism, I prefer to use the words *representation* or *representation of reality*, and let the word *mimesis* connote the mimetic illusion.

Representation redefined in this manner is crucial to writing realism, because it accentuates relations among the words rather than between the word and the thing, the Platonic real referent. Modern representation foregrounds writing. Barthes, in *Le Plaisir du texte*, speaks of one sort of representation as a kind of nominalism, the mere naming of things in their material state, a naming that cannot be ignored, overcome, or transacted, something like the "reality effect" or the Nietzschean "That's it!" It does not try to fashion a motivated link between the word and the thing. Such representation is comparable to a notion of strict nominalism, which would accentuate the links among the names for things, rather than among things. Nothing makes this mode more apparent than the writing of a geography with which one is not familiar. While the places identified in a geography ("writing of the earth") have a certain relation to each other, one cannot know this relation in the slightest without knowing the places themselves; what one can know, however, is relations among the names for places. From that knowledge, we then forge a representation of the reality—and this is a mere semblance because we are not *in* the reality. Writing produces this magic creation. Thus, in a provincial novel by Balzac, one can imagine the relations between two cities, or perhaps the relation between upper and lower Alençon, without knowing the cities. Geography plays a role of primordial power in the action of *Les Chouans*: rivers, hills, mountains, cliffs, forests, meadows, narrow roads behind city houses, and so forth are all placed in a relation of significance for the events, the characters, and ultimately, necessarily, the reader; willy-nilly, the reader makes a mental geography. Thus, we enter what Maurice Ménard, in an article on *Les Chouans,* called "the purely nominalist mode, which disconnects the place names from their geographical support and considers only their textual play within the novel."[13]

As I place the accent on writing, I have in mind the relations among the words whose combinations write realism, creating in their performance the representations of reality we are so eager to compose.

Writing

The connection of writing to representation that foregrounds relations among words was established by Roland Barthes: "Writing . . . is the field of the enunciation, it is the text taken as the place where the enunciation is deposited, and thus it is the very contrary of the sociolect."[14] With this simple move Barthes placed the accent on the processes by which a text exists, and foregrounded the activity of writing in the creation of meaning. It is no longer possible to ignore the material presence of text, as if it were the transparent medium of a content. Barthes relegated the signified, in which the speaking of a society keeps its stronghold, to a second place behind the signifier. The consequences for reading literature are enormous. Writing has lost its innocence and in particular its innocent and uncomplicated relation to what the words stand for. Its relation to things lacks the simplicity we believed it once had, its role in our lives has become devious and complex, and it calls attention to itself at the expense of the messages it is supposed to convey. Writing is not merely the linguistic enunciation that expresses an utterance, in spite of Barthes's use of the word *enunciation*; it is "thick." Interestingly, critical parlance has accepted a lax usage whereby *signifier* means *word*, partly because words are no longer considered transparent vehicles of a thought behind them but are instead considered in their material reality, in their relations to other signifiers. Paul de Man simply equates *signifier* with *sign* and *signified* with *meaning*.[15] In 1971, Barthes opposed *écriture* to *écrivance,* the latter a neologism invented to fill a void left when he redefined *écriture* intransitively, when he took it out of the sociolect.[16] (The writer of *écrivance* is naturally called the *écrivant*.) *Écrivance* may continue to behave transparently, revealing (or not) what it is about, but writing, in its functional assertiveness, is that which makes the opposition of the hidden and the not hidden obsolete, thus rejecting both the idea of reflecting an existing reality by putting it into words and the ability to keep it hidden by not describing it or describing it falsely. "[Writing] is not of the order of the message"; "writing does not say something, it is not its task to say something"; "writing is of the order of saying 'almost something' " (*Prétexte: Roland Barthes,* 21, 22, 23).

It is in literature that writing is not of the order of the message. In 1959, Barthes published a "mythology" called "Tables rondes," a text that approaches a rare violence in tone (his gentleness as a person was commonly mentioned by those who knew him).[17] Here he was moved to near rage against the written transcription of that essentially oral and very French intellectual activity known as the "*table ronde*." In such an event, writers discuss their works, and those of others, in response to questions by a moderator-journalist and especially in reaction to the situation in which they find themselves: in the presence of other writers and before an audience. The audience is both in the radio or television studio, not far from the authors, and wherever people are listening or watching. In its dissemination via broadcast, rebroadcast, recording, or satellite transmission, the authors' speaking remains oral. But what Barthes, in this mythology, called the *propos transcrit*—a published text of the *table ronde*—implies a "natural philosophy of Literature, as if a writer were invested with the truth and he could choose the everyday means of expressing it." The presumption that there is one content and several forms is an ideological disaster. Against this abuse stands literature: "Literature is fundamentally an inversion of language, since in it form is single and meanings innumerable. Writing is literally *paradoxical*: it is always coming at truth at a slant." Anti-ideological language survives in literature, where, more often, there is one form and several contents. In *Leçon,* Barthes would so closely identify writing with literature that he claimed he could use the words interchangeably; de Man, discussing Nietzsche, similarly considers literature the place where the rhetorical nature of language is most explicit.[18] Literature as writing is centered on the signifier rather than the signified. It is just this kind of writing that I have in mind, with its ability to create innumerable meanings, its near identity with intertextuality.

But there is more. Writing so defined acquires an ontological status it could not hold as long as it was considered the handmaiden to thought. When Barthes states that literature is "absolutely, categorically realistic: it is reality, that is to say the very light of the real" (*Leçon,* 3: 805), he is granting to writing a privilege to *be* real that goes beyond any question of its ability to *represent* a reality. In pithier form, according to "Tables rondes," "writing is made out of a refusal of all the other languages." Just such a refusal characterizes deconstruction, the mission of which would be to reveal how there has always been an ideology of representation at work in classical notions of imitation. Christopher Norris reminds us that "language is marked through and through by referential (or mimetic) assumptions," which have been greatly simplified by "an *ideology* of representation."[19] The conclusion that writing is the only real, and the ethical consequences this strange assertion entails, are matters for chapter 6, the final chapter of this study.

Semiosis

It will have become apparent that a certain paradox of methodology underlies my approach: while I seek above all to explain the mimetic illusion, the strategic design of that explanation, throughout this study, gives primary importance not to mimesis but to what is often paired with it like its necessary complement, semiosis. Semiosis is not the opposite of mimesis, however. Before discussing that relation, I would like to propose the operative definition I will use.

Semiosis is not complicated: it is the activity of the sign. For my purposes, it covers something comfortable and familiar, not abstruse and unattainable; it is something like Monsieur Jourdain's prose: we have been doing it all the time without knowing it. Signs combine to make meaningful texts; semiosis then represents meaning; in particular, semiosis forges representation or mimesis. It is immediately apparent, then, that explaining the semiosis of a text will lead to the explanation of its mimesis: the mimetic illusion it creates.

Historically, semiology or semiotics is the name given to the science of signs. Versions of semiotics were introduced by Ferdinand de Saussure, Charles Sanders Peirce, and Ernst Cassirer, to explain scientifically the relations among the elements of signification—*icon, index,* and *symbol* for Peirce; *signifier, signified,* and *referent* for Saussure; and so on. From such basic elements, others, such as A. J. Greimas and Roman Jakobson, elaborated complex systems of semiotics and endeavored to apply them to works of literature (for instance, a Maupassant story in the case of Greimas, many poems in the case of Jakobson). In the context of the structuralist project to achieve scientific rigor on a parallel with other areas of inquiry, such studies sought to identify and fully describe the linguistic features of literary works that might be said to construct their meaning. The purpose was often to elaborate a method as much as to provide new understanding of a text such as a Baudelaire poem.

In this study of writing realism, no such "scientific" purpose is intended. My analyses are not semiotic and do not constitute an example of semiology. The structuralist model of semiology, when applied to literature, defines literary language, but inevitably the language itself, not the signification. Rather, the word *semiosis* will identify, as an area for analysis, an activity of the text central to its meaning. Semiosis comes from the Greek *semeiosis,* observation of signs, and is defined as a process in which something functions as a sign to an organism.

Semiosis as an activity describes the domain where relations occur among words, rather than between words and the things they are supposed to refer to. As we saw, the example of geography illustrates a kind of "writing" in which relations are codified both on the level of things (the Missouri River flows into the Mississippi River) and on the level of the signs that name them, their nomination. Barthes felt that in the 1950s, it was the business of writing to separate the signifier from the signified, and he would later affirm the distance of the referent from the sign (for instance in *Sade, Fourier, Loyola*). Bernard Comment observes that semiosis excludes the referent in Barthes's practice.[20] The separation of semiosis from the referent can be illustrated in common experience. It may seem paradoxical to suggest that the semiotic relation is evident in our ability to tolerate ignorance, but the example may be instructive. Anyone who has learned a foreign language with a significant degree of competence can understand the gist of a sentence in that language without knowing all its words. To the extent that our manipulation of information in that language has reached an adequate degree of refinement, we may mentally tell ourselves the part of speech of the unknown word and put a blank token in its place, as it were, to represent its role in the sentence or the semiotic entity in which it is found. The most obvious examples are again those seen especially from a nominalist perspective, such as names for plants, animals, items of clothing or furniture, elements constituting a description of a narrated, represented world for which a corresponding element in another language would exist (*aubépine* for hawthorn). Without knowing the referent, we nevertheless understand the relations among the signifiers—and that is a semiotic relation.

Michael Riffaterre has proposed a refined definition of semiosis in his *Fictional Truth*: "the three-way relationship between a sign, its object, and its *interpretant*" (with a reference to C. S. Peirce). "It is therefore opposed to referentiality, the assumed relationship between a sign and nonverbal objects taken to be reality. Because the interpretant is a sign as well, it in turn needs its own interpretant to achieve anew the three-way relationship. This process continues *ad infinitum,* thus defining unlimited semiosis."[21] In such a definition, the connection of the sign to the object referent has become problematic. The description places the sign at a considerable distance from the referent—without altogether denying the existence of the referent—by placing intermediate steps between the sign and the thing it refers to (which Riffaterre calls "its object"). Signification occurs across the intermediate steps. Barthes, studying the language of Sade's novels, produces just this kind of semiotic analysis. Starting with what he calls an intelligible real, for example, characters who live as if they existed in the real world, the language creates the "crime," say, a condensation of incest. The "reality" that it is supposed to represent becomes unreal; the only real is the discourse. What is impossible in the referent—in effect making the referent nonexistent—is possible for discourse. "Being a writer, and not a realistic author, Sade always chooses the discourse against the referent; he is always situated on the side of *semiosis,* not *mimesis.*"[22] Barthes, along with Kristeva and Sollers, also revised the linguistic term *signifiance,* a substantive related to *signifiant,* the signifier, to place the accent on the signifier, not the signified or the referent of the sign. I find this concept useful for insisting on the semiotic relations in a text.

Yet, one cannot "do an analysis" of semiosis without taking mimesis into account; they are not separable. Nor can they fairly be described, in my opinion and in spite of Barthes, as opposite extremes. Thus, Shlomith Rimmon-Kenan, speaking of characters in a novel, exaggerates when she writes: "Whereas in mimetic theories (i.e. theories which consider literature as, in some sense, an imitation of reality) characters are equated with people, in semiotic theories they dissolve into textuality."[23] Neither extreme is appropriate; characters both imitate real people—what I called the mimetic illusion—and exist fully in textuality. My intent is to maintain the focus on textuality or semiosis and to show how it produces the mimetic illusion. Thus, one can speak of semiosis in the representation process, and then one can study how writing makes semiosis. When writing is also an object of representation—when it is represented in the fiction, as in the cases I am studying here—then one can show how it works to produce the semiosis of that fiction, self-reflectively. In some cases, semiosis can stand in a figural relation to representation; mimesis then figures semiosis, which is what occurs in several novels by Balzac: motifs in the represented story represent also the writing of the story. (I will provide a fuller explanation in chapter 4.)

Other terms related to semiosis may further clarify this understanding of semiosis. To prevent possible confusion, it is necessary to show how semiosis is not identical to Benveniste's term *enunciation,* the act by which an *utterance,* or *énoncé,* is made present. These terms are linguistic and apply to language in any context; the utterance is produced by the enunciation and cannot exist independently of it, in language. In an act of enunciation, language is used to refer to the world. If one adopted this straightforward model, conflating it with semiosis, semiosis would function as the act of enunciation and produce mimesis, like an utterance. This, however, would be a great simplification, and it would also ignore historical usage of the term *semiosis. Enunciation* implies the presence of a speaker—a locutor who proffers the discourse; my conception of semiosis is not limited to such a presence but includes any and all aspects of the writing that produce the realism. The Benveniste model, not unlike the vener-able *form/content* pair, places enunciation in the position of the agency respon-sible for producing the utterance, or *énoncé*. Even if enunciation is broadened to the level of the narration, there is still the implication of agency by an authority producing an utterance, the narrative, defined by reference.[24] To a degree, that is also the model of the *discourse/story* pair. None of these sets of paired terms adequately describes semiosis, which is not opposed to mimesis as something it produces. One might describe semiosis as the *form of content*, applying Hjelmslev's glossematic term to narrative, to oppose it both to the substance of content and to the form of expression; semiosis would be the writing in which the content is made.[25] Liberated from the stricture of an *agent/product* pair, semiosis is available for study in its own right.

Paul de Man's term *rhetoric* provides a useful complement to semiosis. Analyzing Nietzsche's discussion of rhetoric, de Man shows how language is rhetorical rather than representational or expressive of a referential, proper meaning, thus marking "a full reversal of the established priorities which tradi-tionally root the authority of the language in its adequation to an extralinguis-tic referent or meaning, rather than in the intralinguistic resources of figures" (*Allegories of Reading*, 106). In other words, rhetoric refers to the relations among words—the intralinguistic relation—rather than to the relations of words to things—the extralinguistic referent. Semiosis, in this study, embraces the entire range of the intralinguistic use of language.

How semiosis can nevertheless be distinguished from de Man's rhetoricity might be described by the following distinction. One should, strictly speaking, distinguish between *reference*, a function of language that describes its relation to objects outside language (whether fictive or real), and *representation*, which is a construction of reality or of objects outside language by means of language. I use *semiosis* to describe the processes of writing that create the representation, and *representation* refers us to the mimetic illusion. As Ducrot and Todorov write, "One no longer seeks to say how a preexisting reality is described, but how the illusion of such reality is created."[26] I cannot repeat this often enough: the reality represented in the text is a construction, and semiosis is the process of the construction. To be sure, referentiality is a property of representation. Representation functions by establishing a relationship between the writing and the thing the writing constructs, and this relationship is referential—as long as we remember that there is not a thing referred to outside the writing; the constructed reality that is represented by the writing is *in* the writing, and this closed system, this process, is semiosis. De Man does not quite make this distinction between representation and reference, in his language, but does describe fiction in a manner similar to this: "Fiction has nothing to do with representation [I would say *reference*] but is the absence of any link between utterance and a referent [so that] this fiction becomes the disruption of the narrative's referential illusion" (*Allegories of Reading*, 292).

It should be clear that this study is not an example of semiology and that I do not hold to a particular school of semiotics (for example, Russian or Greimassian). What is important to me is the root of the word. Semiosis is simply the activity of the sign, and the semiotic dimension of the text concerns that activity. Reading and writing are semiotic activities. Because letters are instantly semiotic, I will discuss several novels in which letter writing is central, including two epistolary novels. Their suitability for expressing unmediated contraries, in the mimetic realm, comes immediately to mind. Thus, to introduce the term *semiosis* in my analyses is to describe forthrightly that writing of realism, which is my topic.

Texts

In the novels and short stories of this study, writing occurs among the events of the story told and reflects the writing of the novel itself. There are different kinds of writing events in the works of this corpus. Characters write letters to each other in Laclos's *Les Liaisons dangereuses* and in Balzac's *Mémoires de deux jeunes mariées* and *Modeste Mignon.* In Diderot's *La Religieuse,* a nun cloistered against her will addresses the text of her memoirs to a nobleman who may be able to save her. In *Femmes,* Sollers portrays his protagonist in the process of writing a novel whose title is also *Femmes,* the realism of which is anchored in Sollers's life. Serge Doubrovsky in *Le Livre brisé* models his identically named protagonist strictly on himself and portrays him writing an autobiographical novel just as he is. Writing realism is figurative in Balzac's *Ursule Mirouët* and in Marguerite de Navarre's *Heptaméron.* Motifs or figures that occur in the plot represent writing, or stand in its place: a mirror and an epistle in verse in the twenty-fourth tale of the *Heptaméron,* which cast reflection on the entire work;

genealogy and an inheritance in *Ursule Mirouët*. These texts demonstrate, each in their different, interesting ways, how the mimetic illusion functions: the novelists show their hands.

The *Heptaméron*

The *Heptaméron* was written by Marguerite, queen of Navarre, sister of François I, king of France, probably between 1541 and 1546. The work is unfinished. A manuscript was prepared posthumously in 1553, and a defective first edition was published in 1558. The title by which the work is familiarly known is the fabrication of Claude Gruget for his 1559 edition, ten years after Marguerite's death. Edwin Duval has shown that, had she finished it, Marguerite would certainly have called her project of a French Decameron *Les Cent nouvelles*.[27] Her collection of tales resembles the *Decameron* in that ten aristocratic narrators cut off from their usual life by disastrous events agree to tell a tale a day each for the ten days it will take to rebuild a broken bridge. In striking contrast to Boccaccio's tales, however, the frame narrative has prompted more critical commentary than the tales themselves. The seventy-two tales Marguerite completed are introduced by a prologue in which the ten narrators become well-developed characters. As each day's narration unfolds, the reader learns more and more about the narrators, their personalities, their desires, and their usually conflicting opinions on the tales they have told and listened to. Any reader of the *Heptaméron* eventually comes to an opinion on a question inherent in the narrative design: Where does the mimetic illusion work better—in the tales themselves or in the frame story?

The general problem of writing that the *Heptaméron* puts before us stems from its structure, connecting the recounted tales with the frame story and putting into play the difference between fiction and truth or history, narrating and fact. Broadly, the theme of the work as a whole is love; the topic is both illustrated in the stories the narrators tell about other people, some of whom are real and well known, and debated in the commentary following each tale. The "system" of the work thus puts into opposition the story and the discourse on the story, by alternately presenting tales told by its ten *devisants* (or speakers) and their opinions on those tales. Before beginning a tale, the narrator gives its meaning—its signified, its closure, its moral, sometimes—or at least an indication of its purpose, an orientation for the hearers. The narrated tale often serves as an exemplum. After the tale is finished, the hearers (who have, interestingly enough, been scrupulously silent) offer commentary and reaction, in a dialogue that usually includes the narrator. Members of the audience may demolish the truth of the story, dispute its meaning and interpretation, add their approval, or allude to other cases they know of. Then a new narrator takes up the thread. Far from a gathering of tales in the manner of the Burgundian *Cent nouvelles nouvelles* or the *Cent nouvelles ou contes joyeux* of Philippe de Vigneulles, Marguerite de Navarre's work is of an entity, a narrative of the whole with pauses or stopping places only at the end of a day's narration.[28] Editorial interpolations indicate the material division of the work into ten separate stories per day, their separation marked by a heading and summary for each tale told.

The *Heptaméron* is a good place to begin this study of writing realism. Considered in its breadth and depth, the work has presented every problem of fiction and reality for analysis. Because it would be impossible, and beyond the scope of this book, to restate all its meanings and instructions, the analysis will be symptomatic. The twenty-fourth story, analyzed in detail, is built on the theme of pretense (*faire semblant*) or fiction, expressed in terms of hiding or revealing, an opposition of surface to depth or of "countenance" to "heart." Related to these oppositions are questions of truth and falsehood, of honesty and keeping a secret, and ultimately of fiction and reality. The focus on writing serves to explain the writing of realism not only in the tale told but also in the narrative frame, and finally in the work as a whole. Writing in the tale, in the frame narrative, and in the entire book stands as a supplement to experience—hence the title of chapter 2, "Fiction and the Supplement in the *Heptaméron*."

Les Liaisons dangereuses

Laclos's *Les Liaisons dangereuses* may not need introduction. Yet there are compelling reasons for another study of this famous and popular novel published in 1782—primarily the fact that letter writing is its chief focus. By this I mean not only that almost every element of the story reaches us via letters written by the actors in the story, but also that the actors focus on their letter-writing activity: letter writing is among the most important of the things they do and write about. In addition, their letters bring about events and thus determine what happens. Letter writing seamlessly becomes action. As I have said, a letter is instantly semiotic in that it is always a writing of experience, of realism. Therefore the process of writing the real is laid open to the reader's examination at every moment, from start to finish. Among other things, each letter writer creates herself or himself in writing. Emanating from a self, a letter often serves as a mask; letter writing is astonishingly well adapted to lying. The marquise de Merteuil's autobiographical letter (the eighty-first) stands as a model for the narrative of the self, a model of the kind of activity that the other characters engage in with less refinement than the marquise. She and the vicomte de Valmont, the two libertines, pursue their purposes with a tenacity that has been described as characteristic of the libertine ethos: "The libertine is a creature of 'projects.' . . . Energy, lucid volition, and knowledge of the heart make such projects synonymous with action and success."[29] That at least is the theory.

The novel recounts many projects—two or three central ones and a crowd of smaller ones—but most projects do not arrive at their ends. In fact, one could produce an adequate description of the novel simply by charting all the projects and their deviations from their straight course, as other projects interrupt them. If diagrammed, such an analysis would form a branching structure in which straight paths divide or are inflected or deflected repeatedly; the entire novel would consist of plans turned away from their ends. Such a design inheres in the primary feature of the novel's semiosis, its epistolary form. Immediate consequences of the epistolary form include fragmentation of the point of view, lack of a narrating authority, circuitous communications, misdirected letters, disagreements and misunderstandings, gaps and incompletion, and so on. All of these factors I consider central to the understanding of the story—to the way the story reaches the reader and can be interpreted there. Part of the fiction created by this writing concerns the very existence of the letters and how they have come to form a story. The novel is therefore moderately self-reflective. In the construction of realism by the writing, the roles of the "editor" and "publisher" are significant. Some letters are suppressed, it is claimed. Some have been shortened, removing unnecessary verbiage. Others are presented in their inelegant prolixity, such as Cécile's. Claims in the preface regarding truth and reality color our reading of the letters.

As the record of experience, letter writing is always inadequate: either more or less than the experience itself. Motivations, inventions, interpretations, elaborations are added to experience. But the letter remains this side of action: the rape of Cécile by Valmont is never as much in language as in reality; its duration is not that of the night; lacunae, silences, even euphemisms govern its writing. Its expression in language therefore has a certain sort of reality that cannot be the same as the reality it purports to recount. We can follow this stumbling construction of reality through a symptomatic theme, that of consolation. Starting with the last word of the text, the verb *consoler,* this concept allied with reason and *sagesse,* or sage wisdom, dominates the novel's tragic conclusion precisely because it is absent. Consolation weaves a thread among the various intrigues: all characters except the marquise seek it; none, in the end, obtains it.

Letters are acts. They have an astonishing motility in this novel (unlike, for instance, the letters in Balzac's *Mémoires de deux jeunes mariées*), and their movements are sometimes as effective as actions. In chapter 3, I will examine two particular cases of letters as acts and their construction of reality in *Les Liaisons dangereuses.*

La Religieuse

Suzanne Simonin faces similar constraints in *La Religieuse.* Diderot's novel was written and rewritten about 1760, 1770, and 1780–82 and finally published in a volume, like much of his work, including *Jacques le fataliste,* only posthumously in 1796. This novel poses the case in which the sense of truth coming from realism is motivated by reality itself. The nun, the very fictive Suzanne Simonin, narrates her unhappy life in three convents; the man to whom she addresses this long missive, essentially the bulk of the novel, exists in the real world. Exceptionally, therefore, when the reader puts herself in the place of a character, to feel as he does, to know his experience, she can put herself in the place of a real person: the marquis dè Croismare to whom the nun speaks in her writing. Because the model of the receiver or narratee is a real man, the novel's messages reach the real reader more easily; the mimetic illusion comes all the more smoothly. *La Religieuse* is an unusual work (in fact like most of Diderot's writing), which took birth in a project to bring the "charming" marquis back to Paris from his Normandy lands, and quickly engaged Diderot's passions in a plea against the forced taking of the veil and the social problem of involuntary confinement in convents. In the several years of revision, tinkering, and reorientation that followed, the work became highly self-reflective.

This would not be so if the novel had not been framed by its famous preface, called, in the nineteenth century, the "*préface-annexe*" and published sometimes before, sometimes after the text of the novel (or sometimes only in the notes). Here the initial purpose of the text is revealed: a mystification perpetrated on the marquis de Croismare by Diderot with the help of friends. Diderot and company hoped to persuade Croismare that Suzanne really existed and needed to be rescued by him; they hoped to move him with her plight much as he had been moved before to help a real nun, Marguerite Delamarre, who wished to annul her vows. Included in the preface with the account of this mystification are letters Suzanne wrote and others written on her behalf, which have the curious role of validating retrospectively the realism of the text of Suzanne's long narrative. The author of the preface purports to be Melchior Grimm, who first published the preface in the *Correspondance littéraire* in 1770. Meister then published the novel in the *Correspondance littéraire* in nine installments in 1780–82, accompanied by this preface, about the same time *Les Liaisons dangereuses* appeared. At that time Diderot revised the novel originally written in 1760, revised the preface Grimm had written, and added the letters written by Suzanne to the marquis and others. The marquis replied with what can only be called real letters, which are printed chronologically in the preface, somewhat revised by Diderot, muddying the confusion of fiction and reality even further. As Lucette Pérol has shown in a study focusing on the marquis de Croismare, he is first a real man in the 1760 text, which is a correspondence real on one side and fictive on the other; then a character in a "novel" in the version Grimm published in 1770, when Grimm recounts the mystification; then something like a coauthor because his reticence about coming to Paris to save the nun influenced Diderot and company to kill off their heroine; and finally a reader, when Diderot prepares the text in 1780–82 for publication as a novel among his *Œuvres complètes.*[30]

Illusion is so well created that it becomes reality: this is a familiar Diderotian claim, a theme replayed many times in his fictions and essays. The story of Mme de La Pommeraye in *Jacques le fataliste* is the ideal illustration. To obtain revenge on the marquis des Arcis who has ceased to love her, she schemes to make him fall in love with a courtesan whom she presents to him as an honest woman, by means of an elaborate plot conceived in its every detail to forge an illusion of a virginal life. Only on the morning following the marquis' wedding to the courtesan does she reveal the true origin of his wife. But far from destroying the marquis, the marriage will be happy: the young woman has effectively *become* the honest woman that Mme de La Pommeraye's fiction created. Similarly, Suzanne Simonin hopes to use her writing to forge the reality of her experience; she has a naïve belief in the power of words to represent—which is to create. But naïve representation does not exist alone. Like Suzanne, and through her, Diderot calls attention to the mimetic illusion in so many words. My analysis will begin with the question concerning the mimetic illusion, which Diderot formulates in the short final paragraph of the preface (most often published last, as it was in 1796). As Carol Sherman concludes her excellent summary of the self-reflective tourniquets of the work, "The entire phenomenon of this so-called *novel* insistently poses the question of the limits or boundaries between literary and non-literary spaces and ends by subverting the opposition itself."[31]

For both of these eighteenth-century novels, our good understanding transits the characters' misunderstanding. That is why I have called chapter 3 "Listen, Hear: Dialogues of the Deaf."

Mémoires de deux jeunes mariées, Modeste Mignon, and *Ursule Mirouët*

Typically, Balzac has been thought of as a retreat with respect to the modernity of Diderot. His prose was the scapegoat of the new novelists of the 1950s and 1960s, for instance, who cast it in the role of un-self-conscious representation and imitation of life, a dishonesty it was no longer possible to perpetrate. Lucien Dällenbach, one among many, has forcefully reiterated the "error" of these views in his recent book, *La Canne de Balzac,* taking the new novelists to task for describing Balzac's text as " 'complete,' 'full,' without openings, continuous, smooth, not fragmentary, monolithic, wordy, homogeneous, *readable.*"[32] Rather, Dällenbach maintains totality is fragmentary, fullness is merely an inconsistent theoretical notion, order is inextricably tied to disorder (13); nor should Balzac's books remain fixed in the era he describes, bourgeois society of the first half of the nineteenth century (14). I agree with this view. Concomitant with Balzac's goal of a totality to be described and a profound belief in the unity of composition, the writing has as much to say about its own existence as about the total world it wishes to describe. The self-consciousness of writing is *masked,* in Balzac, but the writing *is* powerfully self-conscious in its rhetoric. Figures of semiosis, found in the mimesis, which I call mimetic figures of semiosis, lend the writing an artful duplicity.

Three novels illustrate this theme through letter writing and other semiotic figures of writing. It is perhaps no accident that all three are founded on structures of duality. In the epistolary novel *Mémoires de deux jeunes mariées,* the only novel by letters in *La Comédie humaine,* only two voices speak (with minor exceptions), and no putative editor gives even as much guidance as Laclos's editor. The result is a kind of bipolar autobiography alternately narrated by Louise and Renée, as each recounts her life to the other over the course of several years, through marriages, children, deaths, and remarriages. Not unlike Suzanne Simonin's writing in *La Religieuse,* the letter-writers create themselves in their narrative according to a system of naïve representation. As the novel progresses, the two authors of its dual narrative accentuate their differences. It is interesting that Balzac gave this most indecisive of books the position of first novel in *La Comédie humaine* (although it was not the first novel in order of composition), as if to alert the reader to the task of reconciling opposites throughout the larger work, a task that was often destined to fail.

Modeste Mignon, the heroine of the romantic novel of this name, carries such a task within herself, and she achieves, almost in spite of herself, a marvelous union of romantic ideals with reality. Enamored of literature, inclined to dream but exceptionally aware of the hideous reality of a young woman's destiny (marriage), Modeste sends an anonymous letter of gushing admiration to the famous poet Canalis, who tosses the letter aside with a sigh of disdain and boredom. The letter's sincerity nevertheless reaches a kindred spirit in the form of the poet's secretary, Ernest de La Brière, and he replies in writing that reveals his own sincere self-portrait, even though he writes in the name of Canalis. During the course of this anonymous correspondence with a man she does not know, Modeste creates her self in her writing, in the first half of the novel. In the process she also reads La Brière into existence as her ideal mate. Because the novel includes the text of these letters, it puts these processes of composition before us in their full detail. The latter half of the novel, a comedy of marriage, pits reality against the fantasy Modeste did not know she was living, and she must adapt to the truth that pierces the masks created by the letter writing. There is a kind of lost illusion for the young woman that parallels the lost illusions of young men in several other Balzac novels, but what arises out of that loss is truth.

It would not be excessive to consider *Modeste Mignon* an updated discussion of the questions of representation posed by *La Religieuse*. The heroines of both novels write themselves into existence, but Balzac includes the effect on the reader of both letter-writers' naïve representations.

A drama of inheritance occurs in *Ursule Mirouët* too and ends happily, like a comedy, with marriage, thanks to the somnambulistic powers Ursule Mirouët possesses. In this 1840–41 novel, Balzac opposes the spiritualism of his pure, young heroine to the crass materialism of the bourgeois relatives who despoil her. While the actual writing events in *Ursule Mirouët* are less copious than in the other two novels, they are nonetheless significant: papers that represent a large sum of money that Ursule's loving guardian, the doctor Denis Minoret, wishes to leave her. But I include this analysis primarily to illustrate the relation of the represented narrative to its semiosis, to show how we may glean information about the writing of the story from the story itself. The novel includes a dual system of meaning that provides both the mimetic frame of the narrative and the semiotic structure of our reading. Like *Modeste Mignon* and *Mémoires de deux jeunes mariées*, *Ursule Mirouët* struggles to find unity in the midst of opposition. The opposed terms, mimetic figures of the writing, are *genealogy* and *inheritance*, the first linked with materialism and the second with spiritualism. Genealogy, a writing of the relationships among four intermarried families, represents the noxious elements of the plot—a mediocre capitalism of evil, of low-minded cupidity—whereas inheritance, linking Ursule with her guardian and a small, select society of intellectuals, writes the good elements of the story—the spiritual in the intellectual sense, order, justice, light, and above all love. The ultimate purpose of the plot is to return the money to its rightful owner, Ursule. One can admire the ingenuity that Balzac musters to combine an affair of succession with an act of somnambulism; the fact that spirituality wins Ursule a material gain indexes the overcoming of contradiction by means of the writing.

Not unlike the mutation of Modeste Mignon's "novel" of love into an almost satirical comedy of "the heiress," the two parts of which are needed as ingredients in the happy ending, *Ursule Mirouët* evolves into a story of the extraordinary ability of a pure, innocent young girl to focus her mind so that she can see beyond the visible, to see the evil acts that robbed her of her succession. Only by this means does the story come to its happy end.

Underlying all these novels is the notion of the "unity of composition," which I include in the title of chapter 4. The unity of composition is the goal of Balzac's writing—a goal that remains only an ideal, never reached. Such a focus is not inconsistent with a view of Balzac's writing as self-reflective and displaying the mechanisms of its construction.

Femmes and *Le Livre brisé*

The strong French tradition of the representation of reality (I am thinking of the extraordinary fortune of the word *vraisemblance,* verisimilitude) has developed through stages, the last of which, in our time, is ironic. In chapter 5, two striking, successful novels by living authors will illustrate how writing represents reality in our time. When Philippe Sollers published *Femmes* in 1983, his first novel *chez* Gallimard (alias "La Banque Centrale"), it was to be the first of now nine novels in a new, so-called readable style. Unlike the radical structuralist or semiotic experimentation of *Drame, Nombres,* and *Lois,* from the 1960s and 1970s, *Femmes* and the later novels resort to some of the standard features of novelistic writing: characters with recognizable personalities and psychologies, events, locations, chronology, a narrator persona, dialogue, and a degree of development and change. Also unlike *H* (1973) and the two volumes of *Paradis* (1981, 1986), there is punctuation, capitalization, and paragraphing, in support of a plot or story line. And the outstanding feature of the story is writing: writing is the central, omnipresent topic of *Femmes.*

From the beginning to the end, a manuscript of a novel is being written before our eyes. Its title is *Femmes,* and it recounts, among other things, the conditions of its own existence. The novel being written by its first-person narrator persona, an American journalist named Will, doubles Sollers's novel, as a lining doubles a coat; the novels are coextensive. The writing process could scarcely be more self-reflective, a *mise en abyme* carried to its logical extreme. This is raw writing, the inscription of writing at the moment of its production, and the time of writing is the same as the time of events.

This conflation of times also occurs in Serge Doubrovsky's 1989 book *Le Livre brisé,* with many additional chronological complications. Here the narrator and writer is called Serge Doubrovsky; he recounts his own life, and writes about writing his life in his several books. Although *Le Livre brisé* is published with the designation "novel," Doubrovsky has invented a term for its unique blend of real events recounted as if in a fiction, the term *autofiction* already adopted and as often adapted for use by many others. Like Sollers in *Femmes,* writing is the omnipresent topic of the novel's representation of reality. Both novels insistently pose questions of genre, but Doubrovsky's more acutely than Sollers's. When Doubrovsky's writing brings about an event of intensely real repercussions, the generic designation distinguishing fiction from reality acquires an unheard-of urgency, and, simultaneously, a pitiful fragility.

I call chapter 5 "Breaking the Book" because both Sollers and Doubrovsky, in different ways, put into question models of the book, a fitting end for representations of reality in French literature.

Two

Fiction and the Supplement
in the *Heptaméron*

The tales of the *Heptaméron* each come to an end when "the voice" passes from one speaker to another. In borrowing the structure of the *Decameron,* to which her posthumous readers owe the invented title by which the work is commonly known, Marguerite de Navarre sought to make the agglomeration of oral tales realistic and natural. The narrative of the situation from which the seventy-two tales emerged does achieve a convincing realism and coherence: the flood near Cauterets from which five noble men and five noble women barely escaped; the need to await the construction of a new bridge over the water; and the decision to pass the time in storytelling, each telling one story each day on a theme agreed upon by all, alternating male and female speakers. The plot and the finely drawn characters of this frame story have been the object of much critical attention: the setting and the characters have been analyzed in consummate detail, their opinions inventoried and categorized as they comment on the tales they have just heard, their thematic preferences duly recorded based on the stories of which they are the authors, and so on. Only a few readers have commented on the act of passing the speaking voice from one character to another.

This transmission of narrative authority is never lacking, so great is Marguerite de Navarre's care to maintain the realism of her narrative frame, the setting that allows tales to be told. If my experience is a common one, as I suspect, most readers are likely to forget the details of the stories the *devisants,* or narrators, have told, unless reminded by the names of the characters in the tales or by short summaries of the plots. Yet, after time has eroded one's memory of the stories' contents, the language of the transmission of authority nevertheless remains, as familiar as a refrain in a ballad. In short, while one may need to reread the book to recall the plots of the seventy-two stories, who told them, or the topics chosen for each day's narration, one does not need to be reminded how narrative authority circulates. Without fail, before each tale, a particular moment occurs when narrating is "handed off," and these moments are so formulaic that they command attention. In fact, with very few exceptions, the author uses only two phrases (with slight variants): "je vous donne ma voix" [I give you my voice] and "prenez ma place" [take my place], to mark the moment where the right and requirement to speak pass to another narrator. By comparison, the transmission of letters in *Les Liaisons dangereuses,* while also the object of scrupulous care, takes complex forms, because the chronology is elaborate and the origins and end points of the letters are multiple. In the *Heptaméron,* the two phrases, tabulated in appendix A, return like myths and persist like echoes. Yet, surely, dwelling on these moments of passage is to engage in a devious reading, one that perversely pays attention to what is *not* story. The passing of the voice indicates where the text turns momentarily away from the mimetic activity of tale-telling. Because it marks the limits that define the mimetic activity, it is a moment that merits particular attention, in the *Heptaméron,* for I believe that the modernity of the work lies in the demands it makes on the reader to define it. In other words, I am beginning from this reading effect, one that involves memory in the signifying process, to discover the semiotic processes of writing realism in the *Heptaméron.* Whereas story is mimesis, an illusion of reality, the attention to its beginning and ending and to its conditions of existence concerns semiosis.

The gift of the voice naturally marks the moment of yielding up authority to another, but it also propels the narrative forward and, significantly, disallows any break in the flow of reading. (Only when vespers come, and the characters must leave the meadow, do we too get a chance to quit our reading, once every ten tales.) This raises a basic question: Where do the tales begin? Modern editions place a heading with the number of the tale and the short summary devised by Adrien de Thou in 1553 or by Claude Gruget for the 1559 edition at the point where one of the ten *devisants* begins the embedded narration. Thus, for the twenty-fourth story, this heading and summary are found in the François edition:

VINGT QUATRIESME NOUVELLE

Elisor, pour s'estre trop advancé de decouvrir son amour à la Royne de Castille, fut si cruellement traité d'elle, en l'esprouvant, qu'elle luy apporta nuysance, puis profit.[1]

[TWENTY-FOURTH TALE

Elisor, having been too forward in uncovering his love to the Queen of Castille, was treated so cruelly by her, as a test, that she brought him harm, and then profit.]

The tale itself begins next. In the logic of the narrative structure, however, no such break occurs; these headings are merely editorial interpolations in an unbroken text. The point is important because the number of the tale and the summary are not in fact the place where the writing of each tale starts. If anything could be said to designate, in the *writing* of the text, the real beginning of the next numbered tale (the second, after the first, and so on), it would be the change indicated by the gift of the voice, at which point the new speaker introduces the next tale. I call this beginning real because the focus of attention (the *devisants'* and ours) passes from one tale to the next at that point.

The François edition gives the number of the tale and the plot summary just before the tale or the embedded narration begins. The gift of the voice and the short speech or dialogue introducing the tale therefore occur before the interpolated heading. As François explains, the manuscript history and the facts of publication are quite complex. The first nearly complete edition was published ten years after Marguerite de Navarre's death, in 1559, by Claude Gruget, with plot summaries and other interpolations and expurgations. Adrian de Thou had devised other plot summaries in his complete 1553 manuscript (four years after Marguerite's death), and the plot summaries were presented in a table before the beginning of the prologue, rather than interpolated in the text as they are in the François edition I am using. Unlike François's edition, de Thou's manuscript "edition" usually marks the beginning of the tale just before the voice is given to the next narrator, except in tales 1 through 6, 8, 9, 11, and 12, which begin at the point where the narrator begins speaking—introducing the story. Yves Le Hir's rhetoric, in his edition of this manuscript, obscures his observations about how the manuscript marked the division between tales; in any case, his purpose differs considerably from my point, which is that the passage to the next story is marked in the writing, independently of any interpolated break or heading.[2]

Yet, I believe modern editors such as Michel François have chosen well to place the breaks where they did, assuming interpolations were necessary at all, because the passage of the voice is truly not a good spot to tear the fabric of the narrative discourse. On the contrary, it is remarkable with what effortless skill Marguerite de Navarre brings the telling phrase ("I give you my voice" and so on) into the exchange of opinions on the previous tale, so that the passage to the next one is nearly seamless. The point is that each story materializes because a *devisant* has listened to another person speaking and receives the voice because of that listening; tale-telling partakes of commentary as the taker of the word elaborates upon an opinion provoked by the previous tale and illustrates it via a fresh tale. Much as remembering and forgetting characterize the reader's position in the face of the work as a whole, the stories are often told because the *devisants* are reminded of similar—or different—cases: "Vous me faictes souvenir, dist Parlamente, de celluy qui . . ." [you remind me, said Parlamente, of the man who . . .] (353). It is such a phrase that invites the gift of the voice, prompting the previous speaker to pass the word to the one so reminded. If the frame story and its characters have captivated the majority of readers, to the detriment of the tales themselves, it is because this orderly movement of voices takes one up into the seamless structure of each day. M.-M. de La Garanderie and others before and since admire the spontaneous style and the interesting characterization of the narrators. She writes that the group of *devisants* is "the most important and the most original creation."[3] Because the sex of the narrators always alternates, this seamless structure simulates a microcosm of the heterosexual world order, as representing order itself.

Always present in the gift of the voice, however, is the threat of its loss, by censure or silence. If the chosen recipient of the voice refused the gift, in fear of not pleasing a member of the audience, for instance, or because the story the speaker has in mind should not be told, disorder would intervene. When the voice is passed, it is most vulnerable to being "dropped." It is a measure of the power of the narrative design that this loss remains only a virtuality, never a reality. Nobody who is given the voice refuses to speak next. While speaking is a defense against silence, to assume one's share of narrative authority entails significant risks. The exchange of the word is in principle subject to censure, because to speak is also to choose to reveal.

What I wish to analyze, in this reading, is the necessary strategy that keeps the word going by supplying a structure that is essentially semiotic. This strategy is the deployment of a *third term,* which engages the logic of the *supplement.* I will focus on the twenty-fourth story, told by Dagoucin, because it exemplifies this problematic, and does so via an embedded writing. Elisor, hero of the tale, invents two supplements, a mirror and an epistle in verse; his task of explaining via these writings parallels Dagoucin's, when he recounts the story, and Marguerite de Navarre's when she writes the *Heptaméron.* When Elisor "speaks" in mirrors and epistles, the voices that we hear are not only his but also Dagoucin's and Marguerite's, for the twenty-fourth tale is a specular narrative that reflects and reflects on the entire *Heptaméron.* I would add that my use of the term *supplement* does not adhere to a strictly Derridean definition, as the concept is first analyzed in *Of Grammatology* with respect to Rousseau, because the effects of the supplement are not necessarily negative.

Dagoucin I

Dagoucin, chief exponent of Platonic love and a suitor, or *serviteur,* of Parlamente, finds his opinions called into question by the tragic events of the twenty-third tale. In that account, a Cordelier monk rapes a woman, who kills herself in shame. The woman's brother, thinking her husband is the murderer, slays the husband in revenge. The animated conversation following it concerns the evil of certain priests, until Saffredent urges the company to abandon this disgusting topic: "'parquoy, *sinite eos* [laissez-les]; et sçachons qui aura la voix d'Oisille.' La compaignie trouva l'oppinion de Saffredent très bonne, et, laissant là les prebstres, pour changer de propos, pria madame Oisille de donner sa voix à quelqu'un" ["therefore, *sinite eos* [let them be]; and let's find out who will have Oisille's voice." The company found Saffredent's opinion very good, and, leaving the priests behind, to change the topic, begged madam Oisille to give her voice to somebody]. Dagoucin has had no chance to speak his mind about the twenty-third tale, but it has cast him into such contemplation that Oisille thinks he must be "preparé à dire quelque bonne chose" [ready to say some good thing], and she gives him her voice. Yet Dagoucin accepts the voice only as a fall-back: "Puis que je ne puis ne n'ose, respondit Dagoucin, dire ce que je pense, à tout le moins parleray-je d'un à qui telle cruaulté porta nuysance et puis proffict" [Since I cannot and do not dare say what I think, Dagoucin replied, at the very least I will speak of one to whom such cruelty brought harm and then profit]. Censuring his actual opinion, which remains unspoken, Dagoucin will produce a substitute for the lacking commentary, of which "such cruelty" leaves only the slightest hint. Gisèle Mathieu-Castellani writes: "When a narrator *cannot and dare not say* what he is thinking, . . . the tale offers itself as a way to satisfy his desire."[4] Already in this brief dialogue in which the voice is given and taken, the threat to its continuing circulation is inscribed, and Dagoucin's acceptance of the voice in spite of the need to censure his real thoughts (but why, and will the reader find out?) requires that he resort to a supplement, as I will show more fully later.

"Nuysance," or harm, stems from an abuse of love's power, as Dagoucin explains in his introductory moral:

Combien que Amour fort et puissant s'estime tant qu'il veult aller tout nud, et luy est chose très ennuyeuse et à la fin importable [insupportable] d'estre couvert, si est-ce, mes dames, que bien souvent ceulx qui, pour obeyr à son conseil, se advanceans trop de le descouvrir, s'en trouvent mauvais marchans.

[Even though Love, strong and powerful, has such a high regard for himself that he wishes to go entirely naked, and it is a very disagreeable and in the end insupportable thing for him to be covered, nevertheless, ladies, very often those who, obeying his counsel, are too forward in uncovering it, find themselves to be bad merchants.]

Playing on "entirely naked," "covered," and "uncover," Dagoucin suggests both the story's theme—the cruelty and harm of love and its paradoxical outcome in profit—and his narrative strategy—the desire to reveal while keeping the secret. The moral will apply to both the hero and the narrator, as we will find out; both, if they speak too much, risk becoming "bad merchants." In telling about one who suffered harm and then profit from a woman's cruelty, Dagoucin will repay himself "at the very least" for the lost words he dared not speak. The profit to his listeners and to Marguerite's readers resides in this supplementarity of his storytelling, to which we will return. Dagoucin's introduction, with its elliptical metaphors, poses the terms of our close reading of his tale.

Elisor

The story begins under the sign of the secret, in keeping with its theme of courtly love. Elisor, a perfect gentleman at the court of the King and Queen of Castille (whose names are not revealed), is the object of universal admiration, not only for his "beaultez et bonnes conditions" [handsomeness and noble status] and his virtues, but also for his strangeness, for he is not known to love or serve any woman, in spite of the great numbers of beauties who might have "melted his ice." The queen, who is virtuous but "non du tout exempte de la flambe laquelle moins est congneue et plus brusle" [not at all exempt from the flame that, the less it is known, the more it burns], accuses Elisor of deception or pretense ("s'il estoit possible qu'il aymast aussy peu qu'il en faisoit le semblant" [if it was possible that he loved as little as he pretended]). To this he replies in self-defense: "Si elle voyoit son cueur comme sa contenance, elle ne luy feroit poinct ceste question" [If she could see his heart as well as his countenance, she would never ask this question]. The physiology of hiding suggests that the surface symbolizes deception or pretense whereas depth represents honesty and honor: if a secret must be uncovered to acquit the knight of deceit, it can be found only in the heart, not on the countenance.[5] While his countenance is among his instances of "strangeness," his heart is among his "virtues," and matches his handsomeness and noble condition. For the reader, and probably the queen, Elisor's reply already reveals the identity of his mistress, and that it is secret. To keep it silent is to follow the courtly norm.

Elisor's self-defense, alluding as it does to an opposition between hidden and not hidden, adds a layer to the secret because its symbolic language invites further inquiry. To be sure, the word *heart* is such a dead metaphor for love that Dagoucin's audience may not give it a second thought; they will assume that the queen will have understood its significance instantaneously. Yet the queen asks for a "translation" of his metaphor: "Elle, desirant sçavoir ce qu'il voulloit dire, le pressa si fort . . ." [She, wishing to know what he meant, pressured him so strongly . . .]. Guided by the queen's insistence on knowing, the listeners (and readers too) quickly realize that a dead metaphor is not involved here. The symbolic word does not refer to something so well known that it is without value as information; it is the intimate index of a secret. And if we read more carefully, we see immediately that she does not want to know what he means by "heart" but rather why he says she would not ask if she could see into his heart. The queen may have guessed that she is in his heart, and she seeks his wanting to say, his "vouloir dire," in the literal way: she wants him to want to say his hidden thought. She is asking him to break his self-imposed censure; she is asking him to have the courage to expose his thought whatever the risk—and she has probably guessed just what risk Elisor faces.

The queen's insistence leads to a confession, the most acute form that the revelation of a secret can take, particularly in the resiliently Catholic country of

Spain: "Il confessa qu'il aymoit une dame qu'il pensoit estre la plus vertueuse de toute la chrestienté" [He confessed that he loved a lady whom he considered the most virtuous of all Christianity]. The confession marks the start of the abuse of love's power that Dagoucin spoke of in his introduction: wanting to go naked, love begins to force the unspoken, censured truth to the surface. There it may perhaps be seeking absolution, in what form we are yet to find out.

Not content with this partial confession (which continues to hide by using periphrasis), the queen offers continued conversation, or what is ambiguously called "commerce," in exchange for completely uncovering the secret: "Elle ne parleroit jamais à luy, s'il ne luy nommoit celle qu'il aymoit tant" [She would never speak to him, if he did not name the one he loved so much]. Naming the woman is her price. "Commerce" is later glossed by "sa veue et bonne grace" [seeing her and having her good graces], specifying the intimacy with the queen that Elisor stands to lose. Beyond its commercial sense, *commerce* means conversation, but, not unlike the English word *intercourse*, certain contexts suggest sexual relations.[6] Simulated anger hardens the queen's unequal bargain: "Elle feit semblant d'estre fort courroucée contre luy" [She pretended to be very infuriated at him]; but Elisor's counteroffer, so to speak, comes from the heart, as underscored by the verb *aimer:* "Il aymeroit autant mourir que s'il falloit qu'il luy confessast" [He would prefer to die than if he were obliged to confess to her]. If it is true that the allusion to death appropriately lends rhetorical strength to the desire to keep the woman's name secret, is it not also possible that rhetoric risks being taken literally? For Elisor, speaking is rigorously equivalent to dying: "he would prefer to die" expresses the truth, not a mere rhetorical pretense. As for the queen, her devious questioning tactics are roundabout in a way that the *Heptaméron* defines as "feminine": dissimulating her interest but seeking Elisor's spoken declaration of his love. One can compare this to the intermittent debate among the narrators about the woman's need to dissimulate her interest in a man under a mask of virtue and honor— for instance, in the comments following the forty-second tale. As paradoxical as it may sound, what the queen wants is exactly what she threatens to take away: "commerce" with Elisor, for not only does she suspect that Elisor loves her, she also is disposed to love him. Her behavior can be qualified as neurotic, displaying simultaneously what Mathieu-Castellani calls a "drive to dissimulate" and a "desire to denude and uncover" (*La Conversation conteuse,* 203).

The language of the marketplace (giving, taking, losing), however inappropriate for a queen and a perfect handsome nobleman, already illustrates Dagoucin's introductory moral about "bad merchants." In this exchange of values, Elisor will be the weaker bargainer if he uncovers his love in exchange for speech; the dilemma for him is that he will lose that love by not speaking, because, as we already suspect, the perfectly virtuous woman he loves is the queen herself. Elisor has entered into a negotiation in which he is inevitably the loser: he will lose her if he speaks, according to the constraints of courtly behavior, just as surely as if he does not speak.

One cannot name pleasure without also provoking its censure. Elisor resolves the dilemma by resorting to a third term, which is, as Barthes says in *Le Plaisir du texte*, "different from pleasure and from its censure."[7] A subtle subversion eschews the paradigm and finds a third term (87). Not a synthesis but "an eccentric, unheard-of term" (87), the third term is the verb *to see* in the causative "faire voir" [make one see]. This term avoids the dialectic of speaking/not speaking. "To see" is not a compromise but a way out: "Ma dame, je n'ay la force, puissance ne hardiesse de le vous dire, mais la premiere fois que vous irez à la chasse, je vous la *feray veoir;* et suis seur que vous jugerez que c'est la plus belle et parfaicte dame du monde" [My lady, I have neither the strength, the power, nor the boldness to tell you, but the next time you go hunting, I will *make you see* her; and I am sure you will judge her the most beautiful and perfect lady in the world] (emphasis added). Clearly, speaking demands power and boldness, the very qualities Dagoucin lacked ("I cannot and dare not"), while "to see" occurs in another realm and requires neither. There are no courtly rules governing "make one see" as there are for speaking and silence.

The queen hastens to go hunting and Elisor with her as is his custom. Fourteen lines dwell on his spectacular accoutrement. The motif of "make one see" first occurs in a reflexive version, "se faire voir" [make oneself be seen], not only in Elisor's attire but also in "les cources et les saulx que faisoit faire Elisor à son cheval" [the races and jumps that Elisor had his horse accomplish]. His black silk hat sports a rich insignia "où y avoit pour devise ung Amour, couvert par force" [where there was an insignia of Love, covered by necessity], as if decorum forbids displaying a naked child on one's head covering. The covering of Love also recalls Dagoucin's complex statement of the introductory moral, according to which it is the nature of love to want to go without covering, thus causing "nuysance," or harm. The hat and insignia stubbornly insist on silence in continued defiance of the queen's commands, while Elisor is preparing to avoid both speech and censure. The elaborate accoutrement has a most un-usual feature, the point of which is to make her see, without naming her, the image of his lady: "Et feit faire un grand mirouer d'acier en façon de hallecret [a piece of armor], et, le mectant devant son estomac, le couvrit très bien d'ung grand manteau de frise noire" [And he had a great steel mirror made in the shape of a shield, and, placing it before his stomach, covered it very well with a large mantle of black cloth].

Let us focus on this mirror and its strategic emplacement. Having satisfac-torily displayed his prowess on his horse, he helps the queen down from hers: "Et, ainsy qu'elle luy tendoit les bras, il ouvrit son manteau de devant son estomac, et la prenant entre les siens, luy monstrant son hallecret de mirouer, luy dist: 'Ma dame, je vous supplie regarder icy!'" [And, as she stretched her arms out to him, he opened his mantle in front of his stomach, and taking her in his arms, showing her his shield of a mirror, said to her: "My lady, I beg you to look here!"]. These are the only words that accompany this act of "making one see"; following it, parallel privative constructions underscore the mutual censuring of speech. The gesture and the word *here* point toward a physiologi-cal emblem of insight more complex than the countenance and the heart mentioned earlier. The seat of our feelings, desires, and ideas, the anatomical "estomac" designates a symbolic locus from which a voice cries out to reveal hidden thoughts. Huguet's dictionary observes: "C'est de l'estomac que sortent les soupirs, les cris, les paroles" [It is from the stomach that sighs, cries, words emanate]. Although surface is semblance, the mirror on the dazzlingly arrayed stomach covers speaking but allows insight into the "so honorable truth" of Elisor's love, like a window into the heart.

The mirror thus has properties unique among all the knight's coverings. It is both internal and external, surface and depth, covered and uncovered. One might almost say it is both opaque and transparent. Granting vision yet allow-ing silence to continue, it is a medium of the third term. The mirror translates the internal to the external; it is the objective symbol of the passage to seeing and knowing. Because mirrors into lovers' hearts reveal love by showing the object they reflect, Elisor's mirror is also a fine symbol of potential parity in love. But we have temporarily lost touch with the queen's point of view; the narrative voice has ceased to give clues to her thoughts.[8] We are soon to find out that "make one see," as a method of telling, does not satisfy the queen, at least not here. Dissimulating her interest, she is not content to see her image; she would bring what is hidden in the stomach to the surface covering it. Here she is true to the Renaissance belief in the presence conveyed in the spoken word, as if she would refuse to interpret until she has heard speech. It is speech that she had commanded and it is speech that she will now resort to, after supper, in the longest part of the tale. If the mirror is the "text," the conversation following performs an *explication de texte*—critical commentary.

The queen protests that Elisor "estoit le plus grand menteur qu'elle avoit jamais veu, car il luy avoit promis de luy monstrer à la chasse celle qu'il aymoit le plus, ce qu'il n'avoit faict: parquoy, elle avoit deliberé de jamais ne faire cas n'estime de luy" [was the greatest liar that she had ever seen, because he had promised to show her during the hunt the woman he loved the most, which he had not done; because of which, she had decided not to grant him her consideration or esteem]. This is sheer deception, an intensification of the first dialogue, in which "elle feit semblant d'estre fort courroucée contre luy, et jura qu'elle ne parleroit jamais à luy, s'il ne luy nommoit celle qu'il aymoit tant" [she pretended to be very infuriated at him, and swore that she would never speak to him, if he did not name the woman he loved so much]. In describing the queen's speech in this dialogue after the mirror episode, the narrative voice inserts the phrase "faisant la mescongneue" [pretending to be misunderstood], affording insight into the queen's mind and alerting the reader that she is still in the mode of the *faire semblant*, a mere feint. Her dissimulation is designed to obtain speech.

Elisor foresees that she refuses his strategy ("ayant paour que la Royne n'eust entendu ce qu'il luy avoit dict" [fearing that the Queen had not understood what he had said to her]); he affirms he has shown her not only the woman, but "la chose du monde qu'il aymoit le plus" [the object that he loved the most in the world]. Still refusing to understand anything so devious, she replies "qu'elle n'avoit poinct entendu qu'il luy eust monstré une seulle de ses femmes" [that she had not in the least understood that he had shown her a single one of her ladies]. True, but whom did he show her while helping her down from her horse? "Rien, dist la Royne, sinon ung mirouer devant vostre estomach" ["Nothing," said the Queen, "except a mirror in front of your stomach"]. Pretending she has seen only the surface, still she refuses to see into the mirror. Essentially, she refuses to collaborate in the fabrication of the supplement. Elisor next forces her vision inside the mirror: "En ce mirouer, Madame, dist

Elisor, qu'est-ce que vous avez veu? —Je n'y ay veu que moy seulle!" ["In this mirror, Madame," said Elisor, "what did you see?" "I saw only myself alone!"] she replies. "Doncques, ma dame, pour obeyr à vostre commandement, vous ay-je tenu promesse, car il n'y a ne aura jamais aultre ymaige en mon cueur, que celle que vous avez veue au dehors de mon estomach" [Therefore, my lady, to obey your command, I have kept my promise to you, for there is not nor will ever be any other image in my heart than the one you saw on the outside of my stomach]. "Image in my heart," a noble periphrasis, both speaks love and obeys the censure, because the general property of the figure of periphrasis is to show without saying, precisely by creating an image. The opposition of the image in the heart to the "outside of my stomach" again reproduces that of depth to surface. The device of the mirror as an objective and concrete realization of insight or knowledge, transcending or negating the opposition of speaking to censure, would maintain love on the idealistic plane; it functions much like rhetoric. Elisor uses the mirror to avoid both speaking and silence, but willy-nilly rhetoric carries him forward into speech—and potential harm.[9]

The mirror, index of love's harm, is one of two foci in the story, which has some of the curious properties of the ellipse. (Its second focus, on the verse epistle, will nicely index profit.) The events centered on the mirror concern the dialectic of covered/uncovered, and their outcome will soon prove Dagoucin's thesis that on the side of the uncovered there lies harm. At the center of the ellipse and of the tale occurs an extended conversation (more than two pages) in which Elisor gives voice to his love, in a speech remarkable for very long sentences and the proper, nonperiphrastic terms *to love, to revere*, and *to adore*, with rhetorical expansions thereon. He accepts the risks inherent in speaking, which Dagoucin had succinctly outlined and the critical reader must also take, for his life is in the hands of the image he adores: "vous suppliant que ma parfaicte et grande affection, qui a esté ma vie tant que je l'ay portée couverte, ne soit ma mort en la descouvrant" [begging you that my perfect and great affection, which has been my life as long as I have carried it covered, should not be my death by uncovering it]. (In the twelfth tale, also told by Dagoucin, the recourse to speech spells death for the lover.)

The courtly model degenerates not only because Elisor has recourse to speech, but also because this dialogue, under cover of a courtly manner, fully deploys the mercantile metaphor of the introduction. Elisor negotiates as follows:

Et, s'il ne vous plaist, pour la congnoissance de ceste grande amour, m'avoir plus agreable que vous n'avez accoustumé, au moins ne m'ostez la vie, qui consiste au bien que j'ay de vous veoir comme j'ay accoustumé. Car je n'ay de vous nul bien que autant qu'il en fault pour mon extreme necessité, et, si j'en ay moins, vous avez moins de serviteurs, en perdant le meilleur et le plus affectionné que vous eustes oncques ny pourriez jamais avoir.

[And if, because of the knowledge of this great love, it does not please you to find me more amiable than you have been accustomed, at least do not take away my life, which consists in the good I have from seeing you as I am accustomed. For I have from you no property except as much as required for my barest needs, and, if I have less, you have fewer admirers, by losing the best and the most affectionate that you have ever had nor will ever have one day.]

The language of quantity is consistent: as much, more, less, none; the verb *to have* occurs no fewer than eight times, not counting its use as an auxiliary. The structure of the argumentation poses equivalences, compensations, conse-quences, even in the grammatical terms articulating its syntax (and if, because of, at least, for, as much as). The "bien," or property, Elisor enjoys, thanks to the queen, is that "commerce" rendered here by the verb *to see* ("from seeing you") and in the earlier negotiation by "sa veue et bonne grace" [seeing her and having her good graces]. He proposes to keep the same quantity of "good," in exchange for which he will continue to *count* among her "admirers" "the best and the most affectionate." And he does indeed prove himself a "bad merchant," for he implies that the queen has no other admirer as good as he, nor will she ever be able to: "ny pourriez jamais avoir." Upon these inept propositions Elisor's long speech, its length being part of its defensiveness, comes to a precarious end.

The queen strikes a vicious bargain in reply, an egregious exaggeration of the courtly model: she requires him to endure seven years' absence, silence, and fidelity before she will accept him as her suitor. In courtly literature, the test qualifies the hero; if, as some readers have shown, the *Heptaméron* mocks and parodies the courtly tradition while borrowing its armature, here is an excellent illustration of that contradictory status, by which one may appre-ciate the work's modernity. Like the quantified equivalences and compensa-tions of Elisor's language, an apparently frivolous symmetry again activates the covered/uncovered dialectic: because he has spoken of his love after hiding it for seven years, keeping it silent for seven more will reveal it to her all the better, she claims. No fewer than four possible reasons are maliciously proposed by the narrative voice, which suddenly fails in its task of affording reliable insight into the queen's thoughts:

La Royne, ou pour se monstrer autre qu'elle n'estoit, ou pour experimenter à la longue l'amour qu'il luy portoit, ou pour en aymer quelque autre qu'elle ne voulloit laisser pour luy, ou bien le reservant, quand celluy qu'elle aymoit feroit quelque faulte, pour luy bailler sa place, dist. . .

[The Queen, either to show herself other than she was, or to put the love he bore her to a long test, or for loving some other man whom she did not want to abandon for him, or else reserving him for when the one she loved would commit some mistake, to give him his place, said . . .]

These clauses, underscored by the repeated "ou" and commanding the reader's attention because they precede the main verb, suggest in turn her deceptiveness, her cruelty (implied in the long test), her fickleness, and her narcissism—all harmful to Elisor. The poor knight tries to judge from her "visage ne content ne courroucé" [neither content nor angered face] (a literal description of a poker face) what her heart contains, and alternately or simultaneously hopes and fears:

Elisor, regardant son visaige tant beau, et voyant qu'elle s'enqueroit de sa malladye, espera qu'elle y voulloit donner quelque remede. Mais, voyant sa contenance si grave et si saige qui l'interrogeoit, d'autre part tumboit en une craincte, pensant estre devant le juge dont il doubtoit sentence estre contre luy donnée.

[Elisor, looking at her very beautiful face, and seeing that she was asking him about his malady, hoped that she wished to bring him some remedy. But, seeing the serious and virtuous countenance that was interrogating him, on the other hand fell to fearing, thinking that he stood before the judge from whom he was afraid a sentence would be given against him.]

For the queen dwells on her need for proof by experience as a confirmation of speech, in a passage in which the predominant terms are *test, say, proof, to swear,* and *to know.* She now discounts speaking and forces action:

Vous, qui avez passé sept ans en cest amour, sçavez bien que m'aymez; mais, quant j'auray faict ceste experience sept ans durans, je sçauray à l'heure et croiray ce que vostre parolle ne me peult faire croyre ne entendre.

[You, having spent seven years in this love, well know that you love me, but when I have made this test for the space of seven years, at that hour I will know and will believe what your speech cannot make me believe or understand.]

Although this evolution is an abusive perversion of the rules of the game, Elisor, "esperant que la preuve parleroit mieulx pour luy que sa parolle, accepta son commandement" [hoping that the proof would speak better for him than his speech, accepted her command]. A ring is diverted from its customary significance; broken in two, it symbolizes separation more than alliance or even potential reunion, and it is the queen's only reply to Elisor's hope that after seven years she will recognize him "plus fidelle et loyal serviteur" [the most faithful and loyal admirer]. Taking leave of the queen, Elisor is "plus mort que ceulx qui ont rendu l'ame" [more dead than those who have given up the ghost].

When the test is over, Elisor returns his half of the ring with a long letter in verse. The intervening years have, in one sentence, been assigned to the unknowable and hence untellable: "De la vie qu'il mena durant ce temps et de l'ennuy qu'il porta pour ceste absence, ne s'en peut rien sçavoir, mais ceulx qui ayment ne le peuvent ignorer" [Of the life that he led during this time and the suffering he endured because of this absence, we can know nothing, but those who are in love cannot be ignorant of it]. The litotes addressed to those who know worldly love richly suffices.

For this second focus of the ellipse, the staging, or *mise en scène,* appropriately signifies the change we are about to witness: instead of the courtly hunt, we are now in church hearing mass, during which the queen normally accepts written requests from all and sundry. The hermit—none other than Elisor—who approaches her, kisses her hand, and presents his letter wears an accoutrement in which a now unremarkable covering, a large beard, supplants the erstwhile courtly splendor of the knight and indexes his new life as a saintly hermit. There is no chance that this completely unreflective covering will remove itself from Elisor's countenance, nor that it will "make one see" any object of love hidden in the heart. His new moral is to keep his heart hidden, and there is no naughty Eros wanting to go naked. The epistle itself now plays the part of the mirror earlier, a supplement for speaking. The substance of its message is that the latter seven years are unlike the former seven years, which were characterized by constancy and fidelity, while the sixty-eight lines of the text remain as the written sign of this change wrought by time. Artfully contrasting the time during which Elisor kept his love silent in his heart to the time of his forced silence and travail, exploiting the parallel the queen had already established, Elisor relates the two times to two loves, the profane and the sacred, revealing the emptiness of the profane love. In the condensed semantics of poetic language, the epistle reprises the themes of harm and profit. Time allowed Elisor to see that he loved the queen because of her beauty, under which her cruelty lay hidden, and that beauty is nothing, "Et cruaulté cause de tout mon bien" [And cruelty cause of all my good]. Regretting the first seven years given to the deceptive love for the queen, the harm, he has now come to know "true love," his profit, to which he now makes his entire sacrifice. Profane love he abandons altogether to the queen. The ending realizes a variant on the topos "to prefer to die" rather than speak, for Elisor prefers to "mourir au monde" [die to the world] rather than be present before the queen.

In addition to the realization that profane love is a waste of time, Dagoucin (and Marguerite) would have the audience (and the reader) understand that Elisor is also a bad merchant in that he did not recognize a good deal when the queen sent him away; he was a bad merchant when he failed to see that he was buying his sacred life cheaply, an interpretation supported by a quotation in Huguet's dictionary illustrating "mauvais marchand": "If such duchies and lordships could be acquired by purchase, it would be a very bad merchant who would refuse to buy any, at the price the conquest of them has cost."[10] This, then, would be the final sense of Dagoucin's ambiguous idiom. Meanwhile, though Elisor is beyond accounting in this world, the queen is "la plus pauvre et miserable dame du monde" [the poorest and the most impoverished lady in the world], in which both adjectives remind us of their economic meaning doubling the emotional. Neither treasure nor kingdom would buy back what she has lost, bizarrely fulfilling the very terms Elisor had ineptly bargained with: "vous avez *moins de* serviteurs, en *perdant* le meilleur et le plus affectionné que vous eustes oncques ny pourriez jamais *avoir*" [you have *fewer* admirers, by *losing* the best and the most affectionate that you ever had nor will ever *have* one day] (emphasis added).

The verse epistle, second focus of the ellipse, replaces speaking as presence; indeed, the episode concerns a dialectic of presence and absence. Though momentarily present in the church, Elisor is not present as a lover and does not make himself be seen; there is no "make oneself be seen." Quite to the contrary, he disappears so entirely that "il ne fut possible d'en sçavoir nouvelles" [it was not possible to find out anything about him]. Instead of the earlier encounters, which put into dynamic play the opposition of speaking to silence or censure, the verse epistle stands in lieu of oral exchange. It closes on the exact contrary to that "commerce"—"seeing her and having her good graces"—the knight had sought to keep: "Sans nul espoir . . . / Que je vous voye ne que plus me voyez" [With no hope . . . / That I may see you nor you see me again]. A new third term, writing, transcends silence by avoiding the opposition between presence and absence. Its role as a replacement to speaking is announced near the middle of the poem: "Je n'ay eu desir de ce retour / Fors seullement pour vous dire en ce lieu / Non ung bonjour, mais un parfaict adieu" [I desired this return / Only to say to you in this place / Not a hello, but a perfect goodbye]. The "adieu" is performed just before the end: "Je ne puis mieulx dire adieu à tous maulx / . . . / Qu'en ung seul mot vous dire: *Adieu, madame!*" [I can no better say "adieu" to all evils / . . . / Than by saying a single word to you: *Adieu, madame!*]. This "adieu" summarizes multiple leave-takings in the previous approximately twenty lines. Accepting the life given by true, sacred love, it abandons the death-giving love of the queen: "Je le vous quicte et rendz du tout entier" [I abandon it and give it back to you in its entirety]. We recognize in these performatives both a substitute for speech, which is lacking, and an actualization or enhancement of it: a supplement and an actualization of writing realism.

What is more artful, what more rhetorical, than a poem, and what more *evident* rhetoric than a verse epistle when a piece of plain prose letter writing would have served just as well? Dagoucin has "translated" it in spite of the superiority of Castillian in expressing love: "Et, si n'estoit le desir que j'ay de la vous faire entendre, je ne l'eusse jamais osé traduire, vous priant de penser, mes dames, que le langage castillan est sans comparaison mieulx declarant ceste passion que ung autre" [And, if I were not so eager to make you understand it, I would never have dared to translate it, begging you to believe, ladies, that the Castillian language is without comparison better at declaring this passion than any other language]. The putative translation forces our attention onto the poem as written object, alerted as we are by the preterition of Dagoucin's disclaimer, "la *substance* en est telle" [such is its *substance*] (emphasis added). Chief among its many rhetorical devices are figures of repetition, and especially the repetition of "le temps m'a fait voir" [time has made me see], with several expansions.[11] Thanks to time (which the queen gave him, amply), he has come to see "amour pauvre et nud" [love poor and naked]—an ironic reversal of the erotic value associated with nakedness since the introductory moral; thanks to time he has seen "l'amour d'en hault" [love from above]; time has allowed love from above to conquer impoverished worldly love. In spite of the fact that the prologue to the *Heptaméron* had established a generalized suspicion of professional writing, this writing achieves, via its performative rhetoric, what neither speech nor silence would approach and does so by avoiding the presence/absence dialectic. That is also Dagoucin's purpose in telling this tale: his hoped-for profit.

Dagoucin II

Elisor is Dagoucin's double. Dagoucin shares Elisor's virtues and philosophy of love, which are expounded in other parts of the frame story. La Garanderie writes that "Dagoucin projects himself into his masculine character, especially into Elisor" (31); and one can fruitfully compare Elisor's expression of love with Dagoucin's. Was he not the proponent of silence and *covered* love?

Si j'ay aymé . . . j'ayme encores, et aymeray tant que vivray. Mais j'ay si grand paour que la demonstration face tort à la perfection de mon amour, que je crainctz que celle de qui je debvrois desirer l'amityé semblable, l'entende; et mesmes je n'ose penser ma pensée, de paour que mes œilz en revelent quelque chose; car, tant plus je tiens ce feu celé et couvert, et plus en moy croist le plaisir de sçavoir que j'ayme parfaictement. (48)

[If I have loved . . . I still love, and will love as long as I live. But I am so afraid that the demonstration will damage the perfection of my love, that I am fearful lest the person from whom I ought to desire a similar affection hear it; in fact I do not dare to think my thoughts, for fear that my eyes will reveal something of them, for the more I keep this fire hidden and covered, all the more does the pleasure of knowing that I love perfectly grow in me.]

So speaks Dagoucin in comments on the eighth tale, defending Platonic love against a generalized attack by the other men. This earlier expression of his philosophy comes to concrete realization in the figure of Elisor. While Elisor tells the queen "he would prefer to die than to have to confess to her" (194), Dagoucin commenting on the nineteenth tale had said,

Il y en a qui ayment si fort et si parfaictement, qu'ilz aymeroient autant mourir que de sentir ung desir contre l'honneur et la conscience de leur maistresse, et si ne veullent qu'elle ne autres s'en apperçoyvent. (152)

[There are those who love so strongly and so perfectly that they would prefer to die than to feel a desire contrary to the honor and the conscience of their mistress, and even so they do not want her or others to notice it.]

Earlier, Parlamente had warned him to watch out for himself, "car j'en ay veu d'aultres que vous, qui ont mieulx aymé mourir que parler" [for I have seen others besides you, who would prefer to die rather than talk] (48).[12] According to a long tradition that lasted well beyond the sixteenth century, the censured speech of a courtly lover symbolizes the confession of his love. Yet Dagoucin might have wished to pronounce Elisor's marvelously complex sentence found in the conversation at the center of the ellipse:

Et si ne suis digne de vous regarder ny estre accepté pour serviteur, au moins souffrez que je vive, comme j'ay accoustumé, du contentement que j'ay, dont mon cueur a osé choisir pour le fondement de son amour ung si parfaict et digne lieu, duquel je ne puis avoir autre satisfaction que de sçavoir que mon amour est si grande et parfaicte, que je me doibve contanter d'aymer seullement, combien que jamais je ne puisse estre aymé.

[And if I am not worthy of looking at you or being accepted as a suitor, at least suffer me to live, as I am accustomed, from the contentment that I have, for which my heart has dared to choose for the basis of its love a place so perfect and worthy, whence I can have no other satisfaction than to know that my love is so great and perfect, that I must be content to love only, to the extent that I can never be loved.]

We may be struck by the two verbs in "my heart has dared" and "I can" in the negative, verbs that marked the limits of Dagoucin's speaking: "Since I cannot and dare not . . . say what I think." The tale, an explicit supplement for Dagoucin's censured commentary, reflects his idealistic, reverential love, no doubt for Parlamente. As Françoise Charpentier reminds us, "the stories exchanged, . . . sometimes alluding to situations the narrators have lived, can themselves be messages they address to each other, precise messages directed toward a particular man or woman, beyond the generality of their address."[13] But just as an ellipse, by definition, falls short of a parabola, so Dagoucin's elliptical tale risks being defective as parable. Parlamente, unlike the queen of Castille, will have to be a very good reader, in order to "hear" the "demonstration" of his love.

Dagoucin's self-censured opinion arose when he listened to the twenty-third tale. That story concerns a bad monk, while the twenty-fourth castigates a cruel woman. In redressing the balance, Dagoucin has told an opposite tale to the twenty-third (and, what is more, a precise counterexample to the topic of the day: "on devise des dames qui en leur amytié n'ont cerché nulle fin que l'honnesteté, et de l'hypocrisye et mechanceté des religieux" [we are speaking about women who in matters of love have sought no other goal than honesty, and about the hypocrisy and evil of monks] [157]). One might consider his narrative an inverse reflection on the previous tale. If the cruel, frivolous, and narcissistic queen of Castille is an exaggerated portrait of a certain queen of Navarre, at a certain ethical and geographical remove—a doubly mediated and displaced self-portrait—Elisor's trajectory suggests a future course for Dagoucin, an evolution that would hardly be surprising for a Neoplatonist and for the man of religion that Dagoucin probably is. Not wishing to become a "bad merchant," Dagoucin threatens, like Elisor, to seek his profit in the spiritual world as a *good* monk, if the "queen" of the narrative circle continues to be cruel. Many have said that the *Heptaméron* illustrates the difficulty of realizing perfect love. Dagoucin's tale suggests that abusing the idealism of the admirer-lady model might well bring harm and then, paradoxically and on a completely different plane, profit to its hero and to its narrator.

In sum, Dagoucin like Elisor resorts to a third term, telling a tale, but like Elisor's mirror it fails to "speak" for him. The long discussion following his tale is a welter of diverse opinions and suggestive speculations, in which Dagoucin is misunderstood. The message does not "take"; it does not replace his censured thought. Meaning is suspended, proof is yet to come; it is as if the story of Dagoucin's love is also an ellipse, whose second focus is lacking—a parabola, then, in the double meaning of the French word *parabole*. The very necessity of keeping the word going—the structure of Marguerite's writing that I described in the opening paragraphs—causes the lack of resolution of Dagoucin's story in the frame dialogue or narrative. Though a finished *Heptaméron* might have brought a resolution, it is also the nature of Platonic love not to conclude. (Aristocratic storytellers of the seventeenth and eighteenth centuries resorted to the metaphor *conclusion du récit* when they wished to refer politely to that most untellable of real events, sexual union.) Hence the need to tell the tale as a replacement, and its inevitably supplementary nature, which invites further supplements: our reading, wherein we might find an avenue to understanding.

Parlamente

The twenty-fourth tale also has a supplement in the sixty-fourth (383–87), which Parlamente narrates. This narrative of courtly love resembles the story of Elisor and the queen of Castille in many particulars. A demoiselle from Valencia refuses a man to whom she has been promised, after he has sustained honorable love and devotion for five or six years. She is silent on her reasons, though Parlamente offers two possibilities: "mais elle, ou cuydant trouver mieulx, ou voulant dissimuler l'amour qu'elle luy avoit portée, trouva quelque difficulté" [but she, either thinking to find better, or wanting to dissimulate the love she had felt for him, made some difficulty]. For sorrow, the nobleman puts his affairs in order and retreats to a solitary place to forget her and convert his love into a love of God. As time passes with no sign from the woman, he chooses the most disagreeable life he can imagine, that of a monk. Thereupon she, protesting she had not intended to reject him altogether, but merely to "experimenter sa bonne volunté" [test his goodwill] like the queen of Castille, writes him a letter in verse. The epistle mentions her desire to judge his love "by the passage of time" and assures him of her continuing love in spite of the passing time. Regret prompts her to break her silence. He writes no reply, but rejects her in a pointed speech made to the messenger, bearer of the epistle, reported in indirect discourse. Begging her to be content with the cruelty she has already shown him, he asks her to leave him alone, "qu'il n'eust jamais nouvelle d'elle, car la memoire de son nom seullement luy estoit ung importable [insupportable] purgatoire" [that he never hear from her, for the memory of her name alone was an insupportable purgatory to him]. He mentions that mortifying his passion has cost him so dearly that he no longer fears death. Not satisfied with this, and thinking that "la veue et la parolle auroient plus de force que n'avoit eu l'escripture" [sight and speech would have more strength than writing had had], the way the queen of Castille had demanded proof by action rather than words, she encounters him in a chapel of his cloister. From this "plus forte bataille où jamais avoit esté" [hardest battle he had ever fought], a battle with Love, the hard archer, he barely escapes with his saintly life. As Robert D. Cottrell has said, "human love, which in the *Heptameron* is articulated most often in the syntax of sexual desire, is an obstacle that must be annihilated before the Christian can arrive at Christ."[14] Once in the safety of his cell, he offers "some resolution" to their trying tale with two lines of verse in Spanish, which Parlamente does not translate, finding them "of such good substance" that she wishes to avoid diminishing their grace. Thereupon the tale ends with the woman's chagrin and sorrow.

Now, let us not accept any notion that the well was running dry, and that Marguerite found no better inspiration for her narrators than her own tales. Let us instead ask what renewed reflection these (re)writings cast on the entire work.

While some of the themes in the woman's verse epistle repeat those in Elisor's, it is not a supplement or third term; its rhetoric is not performative but exhortatory, dominated by second-person imperatives: "Laisse le gris et son austerité; / Viens recepvoir cette felicité / . . . / Retourne doncq et veulle t'amye croire, / . . . / Viens doncques, amy, prendre ce qui est tien: / Je suis à toy, sois doncques du tout mien" [Give up the gray and its austerity; / Come receive this felicity / . . . /Come back, then, and do believe your lover, / . . . / Come, then, lover, take what is yours: / I am yours, be then all mine]. She realizes that this very direct language belongs to a man's role; it is an "office . . . dont as usé sans vice" [office . . . that you used without vice]. This is the language she now adopts to request his love as he had requested hers—again, exactly the opposite of Elisor's keeping silent and opposite also to the queen of Castille's round-about "feminine" questioning. This taking of the man's word is a striking reversal of gender roles, a key marker of the supplementary relation between the twenty-fourth and the sixty-fourth tales. The structure that puts into play a woman writing in a man's place constitutes a *mise en abyme* of the passing of the voice between a male and a female narrator, the basic structure of the *Heptaméron* in which voice giving is symbolic of the heterosexual ordering of the world. Just as the demoiselle *takes* the word *of* man *from* a man and uses it in the manner of a man, so Parlamente has adopted the language Dagoucin used earlier to communicate his thought, by telling her story via an inserted text as he did. The speech she borrows, a man's "office," is taken from Dagoucin's unspoken declarations; her female speaker actualizes the male speech censored in courtly language. It is as if Parlamente has chosen to illustrate a different possibility of discourse about love, as if to test the results that might come from a masculine speech. At the same time, this move represents Marguerite taking a narrator's or writer's or man's role.

The demoiselle's letter fails to convince. The rhetoric of her lover's refusal, in Spanish, is metaphorical, and its plural ambiguities virtually escape translation: "Volvete don venesti, anima mia, / Que en las tristas vidas es la mia."[15] "Return whence you came, my soul," says the first line, apparently telling the woman to return home, but the syntax of the second is elliptical, starting with the semantically vague connector "que." The double meaning of "anima mia" indexes a conflation of worldly and spiritual love. Though we may translate the second line: "For among the sad lives is mine," we may also understand "la mia" as referring to my soul, giving something like: "For my soul dwells among sad lives." The conventional metaphorical expression for one's mistress, "anima mia," thus becomes literal, as the man's verse addresses his soul and urges it to return whence it came, that is, to God; this, then, is the sense of "anima mia" that prevails. The rhetorical figure thus contains within itself the nobleman's evolution from bodily to spiritual love. Interestingly, it is this writing that possesses power and efficiency in the plot, rather than the woman's imperative, manlike epistle, for it finally persuades her, as the text says laconically, "en voiant l'escripture . . . que toute esperance luy estoit faillye" [seeing the writing . . . that all hope was lost]. The tale rapidly closes four lines after the Spanish couplet. The only explanation for this sudden closure, for this definitive failure of amorous desire, is that the woman reads the spiritual sense of "anima mia" and recognizes the superior power of the love that Elisor had called "love from above."

The story is considerably shorter than the twenty-fourth, and other aspects of its rhetoric similarly convey a sense of haste to arrive at the point or the ending. By comparison, the twenty-fourth proceeds with a certain leisure and amplitude. In introducing the verse epistle, for instance, Parlamente simply echoes in two words—"badly translated"—Dagoucin's gracious sentence of apology and disclaimer for translating Elisor's epistle from the Spanish. The nobleman's speech in indirect discourse vigorously and pointedly refuses the woman's exhortatory letter, in comparison to Elisor's flowery, complex, encumbered syntax, in the long discourse that breaks his courtly silence. Only the scene in the chapel of the cloister seems to offer the possibility of an expressiveness, a fullness of speaking that would reverse the silences and refusals of the story until then and make a happy ending in the worldly sense possible; this scene dwells on the power of such love. The primary emotion is pity—for the nobleman. In hastily escaping, and scribbling what Parlamente calls "three words in Spanish," the nobleman definitively and decisively turns toward the spiritual sense.

At the point where Parlamente takes Dagoucin's place as storyteller, she introduces the tale by chastising in advance women who, like the queen of Castille in the earlier tale, would refuse someone without taking a second look; and she admonishes them to attend to the mutations of time and so give order to the future: "Par ce compte, dist Parlamente, mes dames, vous regarderez deux fois ce que vous vouldrez refuser, et ne vous fier au temps present, qu'il soit tousjours ung; parquoy, congnoissans sa mutation, donnerez ordre à l'advenir" ["By this tale, ladies," said Parlamente, "you will look twice at what you are thinking of refusing, and do not trust in the present time to be always of a piece; for the which, when you know its mutability, you will give order to the future"]. Just as it points to a time not yet available to our understanding, this introductory moral leaves the point of Parlamente's tale in a state of suspension, announcing only that "time" and "order" are the terms of its philosophy. To the reader falls the task of interpreting that philosophy.

Is this tale Parlamente's reply to Dagoucin, at long last? It is as if the considerable similarity of the two stories has no other purpose than to alert their hearers to the relations between the narrators, relations founded on a similarity of their opinions on spiritual love. Is she not saying, as it were, "I hear your complaint, and I sympathize"? Dagoucin may hear Parlamente speaking in the demoiselle's epistle, when she tells him, in so many words, that he has passed the test: "Or ay-je faict de toy l'experience: / Ta fermeté, ta foy, ta patience / Et ton amour, sont cogneuz clairement, / Qui m'ont acquise à toy entierement" [Now my testing of you is complete: / Your constancy, your faith, your patience / And your love are clearly known, / Which have won me to you entirely]. It is interesting, in this regard, to observe how the story comes to be told, when Dagoucin asks Parlamente to take his place. The artful sentence by which Parlamente first alludes to her story, and by which Marguerite ensures the seamless transmission of the voice, contains a metaphorical announcement of her purpose and instantly prompts Dagoucin to beg her to tell it: when Geburon has protested that if a woman were to make him endure suffering for her, he would demand "great recompense" or withdraw his love, Parlamente ripostes: "Vous vouldriez doncques . . . avoir vostre heure, après que vostre dame auroit eu la sienne, comme feit ung gentil homme d'auprès de Valence" [You would therefore . . . want to have your hour, after your lady will have had hers, as did a nobleman from near Valencia] (382). Given the role of time in both Dagoucin's and Parlamente's narratives, and given the evolution of both heroes into saintly characters, we can interpret "to have your hour" for the *man* only in the saintly sense; a turn toward higher love is the proper response to the woman who refuses a man while thinking to find better or pretending to dissimulate her interest. As for the woman, her "hour" would result in her failure to take a second look and to give order to the future because of misplaced trust in the mutable present, the error Parlamente's tale illustrates and castigates. "Order," then, points to the life of the soul, which follows the life of the body.

It is on that plane that Parlamente offers to meet Dagoucin, giving him his "hour" after taking hers. Her tale then completes and takes the place of his, supplementing it, for in the dialogue following, in which sexual love furnishes the terrain for more verbal sparring between the sexes, Dagoucin's silence is eloquent. Once again, like the supplements that replace silence and/or speaking, the narrated tale takes the part of speaking. If we accept that Dagoucin is as good a reader as he had hoped Parlamente was, this unspoken message now closes the loop of communication opened by the twenty-fourth tale.

The Prologue

If diversity of opinion characterizes the dialogues of the *devisants,* the very basis of their storytelling lies in the resolution of conflict. The first "diverse opinions" in the work are found in the Prologue and concern the best way to get out of Cauterets; they result in the French being separated from one another. The object of dispute is the address of the routes (1), the variety of routes that are soon to become metaphors for the diverse opinions the assembled characters will express about how to spend the time in the abbey. Conforming to their respective personalities, Oisille and Hircan propose two known routes to pastime, Bible reading and bodily exercise, at opposite ends of a spectrum. By contrast, Parlamente seeks a "new road," like those that have united the ten privileged men and women in Serrance. The storytelling she proposes strikes a happy medium between these familiar activities and is designed to serve and satisfy all present, not just one or two, and so Parlamente's third term achieves consensus. It reduces the incipient conflict between the spiritual and the corporal; it proposes a mediating activity, conveying truths in a semiotic form we recognize as fiction; and it is itself mediated by its relation to other storytelling activities of note. I am of course speaking of the *Decameron* and the peculiar proto-narrative by which it enters Parlamente's proposal and Marguerite's prologue.

The "hundred tales by Boccaccio" might have furnished a well-known "address of the routes" or a familiar pastime, but what Parlamente proposes is new in a particular way. She makes her suggestion by recounting how notables at the French court intended to write their own *Decameron,* only to be prevented by several important matters (9). Even in this unrealized project, the French had taken their distance from Boccaccio, in one crucial respect: "c'est de n'escripre nulle nouvelle qui ne soit veritable histoire" [that is to write no tale that is not a true story] (9). Putting into play the pinnacle of French nobility for which many readers see the Serrance circle as a stand-in, Parlamente's little account of the French court is identical in its features to the type of tale that will fill the days of the *Heptaméron*. Its characters are real people (François I, Henri, Catherine de Médicis, Marguerite de Navarre) and the story is true, but it is taken in charge by a fiction.[16] Its narrator, a fictive creation, claims to have been a witness to the conversation she reports.

The delightful twist is that the fictive Parlamente places herself into the story on a par with Marguerite: "Et, à l'heure, j'oy les deux dames dessus nommées, avecq plusieurs autres de la cour, qui se delibererent d'en faire autant [que Bocace]" [And at that time I heard the two women named above, with several others of the court, deliberating about doing the same [as Boccaccio]] (9). While Marguerite gives voice to Parlamente, Parlamente here gives speech to Marguerite. When incest bears offspring, the relationships become double. In our interpretive shorthand, we are accustomed to describing this "incestuous" situation by saying that Parlamente is the representation and *porte-parole* of Marguerite de Navarre; Parlamente's speaking is a covering for Marguerite's, a fiction told to hide and reveal a fragment of autobiography.[17] But our shorthand covers a situation of greater complexity. Why not say that Marguerite is the *porte-parole* of Parlamente, that Marguerite speaks for Parlamente? Her speaking not only validates the truth of Parlamente's little fictive narrative, it also takes the precise form of a promise to tell ten true stories each and to assemble seven other people to tell as many. The allusions to historical events of moment that intervene to prevent the realization of this promise only add to the truth that Marguerite's voice lends to Parlamente's. It is she who has Marguerite say here what she would like to say, thus protecting herself, Parlamente, from potential censure.

The ending of this proto-narrative foretells what presumably would have been the ending of the *Heptaméron* had it realized its ambition: a gift of the one hundred *written* stories to Marguerite de Navarre and her circle "en lieu d'ymaiges ou de patenostres" [instead of pictures and paternosters] (10).[18] Thus the circuit of voices arising in a narrated Marguerite would have ended in her as well.

This narrative has naturally been read as Marguerite's devious expression of her debt to Boccaccio and her simultaneous assertion of a conspicuous difference from him (an anxiety of influence): the affirmation of a purely French tradition exemplified, for instance, in Philippe de Vigneulles. Her professed distance from her Italian model, however, is cleverly inscribed not just in these assertions but also in the very structure by which it enters her text, for the project Parlamente now proposes to the group at Serrance is a replacement for the promised but unrealized project, the imitation-with-a-difference of the *Decameron*. It is a replacement for a replacement. Had Parlamente simply proposed that the group write a Decameron, Marguerite and the French court would have had no voice in her speaking. The narratives that follow the prologue replace a text that does not exist except as a voice, a promise. Like Elisor's mirror and epistle, like Dagoucin's tale, the realization of Parlamente's proposal is a supplement, both added to and substituting for a lack or a mere promise of speaking. Protected from censure by Marguerite, Parlamente's proposed supplement is a self-defense analogous to Elisor's and Dagoucin's. It is a supplement to speaking and censure.

Writing Fiction

The actions and themes of the twenty-fourth tale are emblems for the themes of the *Heptaméron* not only as a compendium of ideas about love but also as a *narrative object*. In the Prologue and throughout the work, a fictive narrator tells a true story—that is the claim. However, we cannot objectively assess the claim to truth. We cannot know, for instance, if the small scene at court recounted in a sketch of a narrative actually took place, somewhere and sometime in history. The story is true just as the *Heptaméron*'s tales are true: because the narrators say they are. Thus the stories told in the *Heptaméron* are not real (because they are stories, not events), but they are true (as claimed, and sometimes verified). The stories are not false (because they plausibly mimic reality), but they are fictive (taken in charge by imagined narrators). The elliptical forms, the third terms, the supplements, or what we may call "not silence," are versions of fiction.

The rhetorical form of the tales is heavily marked by both a native tradition and a celebrated, authoritative model. While the historical bridge to the *Decameron* is rhetorically broken by the proto-narrative claiming a conspicuous difference, the literally broken bridge symbolizes the missing link that induces narration. The activity of telling tales becomes a place-holder for time itself;

the break marks a void that narrating fills, in a system separate from but parallel to rhetoric.[19] A rhetorical ellipsis omits something, but leaves a place-holder to mark that feigned absence, to which it draws attention. No less does fiction: it is fictive and hence not real, but it marks the place where truth goes; it supplements truth. It is the third term to both dialectics of presence/absence, speaking/silence. As Barthes has said, "I think the word 'fiction' is the term that constitutes the avoidance of the true/false paradigm. It is a third term: a drifting term, an unheard-of term, a term that undoes a paradigm."[20]

Fiction both replaces a lacking truth and augments it. We readily and naïvely believe the stories are true to the extent that, unlike the queen of Castille, we agree to glance into the mirror and see our own reflections there, when we take Elisor's risk and uncover the word hidden in the heart. Gisèle Mathieu-Castellani draws a significant distinction between the two roles taken by the ten men and women: as tale-tellers and as commentators. She places the *devisants* as narrators squarely in the mimetic camp (telling stories that imitate reality), but as skeptic commentators their suspicions about the stories indicate their refusal of mimesis: "The narrators still need to believe and to make others believe, they require innocent or guilty, vicious or virtuous heroes; the *devisants* [commentators] can no longer believe."[21] Readers in the *Heptaméron's* "era of suspicion" lift the covers and interrogate zones of indecision. Like the *devisants,* we see beyond mimetic illusions when we understand the logic of the supplement and its ability to suspend the dialectics of presence/absence and speaking/silence. Neither the verse epistle nor Dagoucin's tale nor the *Heptaméron* can fail as third terms when the readers addressed exercise their interpretive ingenuity. Fiction awakens such ingenuity best when it proclaims its fictive quality and simultaneously claims to tell the truth. The defects in Dagoucin's narrative—the lapses of omniscience; the places where the narrative voice drifts; its limping, scandalous inconsistencies and perversions—open the door for Parlamente's interpretation, just as the limpings of the conversations that follow provoke a flood of commentary by external readers. Recall the completely arbitrary inclusion of the "Love, covered by necessity" on Elisor's hat, like and unlike the mirror covering the "stomach," a Freudian slip, a talisman protecting its wearer, an adumbration of the hermit's covering and a blatant deconstruction of the mirror's function. According to Mathieu-Castellani, the work as a whole obliquely designates the moment of modern discourse "where the coherence of the logos explodes . . . and where the text becomes, if not illegible, at least differently and contradictorily legible, escaping the grip of a univocal commentary" ("L'Ère du soupçon," 134). The writing calls attention to such effects of the word, prompting a reading like the one Elisor's epistle calls for: by a chastened queen. As Dubois writes, in a stimulating article, "the Word . . . has meaning and a reason for being only if the word is then used to express what the 'Heart' contains."[22] Fiction can not only pretend to imitate reality, it can also narrate a truth, as Elisor hopes the queen will see in spite of his nonpresence, as Dagoucin suggests to Parlamente without daring to speak his mind, as Marguerite proves to her reader in her writing.

The problem is that the term *fiction* had a morally negative connotation for Marguerite de Navarre, and thus her writing faces the risk of being condemned (hence, of course, her rejection of rhetoric and professional writers and the claim to tell only "true" stories). Fiction, meaning hypocrisy, lie, feint, deception, or dissimulation, is glossed in the work by the general and widespread topos that we may call the cruelty of women; an excellent example is found in the important dialogue following the forty-second tale, in which hypocrisy and fiction are renamed "honor" by women who need to dissimulate either their love or their absence of love (294–95). Women need such a covering, or feigned refusal of love, as the female *devisants* passionately and I think successfully argue, but it does constitute a threat to honesty. Speaking may break the code of a woman's honor, but feint and dissimulation are dishonest. Oisille is sternest in nudging the party toward the difficult sustaining of both honesty (a rejection of hypocrisy and dissimulation) and a decent covering; that the struggle is partly won is rendered by the double meaning of "honnêteté," honesty and honor.

Like the feints of honorable women, and like the queen of Castille's devious tactics, it is true fiction's role to cover something we may call (I hope without too much anachronistic distortion) *free speech*, loosely rendering "parler franchement" in contrast to "dissimuler," dissimulate, an opposition found in the debate on the fifty-third tale: "Je vous prie, mes dames, juger s'il n'eut pas mieulx vallu à ceste pauvre dame d'avoir *parlé franchement* à [luy] que de le mectre par *dissimullation* jusques à faire une preuve qui luy fut si honteuse!" [I beg of you, ladies, to judge if it would not have been better for this poor woman to have *spoken frankly* to [him] than to have by *dissimulation* pushed him so far as to offer a proof that was so shameful to him!] (340; emphasis added). Dagoucin's narration does as much to hide as to uncover his thought. According to a tenacious view of the Renaissance engagement with language, which sees writing as a veil covering the "living word," writing is on the side of dissimulation: it hides free speech (see, for instance, Delègue, 271). Simulating a lively oral scene goes only part way toward rescuing the "parler franchement." While Marguerite as author produces a spoken *parole* in an extended written text, the *devisants,* as authors, produce a written word inserted into an extended oral dialogue, for theirs is, as Delègue writes, a "faux narré" [false narrative] (276). To turn harm to profit, to rescue speech from dissimulation, to uncover the thought hidden in the heart, the text makes the reader attentive to its supplementary writing.

I think it does so through resemblance. Whereas speaking engages the symbolic system of language, the third terms depend on and engage resemblance and analogy. Clearly, Elisor's mirror conveys its message by resemblance, not by a symbolic sign; the epistle reprises the "make one see" of the mirror, but in reverse. Dagoucin's resemblance to a courtier who loves highly uncovers his emotion. And resemblance between the *devisants* and members of the French court broadly characterizes the frame narrative, while the proto-narrative of the Prologue resembles the prototype of the stories they will tell. The logic of supplementarity also governs the relations among the three layers of narrated events and the three principal actors in the events told. Elisor stands in for Dagoucin, whose speaking supplements Marguerite's; Marguerite's text seduces via these supplements. Like Elisor and Dagoucin, Marguerite functions in the mode of the "make one see," using the global structure of the work to show rather than tell her meanings, her views on love. The covered word, the heart of the *Heptaméron,* wants to go uncovered, but in uncovering lies danger. Resemblance guides the reader out of harm—the risk of speaking and of being a poor negotiator—toward profit.

I have said the twenty-fourth tale resembles an ellipse. According to the properties of the ellipse, light or sound waves emanating from one focus arrive at the other, bounced off the boundary in any direction. Writing—in the epistle, in Dagoucin's tale, in Marguerite's *Heptaméron*—has all the properties of Elisor's mirror. The function of its surface is to show depth; its countenance hides and reveals its heart—a fair description of rhetoric.[23] Its "faire semblant," or pretense, can make one see, as Marguerite de Navarre well knows. Writing is the medium of the third term; it avoids censure, escapes the contradiction between speaking and silence, covers the seat of the passions, and allows a glance into the thought behind the surface of the stomach. Colette Winn and Philippe de Lajarte have admirably described how the *Heptaméron* forces our attention to the surface features, to the producing act, to the enunciation and the semiosis: the process of making meaning.[24] These semiotic features include, I would add, the way the stories are written into the frame narrative and their link to "sources" or "origins" rejected as such, that is, to a frame outside the text. And perhaps our devious attention to the moments of seamless articulation, the giving of voice, takes us to the essence of the *Heptaméron* after all. The passing of the voice covers the edges, the limits, the stopping points, marking moments of vulnerability. Both joint and suture, or seamless juncture, the passing of voice puts into question the status of the following tale: Is it a continuation of commentary, the opinion of the speaker, or a literary production worthy of an author? Oral expression dissimulates and reveals written text. Slipping in the new start, the gift of the voice strategically dissimulates the absence and presence of a final opinion, leaving a marker to show that something remains hidden and forcing the reader to interpret; saying and not saying, or saying *by* not saying, writing fiction ensures that there is no loss of speaking, no censure.

Finally, the *Heptaméron* is a specular fiction not because of its claim to tell true stories, not because the characters represent real people, not even because the work exemplifies "universal truths"—all of which some readers have proposed and others doubted—but because it reflects the real of writing in action. It tells us as much about semiosis as about mimesis. Mimesis, the illusion of reality, can either stem from a faithful, verifiable reflection of a reality that has taken place, possibly authenticated by historical readers, or allude to a nonverifiable reflection of a social or literary reality (traditions of courtly love, Neoplatonism, and so forth). To the extent that the *devisants* read Dagoucin's tale as representation, as product rather than producing, with inadequate attention to its semiosis, they would not see that writing occults the source of the tale in his love for Parlamente. Beyond resemblance to a real society, beyond reflections of social realities, the tales resemble not only the thought but also the process of writing, the dangerous supplement, by which thought comes to the reader. Dagoucin's profit does not lie merely in reflecting himself in Elisor; Parlamente must hear beyond the mimetic level, not only the "truthful" substance of the story, in the real world, but also its very act of production, its semiotic message. Her good reading depends on ours, in the world beyond the frame. When the queen of Castille gives not voice but silence to Elisor, in exchange for his taking voice to declare his love, it is a bad bargain, in the represented world (life on the earth, which tells a "true" story), but a good one on the metamimetic or semiotic plane, where the real is found. The chivalrous remains in the form of a mimetic reference, whereas the constant, repeated claim made in the name of experience (pretension to truth) opens the fault in which semiosis occurs, in which the reader sees the reality of the word in relation to experience. Like the queen's abusive evolution from an insistence on the word to an insistence on experience (experiment, proof), the entire *Heptaméron* revolves around a risky "nuysance," or harm—giving primacy to experience and represented truth—which the reader turns to profit by attending to semiosis. Having invented a structure to keep the word going, simultaneously recognizing the experience, the censure of the word, and the nature of the covering, Marguerite de Navarre gave such consistency to the project that the reader attentive to semiosis cannot but participate in it, finding profit like Elisor on a different plane. If all three stories of writing close in silence nevertheless, that is the destiny of writing. The ending of the *Heptaméron* may be missing, but its end resides in its readers, as long as we are not "bad merchants."

Three

Listen, Hear
Dialogues of the Deaf

Jacques the fatalist, lying with wounded knee on a poor peasant's bed, over-hears through a thin wall his host and hostess in amorous embrace, then in testy disagreement over the charity she has shown Jacques in spite of their poverty. All the more reason, protests the wife, not to produce a new child—and she is sure to become pregnant because "cela n'a jamais manqué quand l'oreille me démange après, et j'y sens une démangeaison comme jamais" [it has never failed when my ear itches afterwards, and I'm feeling an itch there like never before].[1] "Ton oreille ne sait ce qu'elle dit" [Your ear doesn't know what it's saying], says he, but in spite of his objection, the metaphor lending speech to the ear eroticizes it, as she fully realizes: "Ne me touche pas! Laisse là mon oreille!" [Don't touch me! Leave my ear alone!].

If, as the editors gravely note, the erotic connotations of the ear are a constant of libertine fictions, I think we have here one of the most inventive and beguiling versions of the sexual ear: sexual activity transported to the ear—not only to the woman's, but to Jacques's and ours. The language itself conveys, by its rhythms and its strategies, the action it purports to hide in words that go on "behind" the paper, just as Jacques lies on the other side of a wall of paper. For we can easily read in the text how the couple take their pleasure three times, in Jacques's hearing. The first has already happened during "une assez courte pause" [a rather short pause] (25), before the dispute.[2] The second (after a short moralizing digression whose purpose is to tease the reader) accompanies Jacques's cries of pain: "Je m'écriai: Ah! le genou!... Et le mari s'écria: Ah! ma femme!... Et la femme s'écria: Ah! mon homme!" [I cried out: "Oh! My knee!"... And the husband cried out: "Oh! My wife!"... And the wife cried out:

"Oh! My husband!"] (27)—in all, rather noisier than the first. The third occurs when the woman protests that her ear is worse than ever because "cet homme qui est là" [that man there] will have heard them: "Ah! L'oreille! Ah! L'oreille!" [Oh! My ear! Oh! My ear!] she cries, and her husband replies, again irrationally linking speech to the ear: "L'oreille, l'oreille, cela est bien aisé à dire" [Your ear, your ear, that's easy to say]. Here the writing still pretends to hide what is happening:

Je ne vous dirai point ce qui se passait entre eux, mais la femme après avoir répété l'oreille, l'oreille plusieurs fois de suite à voix basse et précipitée, finit par balbutier à syllabes interrompues l'or . . . eil . . . le, et à la suite de cette or . . . eil . . . le, je ne sais quoi qui joint au silence qui succéda, me fit imaginer que son mal d'oreille s'était appaisé d'une ou d'autre façon; il n'importe, cela me fit plaisir, et à elle donc? (27–28)

[I certainly won't tell you what was happening between them, but the wife, after having repeated my ear, my ear several times in a row in a low and precipitate voice, ended up stammering in broken syllables my . . . ea . . . er, and after this my . . . ea . . . er, I don't know what else, along with the silence that followed, that made me imagine that her earache had gotten better, one way or another; it doesn't matter how, it gave me pleasure, and how about her?]

We receive this mediated communication via Jacques's preterition ("I certainly won't tell you"; "I don't know what") and feigned indifference ("one way or another; it doesn't matter how"): we would not be in a position to overhear this couple making love without Jacques's voluntary or involuntary listening. With his help, we become auditory voyeurs, just as the husband and wife (as Diderot's rhetoric takes pains to suggest) are auditory exhibitionists, whose pleasure is augmented because somebody is listening. About auditory voyeurs, Barthes wrote: "One ought to be able to say *écouteur* for this, the way we say voyeur."[3] In Laclos's *Les Liaisons dangereuses* and Diderot's *La Religieuse,* the reader is placed, like Jacques, in the position of the auditory voyeur and gets pleasure and meaning from an indirect listening.

Diderot called the ear the proudest of the senses.[4] Listening and hearing are not identical, but complementary. Yet these two activities are often confused and hence the verbs misused—they are loosely taken as synonymous, and they are sometimes spoken interchangeably with no serious loss to understanding. For my purposes, however, it will be crucial to keep in mind that to listen is not always to hear, and that hearing does not necessarily imply listening. It would be a further mistake to assume that hearing is a passive activity, and that only listening is active; on the contrary, subjects who hear may define themselves as active, precisely because they hear, and the presumably active subject who listens may be doing so distractedly, not willfully. So much is fairly obvious and hardly needs defending. What does stand to be developed, however, is the interpretation we may give to this complementary relationship of listening to hearing as literary functions.

I have in mind a most unusual description of indirect listening, in which the duad listening/hearing reaches us via a charming comparison. Let us listen to Roland Barthes in a fragment called "Écoute" from his extended discourse on intertextuality, *Le Plaisir du texte:*

To be with the one I love and to think about something else: that is how I have my best ideas, how I best invent what I need for my work. Same for the text: it produces the best pleasure in me if it manages to make itself listened to indirectly; if, while reading it, I am often moved to look up, to hear something else. I am not necessarily *captivated* by the text of pleasure, it can be a slight, complex, tenuous, almost heedless action: a sudden movement of the head, like that of a bird who hears nothing of what we are listening to, who listens to what we do not hear or understand.[5]

The bird—the text—may be listening to something we are unable to hear: a text we do not know, for instance. But the text, on the other hand, cannot possibly hear everything we are listening to as we read; in reading, we listen to something the text does not hear or understand, perhaps a later text. I have claimed that the affirmations in this fragment of *Le Plaisir du texte* pose the conditions of intertextuality, for I consider this passage a compelling though idiosyncratic redefinition of the term.[6] With the indirection of rhetoric, a double mediation of reading pleasure through listening and the movement of the bird's head, Barthes *performs* the pleasure he describes; his definition is "almost heedless" and we are obliged to listen to it indirectly—perhaps incompletely, or even incorrectly. In just such a way does the text have intertexts to which we may not have access. At the same time, we bring our intertexts to the text, and the text cannot know of them—some of them.

Now what this has to do with how literary texts reach us in general lies in our acceptance of the generality of intertextuality (and thus, in part, the pertinence and usefulness of distinguishing this term from allusions, references, sources, and the many other narrower concepts or procedures that contribute to it). Intertextuality understood at its broadest concerns the very conditions of the existence of texts; all texts exist in the textual universe, to which they contribute stars and galaxies, and from which they draw their spatial and temporal definition. Texts are made of other texts, are themselves the "between-texts" of other texts. According to Barthes, the text is

woven entirely of quotations, references, echoes . . . which traverse it through and through in a vast stereophony. The intertextuality in which every text is taken up, since it is itself the between-text of another text, cannot be confused with any sort of origin of the text: to seek the "sources," the "influences" of a work is to gratify the myth of filiation; the quotations from which a text is made are anonymous, unidentifiable, and yet *already read*: they are quotations without quotation marks.[7]

Writing itself depends on and produces intertextuality. It follows that messages the text contains may or may not be heard. We can see that writing may seek to transmit a certain knowledge, but nothing ensures that the writing will be received with the same meaning. This risk is inherent in representational writing. When in *Les Liaisons dangereuses* the two libertines are in agreement, we also understand their designs: "au moins, je parle à quelqu'un qui m'entend" [at least I'm talking to someone who understands me], says the vicomte to the marquise (227, letter 100).[8] Later Valmont will object, "vous avez pris le parti de ne pas entendre" [you have decided not to understand] (343, letter 153); the war that separates them only confirms how ill-founded their "entente" was, and how much our own understanding depends on an uncertain mediation. *Entendre* and its variants, equally meaning hearing and understanding, are the terms in which this problematic is expressed.

This uncertain mediation of events by writing is the first focus of this chapter, beginning with the failure of writing to bring consolation in *Les Liaisons dangereuses*. The second focus concerns a complementary aspect of writing: the belief in writing's ability to effect a change in reality. Such is the belief of Suzanne Simonin in Diderot's *La Religieuse*. When letters are misaddressed, received by the wrong person, written by someone other than the subject who says "I," we may speak of dialogues of the deaf and the role of the accidental in the narrative plot. The reader's understanding, in *Les Liaisons dangereuses*, is mediated by this misunderstanding or *malentendu*, a word that we may read as "bad hearing." *La Religieuse* raises the possibility that uncertain mediation "swindles" the reader, posing the problem of how best to hear what the writing is telling. What I am looking at here, then, is in a sense scandalous, if we consider the etymology of this word: obstacles or stumbling blocks to direct communication. For both of these related acts of writing realism, the level at which the reader's pleasure occurs lies in the expression of representation by semiosis. My purpose is to show that, although writing functions for the characters with different degrees of success, the writing as event forces the reader's attention onto the semiotic level where realism occurs—and there it does not stumble.

The Failure of Consolation in *Les Liaisons dangereuses*

To analyze the semiosis of *Les Liaisons dangereuses,* I propose to begin with the concept of consolation, an overlooked but central theme of the novel. The novel closes on the verb *consoler*: "Adieu, ma chère et digne amie; j'éprouve en ce moment que notre raison, déjà si insuffisante pour prévenir nos malheurs, l'est encore davantage pour nous en consoler" [Adieu, my dear and worthy friend, at this moment I sense how our reason, already so inadequate for preventing our misfortunes, is all the more so to console us for them] (379, letter 175). This last word belongs to Mme de Volanges, conforming to her structural role as a worldly, if obtuse, observer of, rather than intimate actor in, the events that have been recounted in the letters, in spite of her daughter's significant part in them. As Henri Coulet so aptly puts it, "silly Mme de Volanges, the only character authorized to conclude the novel."[9] Nevertheless her assessment is a strong indicator of finality, not only an almost irreversible outcome but also a final meaning. The reader should ask why consolation is impossible for all who desire it, for all the letter-writing characters seek consolation, except Mme de Merteuil. Only Prévan, who does not write, obtains a social consolation when the marquise's letters circulate in society.[10]

It is as if to write is to console oneself, to seek a reply that would console, to recount one's own consolations, or to propose one to another. Like the letters themselves, consolation can be given and taken by writing, much the way the "voice" is given and taken in the *Heptaméron.* But the project of obtaining consolation is bound to fail, not only because different ears hear the word differently, or because writing falls on deaf ears, or because the characters do not "hear ear to ear," as it were. The impossibility of consolation is also inscribed in the defective, limping network of letters that, in narrating experience, do so only imperfectly: always too much or too little, and always after the fact. Judith Spencer describes the need for "an interstitial reading" when signification exceeds the word.[11] Coulet concludes his fine account of occulted letters: "Everything that is denied the reader compels him to a suspicious reading, all the more attentive the less the concealment is emphasized" (614). We saw the need for suspicious reading in the *Heptaméron,* for similar reasons: not everything is spoken, or written. In *Les Liaisons dangereuses,* so extensive and numerous are the faults in the network that to tell them all would be to retell the entire tale, inventorying its scandals. In a sense it is convenient that on the mimetic level Laclos's novel tells scandalous stories, the better to induce the reader into an awareness of the scandals of its semiosis: the *scandalon* that raises obstacles to smooth progress. While the letter-writers tell representational stories like analogues of the author (just as the frame characters of the *Heptaméron* reflect Marguerite de Navarre and her circle), their writing radically subverts the relation between the thing told and writing. Hence, with the characters, we stumble over the impediments to consolation inscribed in the fact that the correspondence does not correspond to experience.

Yet the characters apparently write in the belief that their writing will take over from a defective reality. A striking and famous illustration of this belief, which has the merit of concision as well, can be found in Jean-Jacques Rousseau's *Les Confessions,* in the concert recounted in Book IV in which his music is performed to the unrestrained derision of all present, including the musicians. This nevertheless evokes a consolation of sorts:

Les musiciens étouffaient de rire; les auditeurs ouvraient de grands yeux, et auraient bien voulu fermer les oreilles. . . . Pour ma consolation, j'entendais autour de moi les assistants se dire à leur oreille, ou plutôt à la mienne, l'un: Il n'y a rien là de supportable; un autre: Quelle musique enragée?[12]

[The musicians were dying of laughter; the audience was wide-eyed in amazement and would have liked to shut their ears. . . . For my consolation, I heard the people around me saying to each others' ears, or rather to mine, one: " 'There is nothing bearable in this"; another: "What demented music!"]

This example interests me not only for Rousseau's amusing bewilderment but also for the insistence on ears, particularly the rhetorical device (a kind of zeugma or what has been called *attelage* in French) that focalizes the impossible desire to close them and the indirection by which words reach Rousseau's ears, the "unintended, intended" hearer. These very forces are at play in the representations of letter writing in *Les Liaisons dangereuses.* But if Rousseau *writes* this debacle, it is because a real consolation, not an imaginary or rhetorical one (in this case, ironic), comes from writing it, one that in fact mirrors the consolation Rousseau sought in his entire autobiographical project (and almost certainly did not obtain). For it is only at the moment that he realizes this project—that is, in this same passage from *Les Confessions,* where we now hear the instance of composition and not just the event recounted—that he can write: "Pauvre Jean-Jacques, dans ce cruel moment tu n'espérais guère qu'un jour devant le Roi de France et toute sa cour tes sons exciteraient des murmures de surprise et d'applaudissement" [Poor Jean-Jacques, in that cruel moment you could not have hoped that one day, before the King of France and his entire court, your harmonies would excite murmurs of surprise and applause] (166). In the space of a few lines, a written consolation supplements the humiliation he had suffered in his youth, and it does so by invoking the future anterior of "one day," a manipulation of time made possible only by writing. There is, to be sure, a great irony in Rousseau's apparent faith in the ability of writing to correct a defective reality, but that is just what he expects of his writing in this passage. Both replacing (substituting for) the time of derision, or ironic consolation, and adding to (filling in) a lack of success, or real consolation, the writing wipes out the bad sounds: it closes our ears to the mimesis of humiliation and opens them to the semiosis of consolation. I take this effect as emblematic of what I wish to develop in this chapter.

Rousseau's writing does what the writer wants it to do: it is not defective (in this case). That would be the correspondents' consolation in *Les Liaisons dangereuses.* To be sure, "consoler" means to alleviate suffering (see, for instance, the article "Pain béni" in *L'Encyclopédie*),[13] but by a deflection of language that is characteristic of libertine discourse, the "sufferings" to be alleviated, in this novel, are often sexual. Valmont, playing on the ambivalence of the word, imposes this second meaning: the sexual act is a consolation, and the "consolateurs" are the lovers taken by forsaken women (265, letter 115; 325, letter 144). It is a measure of his influence on Mme de Tourvel that she writes to Mme de Rosemonde, at the moment she escapes from Valmont's company at his aunt's country estate: "Condamnée . . . à n'oser ni me plaindre, ni le consoler" [Condemned . . . neither to dare take pity on myself, nor to dare console him] (230, letter 102), a usage in which we must read the sexual sense in spite of the writer. It is further a measure of misunderstandings in this novel that Mme de Rosemonde replies offering *moral* consolations: "Réservez-vous au moins la consolation d'avoir combattu"; "je me réserve de vous soutenir et vous consoler autant qu'il sera en moi. Je ne soulagerai pas vos peines, mais je les partagerai" [At least reserve for yourself the consolation of having fought back; I reserve for myself to support you and console you as much as I can. I shall not alleviate your suffering, but I will share it] (232, letter 103). So much for her experience in love; perhaps Laclos yields to the commonplace that an old woman no longer knows desire, in spite of Mme de Rosemonde's rose-colored worldliness.

The marquise for her part finds it pleasing and amusing to "console for and against" (127)—both the apparently moral "consoling angel" (128) of Mme de Volanges in her distress and the sexual seductress of her daughter, according to the scandalous letter 63: "je ne lui donnai d'abord que ces consolations gauches, qui augmentent plus les peines qu'elles ne les soulagent"; "Quand la belle désolée fut au lit, je me mis à la consoler de bonne foi" [at first I gave her only those awkward consolations that augment suffering more than they diminish it; When the disconsolate beauty was in bed, I began to console her in earnest] (128). Apparently "console for" is meant to suggest the alleviation of moral suffering, whereas "console against" would define the libertine's stance against society. Writing to Mme de Volanges, however, the marquise forbids herself the sexual sense of the word, and the vicomte de Valmont for his part knows how to lie adroitly to the présidente de Tourvel by feigning the moral register with which he is familiar: "Vous vous occupez de punir! et moi, je vous demande des consolations: non que je les mérite; mais parce qu'elles me sont nécessaires, et qu'elles ne peuvent me venir que de vous" [You are concerned with punishing! And I am asking you for consolation: not that I deserve it, but because it is necessary for me, and it can only come from you] (314). No surprise that moral consolation is not the same as the physical; in the enlightened context of "Reason," only by duplicity or irony can one describe sexual "suffering" as a moral ill to be alleviated.

The letter full of double entendres that Valmont writes to the présidente while using the body of the courtesan Émilie as a desk (103–4, letter 48) is the striking emblem of this ironic duplicity, typical of Valmont's prose. It is interesting that Valmont, in the midst of his sexual consolations during this brilliant act of writing deflected from experience, speaks no more of seeking consolation from Tourvel, but deplores instead her "rigueurs désolantes [qui] ne m'empêchent point de m'abandonner entièrement à l'amour et d'oublier, dans le délire qu'il me cause, le désespoir auquel vous me livrez" [disconsoling rigors [which] do not in the least prevent me from abandoning myself entirely to love and from forgetting, in the delirium it causes, the despair to which you leave me] (103). (The many commentators who have stated that Valmont writes on Émilie's back have made unwarranted assumptions: Laclos nowhere mentions her back.) It is noteworthy that in her reply to this stormy sexual delirium (in total ignorance of the appropriateness of her words, Tourvel writes of "the fearsome storms" and "this dangerous delirium"), the présidente protests that she should not listen, showing how characters can hear while pretending not to listen (106–7, letter 50).

Finally, in this hasty review of the various meanings of consolation, the topos of the scoundrel punished, illustrated in eighteenth-century theater, would allow one man's suffering to bring consolation to others, but this effect, mentioned in the last uses of the word, is exactly what is missing: "Je vois bien dans tout cela les méchants punis; mais je n'y trouve nulle consolation pour leurs malheureuses victimes" [I can easily see, in all this, how the villains are punished; but I find here no consolation for their unhappy victims] (376, letter 173).[14] On the contrary, Cécile, Danceny, Mme de Volanges, and Mme de Rosemonde find no consolation in the chastisement of the rakes. Taken all together, these simple differences of definition symbolize deeper ones, which undermine the hope for harmony and happiness.

Misunderstandings: Two Examples

I propose, then, a principal theme: consolation sought for in the writing but rendered inaccessible by the misunderstandings of this same writing. This theme will hammer at our eardrums, so little one lends it an ear. Misunderstanding is everywhere; discord reigns. Absence being the condition of correspondence, we are well warned by this sentence of Valmont's: "C'est une chose inconcevable . . . comme aussitôt qu'on s'éloigne, on cesse facilement de s'entendre" [It's inconceivable . . . as soon as we are at a distance how easily we cease to understand each other] (264, letter 115). Because a letter must bridge a distance, which is measured by time, it happens that the temporal separation between the writing of one letter and the reception of its reply reproduces the disagreement between the different values of the word *consolation* and of its application. Thus, as we saw, Mme de Rosemonde thinks she is consoling Mme de Tourvel by exposing Valmont as a libertine, hoping to apply the specific to her malady. She always speaks of consolation in the moral sense, as that which promises her friend the "repose of your conscience," which stems from her "courageous resistance" and from her virtue (292, letter 126). But Mme de Rosemonde does not know yet that Mme de Tourvel has just obtained a sexual consolation, and that she is perfectly lucid about the happiness it brings her. To these letters that cross each other, to which answers are beside the point because they arrive after the reply, we can add those that are missing (indicated in a note by the "rédacteur," or editor), or those that arrive at their destination by indirect routes. For example, Mme de Volanges (345, letter 154) writes that Valmont has written her asking that she "mediate" between him and Mme de Tourvel; the "editor" suppresses this letter because one cannot judge whether Valmont is sincere in it or not. The question is capital, however: What role for love? Coulet (610–14) points out that Laclos had written and then suppressed Valmont's two letters, to Volanges and Tourvel (mentioned in letter 154), as well as an earlier letter from Tourvel to Valmont written at the height of her love for him; no letter of such sincere passion was to subsist in the novel.

Misunderstanding also stems from the particular status of the epistolary narrative. The multiplicity of writers causes impediments: it is difficult to distinguish the lies from the truths because the actors who write and the events they describe are not translated before our eyes and ears by a narrating authority as in a nonepistolary narrative. The fragmentation of point of view generates the fragmentation of values. There is a kind of stereophony: two or several writings recount the same event, partially and usually with partiality; none of the characters knows everything. The written presents itself as a record of the spoken, or the mediation of the voice; but it is a feint—and who is speaking, who listening? The letter is a written speaking, whose status as *graphie* or *phoné* is not certain. Dialogism cuts the voice from its origin. For the event to reach us, another writing must take charge: a third party then recounts what happened, and this filling in of lacks is interposed between the fact and the receiver of the letter. Moreover, the voices one hears are always doubled by the author's, which often says what the writer of the letter does not hear or understand.

To illustrate, let me first consider what Ross Chambers has called the "ingérence" of Valmont between Cécile and Danceny, particularly in one letter, then the interference of Merteuil between Valmont and Tourvel, with the letter that kills the présidente.[15]

Consolation, in Cécile's candid writing, initially connotes a charitable goodness that she seeks in Mme de Merteuil and that she would like to offer to Danceny: she knows of no other consolation yet. When Valmont reads Cécile's letters to Danceny, he scolds: "ce n'est pas ainsi qu'elle consolerait son amant" [that's not how to console her lover] (267, letter 115). Cécile will have understood "to relieve from suffering"; her guileless use of the word invokes only the idea of warmheartedness toward one's neighbor: "Je voudrais bien le consoler; mais je ne voudrais rien faire qui fût mal" [I really would like to console him, but I would not want to do anything that would be bad], she says, after receiving Danceny's first letter (45, letter 16).

To inflect the relationship between the two young people toward a sexual understanding, which we may also call an "entente," Valmont dictates letter 117, the last letter from Cécile to Danceny in which the word *consoler* occurs. Valmont's purpose is to "nourrir l'amour du jeune homme, par un espoir plus certain" [nourish the young man's love with a more certain hope] (267). The tactic consists in suggesting to Danceny that the consolation he hopes for can be more than an alleviation of moral ills: Valmont insinuates a sexual act (for which close proximity is necessary). Thus a voice speaks for her—but it will be misheard. Here is how this sounds, with the voice of Valmont speaking in Cécile's tongue:

Croyez-vous que je ne sache pas que ce que vous voulez est bien mal? Et pourtant, si j'ai déjà tant de peine à vous refuser de loin, que serait-ce donc si vous étiez là? Et puis, pour avoir voulu vous consoler un moment, je resterais affligée toute ma vie. (269)

[Do you think I don't know that what you want is really bad? And yet, if I'm having such trouble refusing you from far away, what would it be like if you were here? And then, for having been willing to console you for a moment, I would be distressed for the rest of my life.]

A pretty maxim in Valmont's own style expresses a similar sentiment: "car vous posséder et vous perdre, c'est acheter un moment de bonheur par une éternité de regrets" [for to possess you and to lose you is to buy a moment of happiness with an eternity of regrets] (267, letter 115). Laclos's stylistic mastery shows in the way sentiment can be expressed in these different tones, precisely in the context of the letter where Valmont explains that he dictated the letter to Danceny to console him. In spite of the hand that holds the pen, the word takes on its sexual connotation, and the verbs suggest that she does wish to console him—but will Danceny hear it, even if Cécile does not? Cécile thinks to repel Danceny's insistent demands through her virtuous refusals ("ne me demandez plus une chose que j'ai de bonnes raisons pour ne pas faire" [don't ask me again for a thing that I have good reasons not to do] [270]): the "thing" insinuates itself into these very refusals.

Yet when he receives this doubly focused letter, Danceny fails to hear a sexual consolation. He listens only to the protestations of honor and honesty that Valmont dictated for plausibility's sake; he is deaf to the tone of the Valmont behind Cécile. This misapprehension may stem from a mistaken notion of the addressee. In this reply to Danceny that Valmont formulates for Cécile in letter 117, the language appears to correspond to an expression of sexual desire on Danceny's part, whereas the younger man's language has been merely conventional, and the consolation he speaks of is never sexual. In the letter just preceding, Danceny had written: "L'espoir que vous m'aviez donné de vous voir à cette campagne, je m'aperçois bien qu'il faut y renoncer. Je n'ai plus de consolation que celle de me persuader qu'en effet cela ne vous est pas possible" [The hope you had given me to see you in that country home—I fully realize that I will have to abandon it. I have no further consolation but to persuade myself that indeed it is not possible for you] (268, letter 116). The correspondence limps because there is, precisely, no correspondence between the request ("don't ask me again for a thing that I have good reasons not to do") and the reply: Danceny follows Cécile's request to the letter—that is, exactly—and asks for nothing more in writing. He is, one could say, hearing something other than what he is listening to. The text written to transmit a message is belied when the text is received with another message; the hearer listens badly. When, at the end of the novel, Mme de Rosemonde advises Mme de Volanges to leave Cécile in the convent to which she has fled, she suggests that far from being the passive victim of a mundane seduction by Danceny, Cécile had made advances. It is Valmont's writing that insinuates this "reality."

This dictated letter is the material, verbal trace of Valmont's entire sexual activity with Cécile: in it, he leaves, as it were, his semiotic seed, encoded in the double entendres. It is the writing of reality for Cécile. His interference in the letter writing of Cécile and Danceny, obviously emblematic of his replacing Danceny in love, will end with his death, with Cécile's and Danceny's deaths to the world, as they take their respective orders, and with the vanishing of any consolation.

When Valmont's seed flourishes, and Cécile becomes pregnant, it is as if Valmont's sexual and textual activity achieves real, concrete form, but she knows as little about it as she knows what consolations she was writing to Danceny. What informs her is an event the text calls an "accident" and an "unforeseen event": "Des maux de reins, de violentes coliques, des symptômes moins équivoques encore, m'ont eu bientôt éclairé sur son état: mais, pour le lui apprendre, il a fallu lui dire d'abord celui où elle était auparavant; car elle ne s'en doutait pas" [Back pains, a violent colic, symptoms even less equivocal had soon enlightened me about her state: but, in order to apprise her of it, I had to first inform her of the one she was in before; for she had no idea] (319, letter 140). Such an accident would not have occurred with Danceny, so that what is significant—the information in this noisy channel—is Valmont's mediation. By metonymy, one may say that the miscarriage stands for Cécile's loss of virginity. As an element of the plot or the utterance, her miscarriage appears as an accident, whereas her loss of virginity is the outcome of Valmont's scheming and planning and so could not be called accidental *in the representation*. As an element of the writing, however, in the semiotic realm, the loss of virginity appears as one of those accidents that constitute an obstacle to consolation. This case of mishearing the nature of the consolation requested or denied shows Cécile entrapped in the semiotic web woven by Valmont.

Unique among all is the letter the marquise writes to the vicomte transmit-ting, by a doubly or triply mediated route, a letter of death. This embedded letter is the one with the refrain "Ce n'est pas ma faute" [It is not my fault] (321–22, letter 141). Feigning to bury her jealous anger against Valmont ("Aussi je n'en veux absolument plus parler" [Therefore I absolutely do not want to talk about it any more]), Merteuil invents a story in which the letter takes its place as a quotation. It is a fiction perhaps prompted by a sentence in a letter just received from Valmont: "Non, je ne suis point amoureux; et ce n'est pas ma faute si les circonstances me forcent d'en jouer le rôle" [No, I am not at all in love, and it is not my fault if circumstances force me to play the part] (315, letter 138). In this fiction told by the marquise, "a man of her acquaintance" "passait ainsi sa vie, ne cessant de faire des sottises, et ne cessant de dire après: *Ce n'est pas ma faute*" [spent his life like that, endlessly playing the fool, and endlessly saying afterward: *It is not my fault*] (321); his "belle amie" sees that he gets a copy of a letter signifying the end of a relationship. Valmont understands perfectly that the marquise intends him to rewrite this letter for Mme de

Tourvel, but this understanding or intelligence arrives by an indirect listening: "Ma foi, ma belle amie, je ne sais si j'ai mal lu ou mal entendu, et votre lettre, et l'histoire que vous m'y faites, et le petit modèle épistolaire qui y était compris" [I say, my pretty friend, I don't know if I've read badly or heard badly both your letter and the story that you made up for me, and the little epistolary model contained in it] (323, letter 142). Valmont's reply thus calls attention to the drift in which the epistolary model lies and the "bad hearing" it provokes. In spite of this, the inserted letter is heard accurately partly because of Valmont's expertise in the libertine code (sacrifice is necessary to obtain a new pleasure), partly because the letter is part of another narration that takes charge of the story. The narrative function guarantees a sure delivery and good reception.

Faithful to an ethic of understanding ("entente")—for Valmont better sustains agreement and understanding than the marquise, who refuses to hear and provokes the war—Valmont pays enough attention to it "to hear it well" (321). As a letter that seems to interpose itself between the event and writing, Valmont has only to copy it to the letter, in order to understand it. As Jean Rousset appropriately describes it, the rewriting is a real quotation of a fictive quotation.[16] His reading of it would match what Barthes called "a third adventure of reading," which is the adventure of writing, in which reading is "conducive to the Desire to write."[17] Because rewriting the letter sends the receiver to her death (rather than to the impossible "consolateur" Valmont callously suggests), this is the only letter that is fully an act, the only one in which the language is exactly the same thing as experience, in which the thing and writing correspond perfectly.

The effect of this letter that kills, and of the correspondence in general, nevertheless cannot arrive to our hearing except by a mediation whose characteristics and consequences remain to be explained. The text of the letter of rupture appears only in the marquise's letter in which it is inserted; never do we see it addressed to Tourvel. Valmont borrows a writing whose origin is suspect and whose status is singular to telegraph death to the présidente. Similarly, Cécile speaks of a consolation that she does not recognize through the writing that Valmont lends her. The interference of Valmont between Cécile and Danceny and of the marquise between Valmont and the présidente has the same effect; in both cases, the source of the letter is not its apparent emitter, and its addressee is double or more than double. The message only transits the letter-writer, whose listening is defective: Cécile cannot see all the hidden sense in her letter, and Valmont rewrites the marquise's letter with only a part of himself—it is the rake's copy. While he dreams of rekindling the présidente's love, the marquise is boasting of directing his blows against her: "Quand une femme frappe dans le cœur d'une autre, elle manque rarement de trouver l'endroit sensible, et la blessure est incurable" [When a woman strikes into the heart of another woman, she rarely misses the sensitive spot, and the wound is incurable] (328, letter 145).

These effects of writing institute an inevitable dialogue of the deaf between the emitter of the text and its reader. But "dialogue of the deaf" does not mean that no one hears; rather, it ensures that another listener achieves understanding. The last letter by Mme de Tourvel fails to obtain the consolation it demands because it is without addressee: "Toute consolation m'est refusée" [All consolation is denied me], she writes, in which the passive construction emphasizes the absence of address (354, letter 161). Aimed toward whoever receives it, this writing does not reach its goal, for who would reply? But it reaches the reader, ultimate receiver, through the flux of its possible multiple addressees. Valmont copies the epistolary model in Merteuil's letter because he is listening to another story and hears his own: he was not listening, but he heard perfectly. Our hearing is analogous to his: we do just what causes Mme de Tourvel's downfall, when she admits: "Je passe mon temps à *écouter* ce que je ne devrais pas *entendre*" [I spend my time *listening to* what I ought not *hear*] (199, letter 90; emphasis added). Accepting the impossibility of consolation, we must wish to listen badly in order to hear everything. The text pushes us toward this bad listening, forcing us to engage in listening elsewhere, if we are to hear well.

Author, Editor, Publisher, Reader

When the author himself speaks to the reader, this too is an indirect address, through the writing of the correspondents. What are the stakes of our listening, and what have we heard? Paul de Man formerly used the visual metaphor opposing "blindness" and "insight" in the writings of critics. "Errors," troubled departures from the critics' methodologies, paradoxically arrive at truth; lucidity is the fruit of sightlessness. De Man notes: "The insight exists only for a reader in the privileged position of being able to observe the blindness as a phenomenon in its own right."[18] The auditory correspondent of this opposition, in French, is "le malentendu" and "l'entendement." That is to say, understanding comes to the reader precisely through the misunderstandings and accidents of the correspondents' writing, mishearings that trouble our listening. By this means does the reader hear well, on the condition of listening elsewhere, of accepting a drifting listening, of listening to disorder. For if understanding, which is allied with Reason, is defective or insufficient among the correspondents, on the level of the representation, it is complete for the reader, on the level of semiosis, where the enunciation is put into play: perpetual misunderstanding, then, for the characters, but, through it, understanding for the readers.

The putative gathering of the entire correspondence in Mme de Rosemonde's hands figures this knowledge or insight, in the end. With an exemplary concern for verisimilitude, Laclos has his characters describe exactly, in their letters, the routes of transmission by which each letter comes to Mme de Rosemonde. I find an interesting parallel, in this painstaking effort to ensure that the letters reach the next level of hearing, with Marguerite de Navarre's insistence on the gift of the voice and the taking of place in the *Heptaméron*. Both are phatic strategies concerned with ensuring the life of the narrative as well as its realism; that is, the care taken to maintain the channel of communication functions on the level of the represented story for the characters, and on the semiotic level for the reader. On the story level, only Rosemonde might enjoy the possibility of knowing what everybody has written; to entomb the secret is then the only consolation that remains available to her. In asking Danceny for Cécile Volanges's letters, she begs him to concur in "la sûreté d'un secret, dont la publicité vous ferait tort à vous-même, et porterait la mort dans un cœur maternel. . . . Enfin, Monsieur, . . . si je pouvais craindre que vous me refusassiez cette consolation, je vous demanderais de songer auparavant que c'est la seule que vous m'ayez laissée" [the assurance of a secret the publication of which would bring harm to yourself, and would carry death into a maternal heart. . . . Finally, Sir, . . . if I were to fear that you would refuse me this consolation, I would ask you first to reflect that it is the only one you have left me] (372). A page later she says to Mme de Volanges that, "dans l'impuissance où je suis d'y joindre aucune consolation, la grâce qui me reste à vous demander, ma chère amie, est de ne plus m'interroger sur rien qui ait rapport à ces tristes événements; laissons-les dans l'oubli qui leur convient" [impotent as I am to join any consolation to it, the remaining favor for me to ask you, my dear friend, is never to question me again about anything having to do with these sad events; let us leave them in the oblivion they deserve] (373), in which the impossibility of consolation may be expressed only by silence. From these papers piled high at Rosemonde's chateau, the real emitter, Laclos, posing as the "editor," can now extract a novel, for our hearing, and the novel we hear includes the gaps and other disturbances to completion and order. Our profit and our consolation, as readers, stem from a kind of forfeit paid by the correspondents, who lost the game—a forfeit one could well call the payment of a consolation. Letter-writers are locked into the mimetic illusion, even though they may be suspicious of it, and their composition does not achieve consolation for them; only the indirectly-addressed reader, placed on the meta-mimetic level, hearing the scandals, achieves understanding.

The "éditeur," who is not the "rédacteur" but the publisher, had projected another consolation for his readers, and it would perhaps be well to admit here that it is he who had the last word, in an appended note, and that Mme de Volanges's summary "adieu" is last only within the fiction of the letters. It is a constant in the eighteenth-century novel that the last words promise to continue it: the text leaves an open door, lays a stepping stone, figures a raised foot. Professing that "des raisons particulières et des considérations que nous nous ferons toujours un devoir de respecter nous forcent de nous arrêter ici" [certain reasons and considerations that we will always take it as our duty to respect force us to stop here], the publisher thus provides an indirect gloss on the word *consoler*, to which the note is appended. The note appears motivated by the need to explain the stopping point to which the letters have come—and to console the reader for the absent future. In postponing to an uncertain future time "la suite des aventures de mademoiselle de Volanges" [the continuation of the adventures of Mlle de Volanges] and "les sinistres événements qui ont comblé les malheurs ou achevé la punition de madame de Merteuil" [the sinister events that have completed the misfortunes or finished the punishment of Mme de Merteuil], the publisher terminates the tragedy "in this moment." Laurent Versini observes that the note is not in Laclos's hand; Joan DeJean believes the note was written by the real *éditeur*, or publisher of the novel, Durand.[19] As such, it would clearly mark an intention for which the real author may not have been responsible. Indeed, whatever the publisher may have claimed, Laclos knew full well that the events of his novel come to a stop because there is no moral or physical consolation. There remains only a coffer enclosing the letters that we read, and in which we hear absent voices bequeathing to us this admonition: "A bon entendeur, salut!" [You have been warned!].

And what exactly do we hear? Letters in *Les Liaisons dangereuses* that pass to secondary or tertiary receivers, "hidden readers" in Peter Conroy's term, carry messages that the writers did not put in them.[20] Accidental meanings are thereby available to the reader. The content of these indirect or deflected messages is always death—including moral death and death to the world. Danceny, secondary receiver, provokes the duel with Valmont because he has in hand the vicomte's letters to Mme de Merteuil (356, letter 162). Mme de Rosemonde, tertiary receiver of Cécile's letters and powerless to "join any consolation to them," requires Mme de Volanges to leave the girl in the convent (373, letter 172). Society, multiple receiver of the letters of the marquise to the vicomte, finishes the disgrace of Mme de Merteuil (365, letter 168). Reading this novel, ultimate receivers, often at the fifth or sixth remove, we accept to receive, through multiple mediations, through the signifiers that circulate like stolen letters, a dangerous signifier: like the présidente, like Cécile, Danceny, Valmont, Merteuil, and Rosemonde, we receive the message of death—the "death" of the book. There is for us as for the characters a correspondence between the publication of the letters and death; that is the price and the sense of our insight as auditory voyeurs. If we are to hear well, we can accept no future, completed book, made whole by a new intent to finish.

In the story told by these letters, Reason fails; consolation is impossible, mishearings proliferate. These failings figure the real against an ideal in which Reason would reign, consolation be provided, and understanding be at hand— an ideal in which writing letters would arrange the world properly. Such a desire for order, translated to the semiotic level, is the familiar task of the "editor," in that his claim to write a work of Reason would consist in putting the heap of letters into logical and chronological order, making judicious selections, arraying them according to criteria of readability, adding necessary explanations in the notes. These are the tasks he outlines for a novelist in the "Préface du rédacteur." A novel containing a plot, suspense, motivations, ironies, destinies can claim the generic status of an "ouvrage" (or "work"), or even a "novel," as the publisher asserts in contrast to the repeated denials by the "rédacteur," who insists rather that the letters are a mere collection (14–18). If, as Derrida describes it, the ideality of a letter resists its division, either because of the ideality of the signifier or because the Lacanian "point de capiton" links the signifier to the signified, the letter is always divisible in its materiality. If then it belongs to the structure of the letter not to arrive at its destination, because of its materiality, one can say that it never really arrives there, or arrives there tormented by an internal drift. And Derrida concludes that "the mail, in all languages, even the most secure, does not always tell the truth."[21] The characters in *Les Liaisons dangereuses* must concur in this observation. The signifier is not always buttoned down to a signified. From the moment one takes up the pen, the marquise reminds us, one "arranges" words to make an "order" reign in writing that cannot plausibly imitate feelings; "le discours [parlé] moins suivi amène plus aisément cet air de trouble et de désordre qui est la véritable éloquence de l'amour" [[spoken] discourse, being less coherent, more readily brings about this appearance of turmoil and disorder that is the true eloquence of love] (73–74, letter 33).

But just as Reason is defective, and disorder and mishearing prevent the characters' understanding, our ears are forcibly attuned to how the writing invents disorder: anachronisms; holes; undeliverable letters; letters without addressees; second, third, or other receivers; secrets; jolts; mysteries; suppressed letters; interruptions; diversity of styles; abrupt cuts. It is precisely this limping of the semiotic order that makes the correspondence into a novel and that constitutes its eloquence and even elegance, not the fashioning of an orderly world. The actual experience of reading may add another level to the scandalous disorder of the correspondence: if we wish to follow a particular narrative thread (one of the several projects or subplots), we have to skip letters, creating our own semiotic (dis)order. Writing thus fulfills a lack or fault for us, when we recognize it as novel; it replaces experience, on the condition we accept that semiotic practice or *signifiance,* the textual play by which a story reaches the reader, has meaning as much as the story does. Then writing is neither too much nor too little, but just right, and that may well be a consolation.

La Religieuse: A Sublime Swindle?

> Lecteur, tandis que ces bonnes gens dorment, j'aurais une petite question à vous proposer, à discuter sur votre oreiller, c'est ce qu'aurait été l'enfant né de l'Abbé Hudson et de la Dame de La Pommeraye.
>
> [Reader, while these good folks are asleep, I would like to ask you a little question, to be discussed on your pillow, it's what would have been the child born of the Abbot Hudson and the lady de La Pommeraye.]
>
> —*Jacques le fataliste*

This query addressed to the reader, never answered, solicits our participation in determining the value of two of the tales certain characters have told in *Jacques le fataliste.* We are asked to produce their *product.* It is quite intentionally that I speak of a product, because I think a mathematical question lurks in this *boutade,* or witticism. If you multiply together the master and mistress of deceit, the Hudson and the La Pommeraye, do you get the most complete negation of their deceitful essence—"Peutêtre un honnête homme" [Perhaps an honest man], according to one possible reply—or the quintessence of their two beings, "Peutêtre un sublime coquin" [Perhaps a sublime rascal] (257)?[22] If an "honest man," would we not recognize this product as a *replacement and substitution* for deceit? And if a "sublime rascal," is it not an *enhancement and augmentation* of deceit? These are the very terms of supplementarity.

Now suppose we were to marry Suzanne Simonin, the nun, and Jacques the fatalist. What would their product be? Apart from the fact that one would talk constantly and the other would write everything down, they would argue obsessively about whether writing can change one's fate. Whatever the outcome, Suzanne's product would purport to relate experience. What the reader would then have to decide is whether the writing of experience must be taken as an integral, symbolic expression, a replacement or substitution for experience that faithfully renders it, or whether it is sublime in swindling its reader. In other words, is Diderot an "honest man" or a "sublime rascal" in writing *La Religieuse?* The material is rich for a discussion. Indeed, as will be evident, it is impossible to approach *La Religieuse* without considering its foundation in this problematic. Of course, Diderot was being sly in his suggestion of a mathematical procedure, for a positive product results from both positive and negative pairs of multipliers. However, while it is plausible that two scoundrels (two negative numbers) will cancel out each other's evil and produce a model of morality (a positive number), to think that way is to think naïvely and according to an ancient definition of mimesis: in short, substitution via resemblance. To listen to semiosis, on the other hand, one would hear the voices of the multiple authorizers of the complex discourse in *La Religieuse,* calling attention to their writing; then writing would stand in an ironic relation to event, and it would be a sublime swindle. In the reading that follows, my purpose is to demonstrate the role semiosis plays as we do combat with the devious strategies of the novel's realism.

Writing to Change Reality

Diderot gave the reader of *Jacques le fataliste* until "tomorrow morning" to reply to his query. Let me use the interval to approach *La Religieuse* via a brief detour through the twenty-second tale of the *Heptaméron*.[23] Like *La Religieuse*, this story portrays the convent as a place where the spoken word does not get out, and it explicitly resolves the relation between speaking and writing and their relation to reality. Sister Marie Heroët's harrowing experience at the hands of a vicious monk finds an outlet in writing in a manner that resonates harmoniously with *La Religieuse*. And like all the other stories embedding written texts, in the *Heptaméron,* this tale calls attention to the semiotic processes by which the writing achieves realism. The prior of Saint-Martin tries every conceivable deception to get Sister Marie into his bed, and takes revenge upon her repeated refusals by degrading her and putting her on a diet of bread and water. Though she cannot *tell* her brother what a struggle she has led against the lecherous priest, she puts everything into a written document that she passes through the convent grill. By this means, the "discourse" of her "pitiful story" finally puts an end to her ordeal. Writing transcends the silences and the censures by which Sister Marie's tormentor has violated her "freedom of speech."

From the outset, speaking plays a large role. What first provokes the prior of Saint-Martin to desire Sister Marie Heroët is her "parolle . . . si doulce et agreable" [speech . . . so sweet and pleasant] during confession—certainly a case of his hearing something her text was not listening to: "Parquoy, seullement pour l'ouyr, fut esmeu en une passion d'amour qui passat toutes celles qu'il avoit eues aux autres religieuses" [Because of which, just hearing her, he was moved to a passion of love that surpassed all the passions he had had for other nuns] (177). While the lines of power are clearly drawn along the doubly reinforced axis of gender and religious hierarchy, giving the prior total authority over Sister Marie, her superiority over him lies in speaking: "Il la trouvoit saige en parolle, et d'un esperit si subtil, qu'il ne povoit avoir grande esperance, et, d'autre part, se voyait si laid et si vieulx, qu'il delibera de ne luy en parler poinct, mais de chercher à la gaingner par craincte" [He found her honest in speech, and of such a subtle mind that he could not have much hope, and, on the other hand, he saw himself so ugly and old that he decided not to speak to her of it, but to try to win her by fear] (177). And so he falsely accuses her of being a bad nun, and the first of his trumped-up charges is that "elle caquette, comme si c'estoit une mondaine" [she gabs like a woman of the world] (178). He attacks her physically; she cries out and faints; the abbess returns, where-upon he proposes never to speak of it again if she will love (!) him; and he promises her an abbey—silence and power in exchange for her love. She coun-ters "qu'il n'eust plus à luy parler de ces propos, ou elle le diroit à la mere abbesse, mais que en se taisant elle s'en tairoit" [that he should cease speaking to her of this matter, or she would tell the mother superior, but for his silence she would keep silent] (179). The verbal sparring, however, continues through several more encounters, in which confessions, true and false, testimony taken or offered, and a judgment or sentence against her by the prior continue to illustrate the contest of corrupt power against speaking.

What drives Sister Marie to writing is the stopping up of her "wise speech." The threat of being put *in pace*—solitary confinement—forces her to choose to be quiet. It is under this sentence of censure that writing blossoms, for when, after years of not hearing from her, her mother sends her brother to the convent, Sister Marie has already written the complete story of her struggle: "tout ce qui est icy dessus, avecq mille autres inventions que le dict prieur avoit trouvées pour la decepvoir, que je laisse à compter pour la longueur" [every-thing mentioned above, with a thousand other inventions that the selfsame prior had invented to deceive her, which I'll omit because of the length] (183). *Verba volant, scripta manent,* as her experience proves, for the written text passes the grill and is carried by the distraught mother to none other than the Queen of Navarre, "à qui elle monstra ce piteux discours" [to whom she showed this pitiful language] (184). The queen's intervention suffices: she calls the prior to appear before her and interrogates him; he withdraws "thoroughly ashamed" (185), retires to his monastery, and soon dies. Marguerite represents herself as making no judgment and passing no sentence on the prior; quite to the contrary, his crimes make her speechless: "La Royne de Navarre, oyant cela, fut tant esmerveillée, qu'elle ne sceut que luy respondre, mais le laissa là" [The Queen of Navarre, hearing this, was so amazed that she didn't know what to answer him, so she left him] (185). Sister Marie's writing, like a magic talisman conveyed to Marguerite's hand, thus brings an end to the vicious priest's dis-honesty. What the queen's presumed speech (to her brother) does achieve, however, is the nomination of Sister Marie Heroët to abbess of another convent, by the gift of the king, a convent that Marie reforms. The gift fulfills honorably the promise dishonorably made by the prior, earlier; it rewards her wise goodness instead of complicity with evil.

Writing covers everything that can be said and more—"everything mentioned above, with a thousand other inventions . . . which I'll omit because of the length"—and moreover it gets out, endures, and effects a modification of reality, a change for the better all around. For just such a belief in the effectiveness of writing will Suzanne Simonin of *La Religieuse* consign her story to paper.

The Preface-Annex

As Jean Catrysse defines it, "*La Religieuse* is the novelistic result of a mystification whose plot was later incorporated into the narration in the form of a Preface-Annex."[24] The admirably convoluted logic of this formula resembles the logic that governs the relation between the novel's utterance (*énoncé*) and the processes of its enunciation. Diderot's strategy reminds one of those drawings by M. C. Escher that create impossible spaces; I am thinking in particular of one that shows two hands each drawing the other. In *La Religieuse,* the novelistic writing is an outcome or result of a process that is openly displayed, a process that becomes part of the novelistic writing—but only after the fact, and under the false appearance of a preface written both later and earlier than the rest and, what is more, located sometimes before, sometimes after the rest, or sometimes only in the notes, in modern editions.[25]

It is here largely in the "Préface" (often called the "Préface-Annexe" but actually titled "Préface du précédent ouvrage" [Preface of the preceding work]) that Diderot's characteristic self-consciousness emphasizes semiotic activity. The most pointed consideration of semiosis lies in the "Question aux gens de lettres" [Question to men of letters] following the narrative of the preface. This short paragraph was written entirely by Diderot in 1781 (that is, during the serial publication of the novel in the *Correspondance littéraire*). It puts into play in anecdotal fashion the fundamental opposition underlying literary invention—between artistic creation and the realistic illusion. It is singularly important: It is last in the text,[26] and thus is not taken up by any further debate; it remains without an answer, leaving entirely unresolved the question it poses; it addresses that question to those practitioners most directly implicated in its problematics; it refers to the entire work at a high level of abstraction, embracing its diegetic themes as well as its narratological ones, in addition to its ethical postures; and finally, it targets the very life of the mimetic illusion. Here is the entire paragraph:

M. Diderot, après avoir passé des matinées à composer des lettres bien écrites, bien pensées, bien pathétiques, bien romanesques, employait des journées à les gâter en supprimant, sur les conseils de sa femme et de ses associés en scélératesse, tout ce qu'elles avaient de saillant, d'exagéré, de contraire à l'extrême simplicité et à la dernière vraisemblance; en sorte que si l'on eût ramassé dans la rue les premières, on eût dit: "Cela est beau, fort beau..." et que si l'on eût ramassé les dernières, on eût dit: "Cela est bien vrai..." Quelles sont les bonnes? Sont-ce celles qui auraient peut-être obtenu l'admiration? Ou celles qui devaient certainement produire l'illusion?[27] (246)

[Mr. Diderot, after having spent his mornings composing well written, well thought out, very pathetic, very romantic letters, spent days spoiling them, on the advice of his wife and his associates in scoundrelry, by eliminating everything about them that was remarkable, exaggerated, or contrary to extreme simplicity and the greatest verisimilitude; so that if the former had been found in the street, people would have said: "This is lovely, very lovely..." and if the latter were found, people would have said: "This is really true..." Which are the good ones? Are they the ones that would perhaps have won our admiration? Or the ones that were certain to produce an illusion?]

Answering the tricky question "Which are the good ones?" would entail eliminating from the game either good writing or plausibility; the alternative apparently forces a choice between aesthetic pleasure (which obtains admiration) and the pleasure that comes with credulity. If we choose the former, we admire the art of manufacture: We see the writer's hand, we hear his procedures, but we also bid farewell to any illusion of reality. Choosing the latter, we forget the creation for the creature, like many a naïve reading. As most readers have observed, the writing in *La Religieuse* often unsettles plausibility, so the realistic illusion, in principle always available, is constantly undermined and lacks the usual consistency of the novelistic. Furthermore, Suzanne herself struggles with this question, from the moment she becomes a writer and writes about herself, and the contradiction between the naïve and the devious reading, to which the reader is constrained, exposes a vein richly deserving exploration.

The question is analogous to the "honest man / sublime rascal" conundrum; it suggests that the illusion of reality is the simple business of mimesis, but we may be smart only if we choose the sublime swindle. A brief comparison with a more stereotypical passage about the style of letter-writers, found in the

"Préface du rédacteur" of *Les Liaisons dangereuses,* reveals how much more "sublime" Diderot's language is, and how subtle the claim. Laclos writes:

D'un autre côté, les personnes d'un goût délicat seront dégoûtées par le style trop simple et trop fautif de plusieurs de ces lettres, tandis que le commun des lecteurs, séduit par l'idée que tout ce qui est imprimé est le fruit d'un travail, croira voir dans quelques autres la manière peinée d'un auteur qui se montre derrière le personnage qu'il fait parler. (18)

[On the other hand, people whose taste is delicate will be disgusted by the too simplistic and too error-filled style of many of these letters, whereas ordinary readers, seduced by the idea that everything printed is the result of an effort, will think they see in some of the others the belabored style of an author who shows himself behind the character to whom he lends speech.]

Although this sentence contains many suggestive layers, including the message encoded in rhetorical devices that the author *is* speaking through his characters, his purpose is largely to point out and gain approval for stylistic variation in the letters. The passage plays the classic part of the *captatio benevolentiae.* Functioning on a deeper semiotic layer, as it were, Diderot's paragraph conveys a different message. Its depth is indexed by the possible meanings of the slippery phrase concerning "good" letters. Does this mean letters that are well done, or letters that are good for something? A purpose may be implied; does "good" mean effective, successful at persuasion? Notice, too, the opposition of "perhaps" to "certain": what is sure is the illusion, whereas admiration of the writing is uncertain. Coupled with the contrasting forms of the two verbs— "would have won," a past conditional, and "were to," an imperfect denoting purpose—it seems clear that the rhetoric of this paragraph seeks our approbation of what is uncertain and conditional, the "lovely, very lovely" of the manufacture, which the text hopes to obtain at the same time as it maintains its already assured verisimilitude and our credulity, our assent to "This is really true."

About the mimetic illusion there is neither doubt nor the need to persuade—such is the implication of the rhetoric. The letters are both realistic in their crude simplicity, their "spoiled" pathetics, and their flattened salience, and admirable for being well written and well thought out. Diderot is telling us that the story is truthful, that we are to see its writing as simple, and that this should not be considered a defect but, in fact, what makes the letters good. As Rosalina de la Carrera nicely puts it, we can forget not to believe the fiction.[28]

Then the illusion of reality is more profoundly complete and more richly signifying. The idea is extraordinarily modern (but then, much of Diderot is) and does a great deal to advance the writing of realism; Balzac will have much the same pretension. In what follows, I attempt to describe how Diderot achieves this remarkable effect.

Naïve Realism and the Semiotic

Although Diderot seems certain the realistic illusion is richly preserved (and he was the first to feel its pathetic nature),[29] almost all readers have pointed out the disruptions in chronology, the contradictions in fact and tone, and other diegetic problems, not to mention the frame-breaking narrative discourse, which upset the illusion. The most serious challenges to the plausibility of the narrative account lie in the lesbian sexual behavior of the mother superior at the convent of Saint-Eutrope. I'll take these challenges as exemplary, for my discussion, of the question of the realistic illusion. This part of the novel has been interpreted on several levels, in view of Diderot's theses. In terms of narrative discourse, many have discussed how the necessary conveying of sexual knowledge through sexual ignorance challenges the plausibility of Suzanne's continued ignorance and innocence in the retrospective account she writes after she has overheard the mother superior's confession—and that account is, of course, virtually the entire book. (Indeed, it is significant that hearing the confession brings her writing to a stop, as I will discuss in a later section.)

It seems to me, however, that the question that has not been put in the pointed form I will put it here—except, thoroughly, by P. W. Byrne, a thesis I shall consider below—concerns not the unlikely innocence of Suzanne the writer, but rather that of the reader. I have in mind the "first" reader, the marquis de Croismare. The question I feel we most need to answer is, How shall the marquis de Croismare deal with the knowledge of the mother superior's sexuality, encoded in Suzanne's rhetoric of ignorance and innocence? This is a challenge to plausibility, but it is also a question of *listening*: What is the nature of the marquis' listening? As Vivienne Mylne has pointed out, all the men in the novel except Suzanne's father show sympathy or try to help.[30] They are listeners. The lawyer Manouri receives all of Suzanne's story to a point, but he fades from the picture. In the last part of the text, the Benedictine monk dom Morel carries on the role of sympathetic listener, the ideal model or reader's guide for the marquis de Croismare. To be sure, the conformity of Morel's situation to Suzanne's allows Diderot to economize on a portrait: his story is the same as hers, and the thesis against convents works just as well against monasteries for men. More important, Morel's intervention prepares Suzanne's passage to the outside. At first, he is the closest model to the ideal receiver of her story, the marquis; she tells her entire history to him, just as she is writing it to the marquis. (If he later becomes her abductor, as is probable, and possibly rapes her in the censured *fiacre* scene, are we to wonder if such a change might potentially occur in the marquis too?) When we learn that Morel "parut m'écouter avec attention et avec intérêt" [seemed to listen to me with attention and interest] (191), we hear her indirect request to Croismare to do as much; Morel's initial posture is the one she hopes the marquis will adopt. What, then, does the marquis hear?

To answer, it is necessary first to accept the interpretation that the "written-Suzanne," the self she presents in writing, is an exhibitionist artist. The image of the innocent virgin that the simple retelling of her story apparently portrays, if one could separate it for a moment from her writing, must be rejected. Although Suzanne "denounces" seduction, in Corinna Gepner's term, that denunciation allows her to claim her innocence as a seductress while sanctioning the presence of seduction.[31] To describe herself, as Gepner has demonstrated, she uses a mediated glance, an indirect mirror, showing herself as other characters must see her. "Involuntary" seduction, then, is the product of strategies and ruses that mask the narcissistic self-portrait. Even the glances, the looks, are written; they do not escape the lying or the manipulation that discourse allows (61). Suffering too is a veil of eroticism (65), as others have also seen, and desire expresses itself in her writing (66).

For instance, Suzanne reports her first meeting and conversation with dom Morel in terms that retrace the beginnings of a love relationship: the conformity of their tastes and experiences, their similarity in character, sentiment, wishes, regrets. Lacking the context—celibates in a confessional—one might mistake this language for the conventional rhetoric of socially sanctioned love:

C'est ainsi que la ressemblance des caractères se joignant à celle des événements, plus nous nous revoyions, plus nous nous plaisions l'un à l'autre; l'histoire de ses moments, c'était l'histoire des miens; l'histoire de ses sentiments, c'était l'histoire des miens; l'histoire de son âme, c'était l'histoire de la mienne. (193)

[Thus it was that the resemblance of our characters combining with the resemblance of events, the more we saw each other, the more we liked each other; the story of his circumstances was the story of mine; the story of his feelings was the story of mine; the story of his soul was the story of mine.]

An interesting example of Suzanne's display of seduction, a small example among many, is in her use of the term *consolation*: she begs Sister Thérèse, "Je ne sais ce qu'a notre mère supérieure, elle est désolée; si vous alliez la trouver, peut-être la consoleriez-vous..." [I don't know what is wrong with our mother superior, she is disconsolate; if you went to her, perhaps you could console her...] (189). Do the suspension points invite the reader to reflect that Thérèse hastening to the superior's side will offer her a "libertine" consolation for the pleasure Suzanne has refused her? And how much of that usage of the word *console* does Suzanne know herself?

We are to understand that such indications of a sexual self are inadvertent. Literally, Suzanne does not hear evil. Byrne calls this the "central contradiction" in her narrative.[32] Having confessed to certain preliminary caresses by her mother superior ("en vérité c'était comme un amant" [truthfully she was like a lover] [151]), she has been forbidden to "lend herself" to more, but she has found it difficult to "se refuser à des choses . . . auxquelles on n'entend soi-même aucun mal" [refuse herself to things . . . which one does not oneself understand as at all evil] (177). After confession she repeats as much to her superior: "les caresses que vous me faites, et auxquelles je vous avoue que je n'entends aucun mal" [your caressing me, which I confess I do not at all understand as evil] (184). Later, after dom Morel has heard her story, he sagely warns her: "C'est votre innocence même qui en a imposé à votre supérieure; plus instruite, elle vous aurait moins respectée" [It is your innocence itself that impressed your mother superior; were you more knowing, she would have respected you less]. Her reply: "Je ne vous entends pas" [I do not understand you] (194); and "Où est donc le mal de s'aimer, de se le dire, de se le témoigner?" [What possible evil can there be in loving one another, in saying it to each other, in demonstrating it to each other?] (195), in which speaking of love is no less natural than hearing it would be. Even her effort at reflection, or intellection, does not lead to understanding ("j'y cherchais un sens, je n'y en trouvais point" [I looked for a meaning, I could not find any] [191]). A defect of her *entendement*—her hearing and her understanding—makes Suzanne unable to grasp the evil of sexuality, leaving her innocence to indicate her desire, in a thoroughly devious fashion.

Already in these mishearings we find much more knowledge as readers than the writer allows. Moreover, what Suzanne does grasp in a general way about the dreadful effects of convents from dom Morel's warnings, she regrets having heard: "Que je suis fâchée de vous avoir entendu!" [How distressed I am at having heard you!] (196). Here, much as the misunderstandings of *Les Liaisons dangereuses* lead to our understanding, Suzanne's inability to "entendre le mal" must guide our good reading. What she does not understand, the evil of the mother superior's behavior, no reader has trouble "getting"; literally, we hear and we understand "(le) mal." We are then exactly in the position of the marquis de Croismare. In a discussion of the relation between the novel and Jacques Rivette's film version made in 1966, famous for being prohibited, Jean-Claude Bonnet comments that there is no marquis in the film, and no first-person point of view. Instead, the combination of the camera's point of view and the aesthetics of the tableau "necessarily makes of the spectator a sort of moral recourse and constrains him to adopt the position of Croismare."[33] We read by supplying what Suzanne Simonin does not understand, and so must the marquis. What in fact she asks Croismare to listen to (after dom Morel) is what she herself does not understand. And Suzanne's text alone conveys the meanings she purports to be ignorant of, and to convey them, *il entend mal.*

Until she has spoken to dom Morel, Suzanne refuses the listening that decodes or deciphers the *obscure*, the *scrambled*, the *mute*, the *hidden*: these are the terms for what Barthes called, in a 1976 essay titled "Écoute," the second type of listening.[34] It is only when she takes the step of voluntarily listening to the mother superior's confession that she hears at last. I am particularly interested in this point of her writing because I feel we can detect in it the passage from the *mimetic* (naïve) account, which claims to relate experience, to *semiotic* inscription, the place where we can best examine the writing of realism for Diderot and answer the "Question to men of letters."

Like Jacques behind the wall of paper listening (voluntarily or involuntarily—must we choose?) to his hosts' lovemaking, Suzanne eavesdrops on the lesbian mother superior's confession. Meticulous preparations and precautions occur in Suzanne's writing before she narrates this event, to the point of calling attention to themselves. After a break in the page, a half-page paragraph focuses on her writing of the eavesdropping and her anxiety about how the marquis will read it; key phrases are the following:

Lorsque les choses peuvent exciter votre estime ou accroître votre commisération, j'écris bien ou mal, mais avec une vitesse et une facilité incroyables; mon âme est gaie, l'expression me vient sans peine, mes larmes coulent avec douceur, il me semble que vous êtes présent, que je vous vois et que vous m'écoutez. Si je suis forcée au contraire de me montrer à vos yeux sous un aspect défavorable, je pense avec difficulté, l'expression se refuse, la plume va mal, le caractère même de mon écriture s'en ressent, et je ne continue que parce que je me flatte secrètement que vous ne lirez pas ces endroits. (197)

[When things may arouse your esteem or augment your commiseration, I write well or poorly, but with an incredible speed and easiness; my soul is gay, the phrasing comes to me without difficulty, my tears flow gently, it seems to me that you are present, that I see you and that you listen to me. If I am forced, on the contrary, to show myself to your eyes in an unfavorable light, I think with difficulty, the phrasing balks, the pen does not write well, the very character of my writing reflects this, and I continue only because I secretly flatter myself that you will not read these places.]

These reflections on her writing serve as seductions and pose problems of interpretation. We are meant to understand, of course, that what is to come is "mal." Although seduction is the effect of both the kinds of writing she describes, it seems clear that the writing that comes readily is the mimetic relation of experience, producing a happy result; this is the writing Suzanne believes in. It is the writing that *represents* without question, without doubt: "il me semble que vous êtes présent, que je vous vois et que vous m'écoutez" [it seems to me that you are present, that I see you and that you listen to me]; it is the writing that is "certain to produce an illusion," the sure and certain option of the "Question to men of letters."

The writing of the "mal," on the other hand, which she is about to produce in the most Rousseauistic moment of the narrative, resembles that difficult and hence uncertain production of "good" writing that Diderot labored at all his days: "the phrasing balks, the pen does not write well." Such writing deserves admiration because it improves upon the mere illusions of mimetic realism, augmenting and enhancing it; Suzanne can only guess at its devious effects when she dreads that the marquis will actually read this part. Surely no better strategy could ensure that he does, for no more pointed language could better direct the marquis to listen. The marquis' task is then to read "le mal," just as Suzanne's is to write it.

The writing that is to follow, then, narrating the overhearing of evil, lies firmly encased in this ironic context: it is devious. A "confessional" strategy that excuses Suzanne's deceitful act of eavesdropping, and also her *writing* of it, is found in this sentence: "Et puis comment supprimer dans ce récit un événement qui n'a pas laissé que d'avoir des suites?" [And also, how can I suppress from this narrative an event that has continued to have consequences?] (197). Rousseau might have written these words in more than one spot of his *Confessions*. This listening event has narratological implications as well as the obvious ethical ones, because it brings an end to the structured narrative of Suzanne's life; what follows are the "réclames," or "announcements," and the "abrégé," or "abstract," of her existence—bits and pieces of narrative not yet put into a structure. The overhearing of the confession thus has an effect of stopping the flow of writing. That this is so seems appropriate, because what can no longer continue is the innocent first-person memoir that has been dependent on Suzanne's ignorance from the start.

It is clear that Suzanne's act of eavesdropping affects her writing: it provokes a new, devious writing. With the opening of her eyes or, rather, ears, comes a new point of view, literally omniscient, which will include conveying evil. Now, as she narrates the conversation she overheard, she becomes the direct mediator of the marquis' hearing and writes about it with significant irony:

Mais s'il est mal d'avoir été surprendre les discours de deux personnes qui se croyaient seules, n'est-il pas plus mal encore de vous les rendre? Voilà encore un de ces endroits que j'écris, parce que je me flatte que vous ne me lirez pas; cependant cela n'est pas vrai, mais il faut que je me le persuade. (198)

[But if it is a bad thing to go snooping on the conversations of two people who thought they were alone, is it not an even worse thing to repeat them to you? Here again is one of those places that I write because I flatter myself that you will not read me; nevertheless it is not true, but I have to persuade myself of it.]

Why write if he is not to read what she writes? In case the irony of "you will not read these places" in the earlier passage (197) has escaped the good marquis, the "nevertheless it is not true" here handily reminds him how to play his role. And that role is to read evil, just as Suzanne's is now to write it like a "sublime rascal"; not only does she know evil in the mimetic story, she also knows the deceit in writing it.

Now too Suzanne knows her future; that is the result of her one act of deliberate listening. As Barthes writes about the listening that decodes or deciphers, "to listen is to seek to know, in an institutional way, what is going to happen" ("Écoute," 222). Quite exactly, Suzanne's future is demarcated by this eavesdropping that uncovers the secret; from that point on, her fragmentary writing brings incomplete closure to the events in the last convent (it narrates fragments of the mother superior's confession [199–201]); it takes her out of the convent; it turns to the present tense, and the historical present. In narratological terms, her eavesdropping begins the very necessary transition that gives plausibility to the exchange of letters with the marquis. Now the text shows its hand. Suzanne becomes the dual subject of an interlocution, "in which the silence of the listener will be as active as the speech of the speaker" ("Écoute," 223).

While the rhetoric surrounding her act of eavesdropping thus suggests that writing is in the service of seduction, this interpretation is not fully available until the final paragraph before the preface closes the loop, as it were, on the meaning of Suzanne's writing about sexuality. This postscript to Suzanne's narrative, which Diderot added late, closely corresponds to the novel's opening paragraph in that the marquis is mentioned in the third person and Suzanne again wonders how he will receive her writing. Now, after rereading what she has written, she fears her self-portrait flatters her:

Serait-ce que nous croyons les hommes moins sensibles à la peinture de nos peines qu'à l'image de nos charmes, et nous promettrions-nous encore plus de facilité à les séduire qu'à les toucher? . . . Cependant si le marquis . . . venait à se persuader que ce n'est pas à sa bienfaisance, mais à son vice que je m'adresse, que penserait-il de moi? (208)

[Could it be that we believe men less sensitive to the portrayal of our sufferings than to the image of our charms, and do we promise ourselves even more facility in seducing them than in moving them? . . . However, if the marquis . . . came to be convinced that I am not addressing myself to his benevolence but to his vice, what would he think of me?]

Nowhere until now had the reader any reason to suppose the marquis had such a thing as a vice, by which Suzanne's writing might seduce him. One may hear

Diderot's opinion about women in general when the postscript continues: "En vérité, il aurait bien tort de m'imputer personnellement un instinct propre à tout mon sexe. Je suis une femme, peut-être un peu coquette, que sais-je? Mais c'est naturellement et sans artifice" [Truthfully, he would be very wrong to attribute to me an instinct proper to my entire sex. I am a woman, perhaps a little flirtatious, how would I know? But naturally and without artifice] (208). By such textual maneuvers the proposition has been insinuated that to a vice corresponds a seduction, and that beneficence responds only to being moved— no doubt by an emotion of an erotic character. Just in case the marquis (object of her address) did not get it by reading her memoir, his vice is now being called to recognize her seduction. In sum, when she is being seductive, she realizes he is listening—lending an ear. And that is exactly the opposite of her naïve claim: "I flatter myself that you will not read me."

Yet Suzanne does not want to have sexual relations with the marquis de Croismare (never mind that it would be literally impossible, unless the real marquis were to become a character in the novel). The rhetoric that shows her as an object of desire while claiming not to is wasted effort, goes for naught, because her text is made to serve a function that it does not know of: to bring the (real) marquis back to Paris. Hence, her request for a position in a distant province (on the next to last page) is a misdirection, an error; thus, her postscript about not being able to write without being seductive marks her recognition of failure in the ultimate moment.

And what did this first reader, this "oyeur," listen to, then? Certainly not the sexuality, according to his letters. The real marquis writes real letters to the fictional Suzanne, and receives replies from her or from Mme Madin on her behalf. (Mme Madin's status is more complex yet: she is neither wholly fictional nor wholly real, because Diderot and friends used her real status and her real mailing address to enhance the reality of the fictional letters they wrote in her name.) Now, it may seem absurd to speak of a man existing in the real world choosing to pay attention to some parts of a fictional autobiographical account addressed to him, and not to hear others. It is, moreover, almost certain that the real marquis de Croismare did not read the text that constitutes this account—essentially, the text not including the preface. But that is precisely the absurd situation of the novel as it remained when Diderot died, perhaps without finishing it. The real replies by the marquis do not satisfactorily answer the account Suzanne has written; he did not hear her appeal to his vice, to his pleasure—at least, that is how he appears in his writing. His incomplete listening, neglecting or refusing sexuality, his failure to hear let Suzanne's innocence endure well beyond the point any ordinary listener would have accepted as plausible, and thus it also let the reader hear Suzanne's seductiveness. The bad listening of the marquis, as it is inscribed in Suzanne's writing, was productive in that it gave existence to both the naïve and devious poles of the "Question to men of letters."

While P. W. Byrne roundly convicts Suzanne of bad faith, I see the needs of the text topmost; taking a stance beyond the represented story, I am looking at the function for Diderot of these episodes, events, and narrative strategies: the purpose of swaying the marquis de Croismare. Byrne's intensely detailed analysis, excellent illustration of Barthes's obsessive reading discussed in *Le Plaisir du texte,* carries conviction; although accepting much I find there, my aim differs. I think the "Question to men of letters" can be construed to address and answer all the contradictions. Diderot claims to win the wager of persuading in spite of the loss of verisimilitude, as the "Question" intimates. In other words, there is a realization of the implied answer to that question, the answer that would claim to persuade while maintaining the illusion. Our task is to "buy" it, overcoming our "problem" with contradictions, including the central contradiction.

The central contradiction—sexual knowledge mediated by sexual innocence—so pertinaciously analyzed by Byrne falls or yields to a higher function: the text as seduction, the creation of the written-Suzanne as object of a reader's desire, which is achieved only at the price of this *invraisemblance*. Interestingly, as Byrne shows repeatedly, Diderot's additions to the "original version" only strengthened the contradictions and further undermined verisimilitude, making Suzanne's narrative more and more an act of bad faith, in Byrne's opinion. Yet is it not possible that Diderot's purpose was to spoil the aesthetic integrity one might expect from a work of art, like those too artfully conceived letters he spent his days spoiling?

In short, it is by Suzanne's *not hearing* and the marquis' *selective listening* that the reader best hears Diderot's text, just as her successful communications pass through a necessary third party before reaching their desired receiver. De la Carrera has carefully demonstrated that indirect, oblique communication is a strategy Suzanne develops; while her direct dialogues and her direct letters fail to communicate, she succeeds with the ternary model (41, 45). Suzanne therefore mirrors the reader of *La Religieuse,* who finds out last what the cause was of the "novelistic result," the term Jean Catrysse used to describe the novel.[35] The reader who engages in the right kind of distracted listening takes in everything, but only by listening against the writer and the first reader. We are to answer the "Question aux gens de lettres" by maintaining both the plausibility of the narrative—against impossible odds—and the aesthetic pleasure of the novelistic. To know the illusion and how it is produced moves the reader better than the mere illusion might, however verisimilar. Writing does not achieve the change Suzanne seeks; her death turns the ending to another purpose, of which she and her writing know nothing. Therein lies the ultimate swindle, and it is sublime.

Écouter-jouir: Lending an Ear

> Lorsqu'on fait un conte, à quelqu'un qui l'écoute, et pour peu que le conte dure, il est rare que le conteur ne soit pas interrompu quelquefois par son auditeur.
>
> [When we tell a tale to someone who is listening, and if the tale is long enough, it is rare for the narrator not to be interrupted sometimes by his listener.]
>
> — *Ceci n'est pas un conte*

This is not true of the *Heptaméron.* For all their vociferous debating, and their eagerness to assume their turns as tale-tellers, the *devisants,* or narrators, are entirely silent while one of their number narrates. This aspect of the design of the *Heptaméron* has intrigued only one critic, to my knowledge: Gisèle Mathieu-Castellani. Showing the work is based on a dialectic of suspicion and semblance, she defines the *devisants'* silence as the locus of belief; suspicion resides in the commentary or the *devis.*[36] This silence contributes to the orderliness of the structure marked by the passing of the voice, creating an exemplary illustration of listening, if not of hearing.

If in *Jacques le fataliste et son maître* Diderot takes pains to ensure that no story is told in such silence and complicity, that interruption is the order of the day, that the listeners' roles are not so well defined, it is because he wants the reader to engage in an active, not silent, listening. "There is no longer," Barthes wrote in his essay "Écoute," "on the one hand the one who speaks, reveals himself, confesses, and on the other the one who listens, keeps silent, judges, and sanctions; . . . his listening is active, it presumes to take its place in the play of desire, of which all language is the theater; it should be repeated: listening speaks" (229). What is explicit in *Jacques le fataliste* is only implicit in *La Religieuse*: the respectful silence of Suzanne's listener is assured by the fact that her story is written, and its transmission to the "editor" remains obscure, but we hear Diderot's text in that overdetermined, multilayered verisimilitude that his "Question to men of letters" requests, when we take our place in the play of desire.

The crossing interferences of the messages contained in the letters of *Les Liaisons dangereuses* contribute to the disorder stemming from the failure of Reason. Yet in spite of its disturbances to narrative authority and point of view, it remains largely a classical novel, because it reserves a role for the reader that is entirely compatible with the authors' role, that is parallel with it. (The word *authors* is in the plural to accommodate Laclos, the editor, and the publisher.) For both roles, Reason's failure is necessary to writing.

Whereas Suzanne's strategy, or rather Diderot's, is not to hear evil, all the better to let us listen to it, Laclos's is to "entendre mal" "hear badly," so we may hear well by listening to the "malentendus." On our side, it is listening, whether indirect or mediated, that is "bad," but productive of good hearing. We are then like Diderot at the theater blocking his ears to "hear" via the gestures of the actors: "Je répondis que chacun avoit sa façon d'écouter, & que la mienne étoit de me boucher les oreilles pour mieux entendre" [I replied that everyone had his way of listening, & that mine was to block my ears to hear better] (*Lettre sur les sourds et muets*, 53). Or we are in the listening utopia Barthes describes, the distracted psychoanalytic listening in its "lay" form, in the mediated communications of literature: "Listening includes in its frame not only the unconscious, in the topical sense of the term, but also, as it were, its lay forms: *the implicit, the indirect, the supplementary, the delayed*: listening is opened to all the forms of polysemia, of overdetermination, of superposition, there is an attrition of the Law that prescribes direct, exclusive listening." ("Écoute," 228–29; emphasis added). Limping, stumbling dialogues make us listen "badly," in contravention to the law of direct listening, but it is at this price *to the characters* that we obtain our pleasure as readers. This is the very action of writing realism.

In this utopia, the reader is in the position of "lire-sourire" [read-to-smile], in Starobinski's happy term (368), because there are characters in the position of "aimer-parler" [love-to-speak], and others convey this pleasure to the reader in the form of "écouter-jouir" [listen-to-enjoy]. When listening becomes erotic, love is vocalized and the ear naturally becomes an erogenous zone, according to Starobinski (374). But the uncertain mediation of the "aimer-parler" in *Les Liaisons dangereuses* forces our understanding to a level in which the "écouter-jouir" is ironic, for the characters. "To make itself listened to indirectly," Barthes had said in *Le Plaisir du texte,* is how the text best procures the reader's pleasure. "Your ear doesn't know what it's talking about," Jacques's host had said. However:

JACQUES. —Vous croyez apparemment que les femmes qui ont une oreille comme la sienne écoutent volontiers?
LE MAÎTRE. —Je crois que cela est écrit là-haut.
JACQUES. —Je crois qu'il est écrit à la suite qu'elles n'écoutent pas longtemps le même, et qu'elles sont tant soit peu sujettes à prêter l'oreille à un autre. (28)

[JACQUES. "Apparently you think that women with ears like hers listen willingly?"
THE MASTER. "I think it is written up above."
JACQUES. "I think it is written after it that they do not listen to the same man for long, and that they are just a bit inclined to lend an ear to another."]

At the risk of refiring the smoldering *querelle des femmes,* I would suggest that although it is written up above that we may listen voluntarily, we are happy to lend an ear to another; we are hearing something else. Our eroticized ear seeks pleasure in unruly listening. Within their fictional, mimetic frames, *Les Liaisons dangereuses* and *La Religieuse* figure this dynamic, which underlies all our reading of fiction, and so they put forward for our attention and enjoyment the processes of their semiosis.

Four

Semiotic Structures and the Unity of Composition

It is a cliché of literature that Balzac's *La Comédie humaine* represents a pinnacle of realism. Strangely enough, it was a pinnacle to which modernist authors of the twentieth century did not wish to aspire: for many of the avant-gardes of this century, the Balzacian novel was a standard, the example of the kind of writing against which the new defined itself. No longer was it possible to write a sentence like "The marquise went out at five," as if unaware of the processes by which such a straightforward description creates an illusion of reality. The twentieth century considers Balzac's prose "politically incorrect," in a sense: to write like Balzac is to ignore the processes of writing, which is no longer possible. Modernist novelists of this century are too self-conscious about their art, have too much to say about the mechanisms of the mimetic creations they foist upon the world. They have taken a militant stand, and in wanting to come clean, they have lost their innocence.

No such "self-consciousness" troubled Balzac. He did rise to a pinnacle of realism, creating a whole world in close imitation of the one he knew. "The nineteenth century, as we know it, is largely an invention of Balzac," wrote Oscar Wilde.[1] It did not bother Balzac that his created reality could only stand beside "true reality," because he thought his model of French society resembled the real world so well that it often surpassed it in truth and realism—and he did not hesitate to say so. Historian of society, secretary to "chance" (the greatest novelist in the world), practically taking the cosmos down in dictation, this realistic novelist had an idea of a complete portrayal, in which all the effects his fertile mind could engender would result from all the causes his keen observation would reveal, governed by all the laws analysis might formulate. All of

Balzac's composition in *La Comédie humaine* tended toward an ideal final form, in theory attainable at the price of an unheard-of effort. Only death prevented him from completing the portrayal; it would have arrived at completion had he had but world enough, and time.

Many prefaces published with first editions of Balzac's novels explained his intentions, giving us a solid basis on which to understand the vast project that became *La Comédie humaine.* From these we learn that the work is realistic because Balzac wanted it to be; at the same time, Balzac spelled out the processes of composition he was using to arrive at that goal. These prefaces and other texts thus indicate a direction for the reader to follow toward apprehending the moment of writing, which leaves traces in the realistic writing itself. Contrary to a long-held view, the text of the Balzac novel does not lack reflection about its semiosis. It is simply wrong to pay attention only to Balzacian mimesis and ignore semiosis, and not only because semiosis is not the opposite of mimesis. Balzacian realism results from a combination of realistic effects and compositional effects, but the reflection about composition lies within the very writing of the realism for which Balzac is famous. The goal of this analysis is to demonstrate how the processes of composition are revealed in the mimetic illusion.

Martin Kanes, in *Balzac's Comedy of Words,* poses in stark theoretical terms the stakes and the outer limits of realistic creation. There is, he writes, "a spectrum ranging from a reader presumed totally ignorant to a reader presumed totally knowing. In the first case the novel would be impossible, since it would entail the establishment of a whole conceptual world. . . . In the second case the novel would be unnecessary, since the presumed reader already knows everything."[2] The components of Balzac's "whole conceptual world" mandate an ignorant though sophisticated reader, one who progressively becomes knowing, while explicative language protects and justifies the fabricated story.[3] Not content to let his characters tell or enact the story, the familiar authorial presence does not hesitate to point out the drama of the scene for which an explanation is necessary for the ignorant reader. The strong voice of the narrator favors theatrical, zoological, architectural, or archeological metaphors to inscribe the mimesis. At the same time, within the very structure of the realistic creation representing events, semiotic features explicate composition: semiosis displays the genotextual process of the story, in addition to the story itself.

Genotext is a useful term introduced by Julia Kristeva, in opposition to *phenotext,* to refer to the activity of the signifying productivity as it exists within the visible, phenomenal text.[4] The phenotext is a signified structure governed by codes; it is the text as phenomenon, as product, with a material existence. The genotext is a signifying productivity, the field of *signifiance*. The phenotext is a structure, whereas the genotext is a process. To adapt this terminology to Balzac, I would say that the genotext refers to what I have been calling composition, the phenotext to the result of that process, the representation of reality. The concept of the genotext, as I use it, does not depend on the historical elaboration of the writing. While genetic criticism claims early versions of a text as its territory and analyzes the historical process of composition and creation, the genotext is that aspect of the phenotext that contains and displays the traces of those complex engendering processes. All the traces of the passage of time are collapsed into the genotext. This is the quality of the text that I am calling semiotic.

The genotextual process is, remarkably, almost always present and usually discernible in the Balzacian phenotext, and it is fascinating to watch Balzac show his hand. A fundamental characteristic of his writing is the skill with which he integrates semiotic explanation into mimetic narrative. In the novels, novellas, and short stories of *La Comédie humaine,* one can describe figures of expression that serve to expose the semiotic, genotextual process as it is seen in the phenotext. Such figures are mimetic because they arise in the plot and generate it, yet they interpret the writing of realism. In using the term *figure* here, I have in mind a general but useful definition from Barthes: "movements of language that are sufficiently formal and repeated that I can call them 'figures.'"[5] Bathes considered figures characteristic of his writing, and he gave them a particularly vital role in the discourse of love. For Balzac, the repeated movements of language that I am describing as mimetic may consist of themes, motifs, or leitmotifs of significant meaning in the narrated story; they are represented images whose role in the plot can be shown to be analogous to their expression on the mimetic level. Mimetic figures thus stand for semiotic structures. In *La Maison Nucingen,* for instance, the narrative circulates, accumulates, is invented or stolen, and so on, in a manner analogous to the way money circulates, accumulates, is invented or stolen in the plot.[6] This motivation of the semiosis by represented realities in the stories makes two functions of language coexist: rhetoric and representation.[7] It is this sense too that the genotext is visible in the phenotext. Because Balzac is the novelist he is, we have little difficulty grasping the connections between the level of events and the level of composition (though these are not really separable levels); the author has done much to make analogy obvious, devising terms of comparison, inventing pointed metaphoric turns, deploying a virtuoso lexicon, and so on. While writing about his characters, Balzac is always writing about his writing too; while telling his story, he takes pains to tell us how it comes to us. His mimetic narrative simultaneously inscribes the conditions and limits of its composition. Jean Ricardou, a notable exponent of the *nouveau roman,* had this to say about fiction: "All fiction, perhaps, at least by intuition, tends to produce an image of the narrative principles that found it."[8] This principle, for all its tentativeness, describes very well what Balzac's writing does, as does this more sweeping assertion by Ricardou: "The great narratives are recognized by this sign, that the fiction they propose is nothing other than the dramatization of their own functioning" (178). For the great explicator who drew *La Comédie humaine* from his own vital substance, the drama of its invention is worth our interest as much as the dramas it recounts—and perhaps the very limits of his vitality dictated such an economy of means.

In a sense, then, Balzac is particularly useful for a study of writing realism because, not unlike Diderot, his reflection guides ours. What I have just described as the replication or reduplication of mimetic figures in semiotic structures might be the subject of a broad study of *La Comédie humaine.* As a symptomatic example, *Modeste Mignon* stands at the center of this chapter; it is a novel in which writing plays a key role. The tourniquets of illusion and reality whirl to a devilish tune at the heart of this romantic and realistic work; sorting them out ranks high among the many pleasures it offers the reader. The example of Balzac's only epistolary novel in *La Comédie humaine, Mémoires de deux jeunes mariées,* serves to introduce the general problematic of how we read a Balzacian narrative: how we come to understand the mimetic world the writer creates. Lacking the familiar narrator who explains everything, *Mémoires* raises this problematic in a particularly pointed way. To close this chapter, the analysis of *Ursule Mirouët* will show two striking mimetic figures of semiosis at work in the composition: genealogy and inheritance. These two figures bring together the mimetic and the semiotic into the unity of composition for Balzac.

Writing and Reading: *Mémoires de deux jeunes mariées*

Written in 1841, the first of the novels in *La Comédie humaine* as it was published poses problems of interpretation arising in differing points of view, like

Les Liaisons dangereuses. Unlike Laclos's novel, however, the difficulty of interpretation concerns so fundamental a matter that an essential question remains
unanswered: What does Balzac think about his characters? Louise de Chaulieu
and Renée de Maucombe, the two heroines, present widely divergent images of
the role of love in a woman's life. As an immediate consequence, the reader
seeks to understand the ethos that each represents. Because only Louise and
Renée tell each other their stories, no single-voiced narration guides our reading or helps us decide between their conflicting fundamental philosophies of
life; direct authorial interventions are entirely lacking. That this is so defies
convention: one might expect at least a framing narration disingenuously
explaining the existence of these letters, commenting on them, or describing
an editor's role—a "Publisher's Note" or an "Editor's Preface," or at least a note
or two, if not a "Preface of the Preceding Work" like Diderot's. Usually such a
prefatory text is motivated by a moral purpose (whether sincere or ironic) or
serves as an interpretive guide. Yet, from the Furne edition on, remarkably,
such mediation was limited to the hand that apparently numbered each letter
and added the names of the sender and receiver. A short preface in the first
edition, however, sketchily followed convention—except that even it gave no
hint of a moral interpretation.

Because there are for the most part only two letter-writers, unlike *Les Liaisons dangereuses,* this largely dual rather than multiple point of view combined
with the more relaxed pace and longer time frame maintains a balanced focus
on the stories of Louise and Renée, unlike any single narrative thread in
Laclos's novel. And other stories do not intervene (except as anecdotes). The
correspondence begins at the moment the two young women leave their convent school, and it continues at first frequently, then more rarely, during their
entire young adulthood, through marriage, Renée's motherhood, and Louise's
widowhood and remarriage. Louise's quasi-suicidal death closes the correspondence. The problems of point of view, in short, are not those that stem from
the accidental, obstacle-strewn structure of letters in *Les Liaisons dangereuses,*
the source of mishearings and the cause of Reason's failure. Rather, as two lives
diverge, the reader falls between them, and cannot choose. A rigorous dialogism rejects dialectical synthesis and sustains opposed values: Paris and the
provinces, Society and Nature, aristocrat and bourgeois (Renée, though not
strictly speaking a *bourgeoise,* makes a bourgeois marriage), illicit passionate
love versus legitimate conjugal love, two parallel but antithetical destinies, a

chiasmic outcome (the "provinciale" finishes in Paris, the "Parisienne" in Nature), and a double morality. Louise's passionate life full of movement, uncertainty, and change contrasts wildly with Renée's calm, secure, but dull existence whose course is traced in advance. Louise clearly represents a Balzacian Ideal, the temptation of the absolute—but that way lies danger and death. Renée stands for the Family, often proclaimed by Balzac as the only solid foundation for society, and some of the warmest pages defend this view—but how proper and insipid! Renée preaches those deep-seated values, whereas Louise wants excitement and risk.

All commentators on the novel necessarily seek to elucidate the philosophies implied by the two life stories, but readers find it difficult to assert unequivocally which of the women conveys Balzac's thought. It is interesting that George Sand suffered little such doubt, and indeed assumed Balzac wished to promote the values represented by Renée. Sand wrote: "I don't come to your conclusions, and it seems to me on the contrary that you prove exactly the opposite of what you want to prove"; "I admire the woman who procreates, but I *adore* the one who dies of love. That is all you have proved, and it is *more* than you wanted to."[9] Sand's significant reading *against* Balzac offers a model for the reader's freedom to choose.

Yet, what *did* Balzac think of the two "solutions" to the "problem" of passion in marriage? Those who have written about this novel resort to some affirmation of both dialogic poles, to avoid misrepresenting Balzac's thought. As Arlette Michel postulates, Balzac is attracted by both Renée and Louise, excluding neither opposed term and trying to operate a mediation between them (*Mémoires*, "Introduction," 32). Michel also writes, in a study of passion in marriage, that for all the seriousness of the Bonaldism Renée represents, Balzac does not give her a triumphant position in the narrative: "How wrong it would be to see in Renée's successes the triumph of the marriage of reason!"[10] No more can Louise's failure be taken to invalidate the morality she represents. It is typical of the results of such analyses of the novel that Michel must resort to the following interesting formula to position the novelist with regard to his creations: "[Renée] thus offers the example of a character that Balzac as a 'philosopher' approves and that, as a novelist, he detests" (192). Only a split subject can hold both sides of the story in his hands, it would seem.

I feel the question of Balzac's philosophy has been adequately dealt with in the critical literature on *Mémoires de deux jeunes mariées* (mainly in the prefaces of different editions), and my purpose is not to bring another brick to that edifice. Rather, I would claim that this duality, this scarcely understandable affirmation of doubleness, stands, for Balzac's writing, in the position of obstacle, of stumbling block—and hence of *boute en train*: a prod. It may well be that Balzac the philosopher casts his vote with Renée, while adoring, like George Sand, a life like Louise's, but I suspect that the novelist is no less involved in this dilemma. It is not so clear that as a novelist he hates Renée and all she represents, because the very existence of the novel depends on her opposition with Louise. And that opposition is put, relentlessly, to good use by the master novelist. It is the figure of his semiosis.

The idea of a double woman initially proposes a vision of unity made from duality; it represents a potentially complete being made of contrary parts, but the image lies in the past and survives, artificially, only a short time. On the first page we find Louise and Renée compared to Siamese twins, an apt symbol of their girlish intimacy in the convent.[11] Through their letters, now separated by more than geography, Louise "lives" with Renée in her Provence valley, Renée "lives" with Louise in Paris (197). They agree to a division of labors. Renée writes, "Tu seras, ma chère Louise, la partie romanesque de mon existence. . . . Tu seras deux à écouter, à danser, à sentir le bout de tes doigts pressé" [You, my dear Louise, will be the romantic part of my existence. . . . There will be two of you, listening, dancing, feeling the tips of your fingers pressed] (222). It is up to Louise to weave "some fine passion"—and she does!—"dans l'intérêt bien entendu de notre double existence" [in the interest, to be sure, of our double existence] (240), while Renée knows all the joys and anguish of having children. But the double woman figure is merely a configuration from the prenovelistic past (the convent school, of which there is properly nothing to be recounted); it is a deceptive misguidance for the reader, an initial condition of unity destined to be upset. Significantly, the Siamese twins of the first page are mentioned in their *death* ("nos âmes soudées l'une à l'autre, comme étaient ces deux filles hongroises dont la mort nous a été racontée" [our souls fused to each other, like those two Hungarian girls whose death was recounted to us] [196]); what the comparison gives, it soon takes away. Repeatedly, Renée and Louise accentuate their differences, sometimes in strong language. Each envies the other, but each also writes freely of her contempt for the life the other has chosen. Never does one change in response to the other's exhortations. No letter mediates between contraries.

Because writing has a double origin in the two correspondents, it readily construes these relentless conflicts; the necessary condition of correspondence, physical separation, provides a mirror of the unrealizable union. The correspondence accentuates unmediated opposition, and because it is virtually limited to the two writers, their opposition is sustained rather than diffuse or multiple. In the mimetic realism of this correspondence, the conflicts and contrasts portrayed or staged for the benefit of Balzac's reader are left entirely up to the writers and readers of the correspondence to express, resolve, or reaffirm. This is the very condition of Balzac himself before his writing: his narratives usually flow from and depend on the oppositional. It is the well-known "secret" of his composition, and the foundation of his philosophy, as if the only way to obtain wholeness and completeness were to add two conflicting parts together. Unity passes through duplicity; diversity would be an avatar of unity. The complete being is made of contrary parts and is naturally, profoundly double, as attested by figures of the androgyne, the transsexual or the ambisexual, and the angel (see *Séraphîta*). Louise and Renée, each representing the connected but opposite activities of reading and writing, never suggest a unitary figure of composition. The irreconcilable nature of the two writings expresses the nostalgia for the whole and the tragedy of incompletion in Balzac's work.

Whatever unity there may be, nevertheless, lies in the reading. The reader who is presumed ignorant, though not the first receiver of the letters, is forced to participate in their interpretation and supplements the absent "explications nécessaires," potentially to combine writing and reading and make the work whole. Through the direct address to its two alternating receivers, the writing portrays the drive to reach the real reader, whose activity is interpretation. Alternately taking the place of Renée and Louise as letter-*readers,* reading over their shoulders, as it were, the interpreter each time completes the fullness of the figure, unites the contraries, and operates the complementariness that the two opposed positions of writer and reader configure. Renée and Louise, in their primary semiotic activity, are our mimetic guides into semiosis. To be the reader presumed ignorant is to undertake the semiosis that supports interpretation: let us not be either Louises or Renées, but a successful combination of both in their semiotic roles. That combination occurs only in the outside writer (Balzac) and reader (us). Each woman by writing places herself with Balzac; each when she reads is an ever contemporary reader.

The lesson, then, concerns how to interpret writing, with what knowledge and with what strategy, in order to grasp Balzac's stance. Some variant of the notion of naïve realism that prevailed in *La Religieuse* operates here, or perhaps more simply put, an identification with the letter-writers, whose writing serves the straightforward function of presenting and re-presenting their selves, again and again, to their reader.

Writing Modeste Mignon

With obvious links to *Mémoires de deux jeunes mariées,* the 1844 novel *Modeste Mignon* carries correspondence into the metarepresentational realm; it offers a fascinating illustration of the writing of realism because the letters it contains are doubly fictional, on two levels, spinning fiction and reality through tourniquets not unlike those in *La Religieuse.*[12] *Modeste Mignon* displays with great comic brio the same naïve representation found in *Mémoires de deux jeunes mariées,* but, like a wily mechanism à la Diderot, the device of the letter writing is devious.

This romantic novel concerns itself with a fundamental problem of marriage, a problem we saw Louise and Renée writing about: what part should be granted to passion in a marriage, as Arlette Michel has put it about the *Mémoires* and *Honorine* ("Balzac juge du féminisme," 183). With *Modeste Mignon,* Balzac wagers that romantic love can coexist with marriage, a program that is both naïve and devious in the frame of *La Comédie humaine.* The key device of the semiosis is a beguiling instance of writing and reading: Modeste's naïvely amorous, anonymous correspondence with the famous poet Canalis whose secretary, Ernest de La Brière, reads her letters and replies in place of Canalis. Immodestly signing herself with the ciphered "Mlle O. d'Este-M.," Modeste writes lyrical, inspired letters that she addresses to Canalis, while La Brière, knowing he is not the glorious poet she thinks she is writing to, signs no name at all in his replies. Reading these letters, Modeste can only ascribe to Canalis the self-representation La Brière produces by his very writing, and she imagines the great poet with La Brière's qualities; La Brière, while writing both for himself and as if for Canalis, struggles to read the real Modeste behind the mask she has chosen. There is thus a real and an imaginary writer and a real and an imaginary reader on both sides of the correspondence. Only the omniscient reader sees all and enjoys the pleasure of knowing more than the writers of the letters do about each other. Here the explanatory material surrounding the correspondence leaves little room for ignorance—but it does raise a central question of interpretation, a kind of "Question to men of letters." To that question this reading seeks to propose an answer. In this artfully constructed novel, writing manipulates the real reader just as it does Modeste. Balzac wins the wager—that love can coexist with marriage—by persuading the reader that the letter writing translates, indeed creates, both the true selves and the ideal addressees of the correspondents.

After eleven letters have been exchanged, the authorial presence writes:

Ces lettres ont paru très originales aux personnes à la bienveillance de qui *La Comédie humaine* les doit; mais leur admiration pour ce duel entre deux esprits croisant la plume, tandis que le plus sévère incognito met un masque sur les visages, pourrait ne pas être partagée. Sur cent spectateurs quatre-vingts peut-être se lasseraient de cet assaut.[13]

[These letters seemed quite original to the persons to whose benevolence *La Comédie humaine* owes them; but their admiration for this duel between two wits crossing pens, while the strictest incognito places a mask on their faces, might not be widespread. Of a hundred spectators, perhaps eighty would find this onslaught fatiguing.]

And out of respect for the "majority" that governs any constitutional country, he "suppresses" eleven further letters. (Bringing the correspondence to a close are three final letters, for a total of twenty-five including the eleven that Balzac suppressed.) This passage adds to the combined real and imaginary writing a new layer of relations between fiction and truth. It is not just a question of deciding if the fictional representation in the letters creates a truthful self-portrait; on a higher level, Balzac creates a "truth" by imposing the fictional reality of the letters. Protesting that they really existed, that there were people who allowed *La Comédie humaine* to use them, in a commodious if common fiction that is strengthened by pretending he has suppressed some of them, Balzac adds this patina of truth to the letters. As a result, we have truthful letters that recount a fiction whose function is to create a truth for the letter-writers, and all of this is embedded inside the great truthful fiction that is *La Comédie humaine*.

It is worth noting that the correspondence evolves in what Barthes called the third type of reading pleasure, in which the reader has the desire to write: "Reading is conducive to the Desire to write."[14] It is, in fact, a remarkable illustration of that principle: nothing succeeds better at prompting each successive letter than reading the writing of each previous one. Furthermore, the correspondence, for Modeste as for us, has all the dangerous attraction of a transgression, because her father has ordered that no man may approach her. The purpose of this interdiction is to prevent the terrible accident that befell her older sister, Bettina-Caroline, who was seduced and abandoned, then died. Thus, Modeste's writing stems as much from the interdiction as from her romantic and *romanesque* temperament, and it is a wily supplement to the interdiction, nicely reminiscent of Elisor's use of the letter in the twenty-fourth tale of the *Heptaméron*. This writing focuses on the question of the representation of reality in narrative.

Situated in 1829, *Modeste Mignon* forges a new alliance between the cynical social realism of marriage, so well illustrated throughout *La Comédie humaine*, and the idealistic romanticism of love. That opposition lies at the heart of the novel. While a fundamental doubleness threatens happiness—"man is double" (541), La Brière blankly states—the ending will unite this and all contraries. The twenty-year-old Modeste's very physiognomy signals her double nature. Purity, transparency, luminosity, the signifiers of modesty, are contradicted by lips that "express voluptuousness," the intimate signifier of immodesty (482). Likewise, "the most knowing mockery" belies the candor of her eye, and "la poésie qui régnait sur le front presque mystique était quasi démentie par la voluptueuse expression de la bouche" [the poetry that reigned on her almost mystic brow was largely negated by the voluptuous expression of her mouth] (482). In addition, her eyes, "limpides comme des yeux d'enfants, en montraient alors toute la malice et toute l'innocence" [limpid like a child's eyes, showed at that time all the malice and all the innocence of a child] (481). Couched in the language of a painting, this physical portrait ends with the euphemistic expression of what one can only call Modeste's sexual potential:

Un observateur aurait pensé que cette jeune fille, à l'oreille alerte et fine que tout bruit éveillait, au nez ouvert aux parfums de la fleur bleue de l'Idéal, devait être le théâtre d'un combat entre les poésies qui se jouent autour de tous les levers de soleil et les labeurs de la journée, entre la Fantaisie et la Réalité. Modeste était la jeune fille curieuse et pudique, sachant sa destinée et pleine de chasteté, la vierge de l'Espagne plutôt que celle de Raphaël. (482)

[An observer would have thought that this young woman, whose alert and sensitive ears awakened to every sound, whose nose received the scents of the blue flower of the

Ideal, must be the theater of a battle between the poems that flutter around every sunrise and the labors of the daytime, between Fantasy and Reality. Modeste was a young woman curious and demure, knowing her destiny and imbued with chastity, a virgin from Spain rather than one by Raphaël.]

Exceptionally familiar with passion because of her sister Bettina's fatal love affair, Modeste is chaste but not pure, devoured by curiosity if not "knowing" (503). Her warm, blond German nature, fanciful and artistic (her mother is German), is opposed to cold French Reason. She is both *bourgeoise* and noble. She is poised on the brink of love, at the poignant, twilight moment between girlhood and womanhood—young enough for candor, old enough to anticipate love: "Modeste eut alors une existence double" [Modeste then knew a double existence] (509)—quite like Renée coupled with Louise in *Mémoires de deux jeunes mariées*. Her double experience contrasts the strictures of humble reality to "le poème de sa vie idéale" [the poem of her ideal life] (509).

In a poetic passage (509–10) opposing marriage to love, some of Balzac's most flowery rhetoric artfully conveys what it hides. Put somewhat crudely, which is just what Balzac did not do, the gist of the passage is something like this: A girl's love is so innocent that it does not include sexual desire; it is Platonic, both in its refusal of carnal passion and in its birth in ideas and its sustaining of ideals; and, without contradicting Platonism, it is romantic, "la première illusion des jeunes filles" [a girl's first illusion]. It is "l'oiseau bleu du paradis des jeunes filles" [the blue bird of girls' paradise], which no hand or bullet can reach, with magic colors and scintillating precious stones that dazzle. In the delicate language that is appropriate for a young woman, Balzac finds a way to express the desires of love, in language so richly suggestive that even a person of Modeste's intelligence would perhaps fail to grasp its import. Already "cet amour platonique si rare, si peu compris" [this Platonic love so rare, so little understood] makes perfection in innocence, chastity, and purity coexist with the thirsty drafts of "l'Inconnu, de l'Impossible, et du Rêve" [the Unknown, the Impossible, and the Dream] that Modeste imbibes. Reality, on the other hand, the destiny of every maid who is not to become an old maid, is "cette hideuse Harpie accompagnée de témoins et de monsieur le Maire" [this hideous Harpy accompanied by witnesses and the justice of the peace], a comic, pseudomythic periphrasis for marriage. (Elsewhere Balzac will write of "les tessons de verre de la Réalité" [the glass shards of Reality] [608].) Reality's opposition to Fantasy, Ideal, poetry, and "pudeur" (modesty) is the operative dichotomy of the entire novel, a struggle played out within Modeste too and ramified throughout the narrative in the opposition of poetry to the positive—this last so handily and so ironically figured by Canalis and La Brière, respectively.

The finality of the novel will consist in reuniting contraries, in unifying the doubleness of Modeste, in preparing and foretelling the persistence and flowering of romance within the hideous reality of marriage. The amorous correspondence, intrinsically double, with its doubled writers (masked and unmasked) and double readers (knowing and unknowing), and replete with double meanings, too, in its address to the reader, is the major operator of this reunification.

Even in its structure, *Modeste Mignon* falls readily into two parts, of roughly similar size (56 percent and 44 percent of the whole, respectively), before and after the moment when her father, Charles Mignon, tells Modeste that she has declared her love by letters to La Brière and not Canalis (606). I characterize the first part as novel, in the double sense of innovative and novelistic, whereas the second is mundane, meaning both commonplace and worldly. Via insistent metaphors of literature, poetry, and theater throughout the novel, the reader is solicited to reflect on artistic representation.

The "novel" of the first part opens convincingly in the novelistic vein with a plot mounted against Modeste, which has all the suspense of a drama whose outcome could be tragic. From the outset "reality" is thus opposed to mere "literature." Modeste's guardians believe that she loves only through literature: "[Modeste] se passionne pour les poésies de celui-ci, pour la prose de celui-là" [[Modeste's] passion is for the poetry of this man or the prose of that one] (495). Only the blind Mme Mignon sees that Modeste loves a real man, and it is at her insistence that they mount a melodramatic stratagem designed to make Modeste reveal her supposed lover, the "real" object of her love, by means of a complex fiction: one of her guardians will pretend to shoot a mysterious stranger in the garden. It is a plot strangely reminiscent of the device by which Raymon de Ramière enters George Sand's novel *Indiana* and its heroine's life. Modeste reacts to this dramatized "real" man "en regardant ses amis d'un air candide et sans aucun effroi" [by looking at her friends with a candid air and without the least fear] (498); she is not convinced of the reality of this fictive representation. What is both a theatrical representation and a mimetic fiction fails to produce the man Mme Mignon insists Modeste loves. In a move that is almost self-parodying, it is as if Balzac plays out this comic plot to introduce the idea that the lover may arise from a fiction. That is precisely the task of the correspondence: it fabricates a suitor for Modeste Mignon. When the second part replays the story of Modeste's love from new premises, it is on the plane of social and economic realities, which until then had little significant part in the story, except as elements of the past. Thus, although the term *roman,* in Balzac's language, initially has ironic connotations, the happy ending will valorize the "novel" Modeste and Ernest have written in the first part without neglecting these mundane and worldly realities.

This romantic reading must arise from our unshaken belief in the success of the representation of self in the letters. That representation has its source in literature, the rather overblown object of Modeste's pleasures. Modeste indulges in continual reading (504), which arouses in her "an absolute admiration for genius" (505). She loves literature and a man whom she takes to be Canalis, "man of letters." With an irony gentler than Flaubert's treatment of Madame Bovary, Balzac's discourse itself becomes fussily lyrical to describe Modeste's literary obsessions: "L'air fut plein de langues de feu. Les arbres lui parurent un plumage" [The air was full of tongues of fire. The trees seemed to her a plumage] (514). Later, when she learns she has been writing to the great poet's secretary: "Le soleil était obscur, la nature se voilait, les fleurs ne lui disaient plus rien" [The sun was dark, nature put on a veil, the flowers no longer said anything to her] (608–9). Balzac is playing with the clichés of romantic poetry (à la Canalis, naturally) to gently mock Modeste's love of glory. Yet it is from such imaginative virtuosity that her happiness arises. Among the pleasures of her imagination there is one that will become a reality: "Son père revenait riche à millions" [her father came back enriched by millions] (506). Like Emma Bovary, she has the

étrange faculté donnée aux *imaginations vives* de *se faire acteur* dans *une vie arrangée* comme dans *un rêve*; de *se représenter* les choses désirées avec une *impression si mordante* qu'elle *touche à la réalité,* de *jouir enfin par la pensée,* de dévorer tout jusqu'aux années, de se marier, de *se voir* vieux, d'assister à son convoi comme Charles-Quint, de *jouer* enfin en soi-même la *comédie* de la vie, et, au besoin celle de la mort. Modeste *jouait,* elle, la *comédie* de l'amour. (505–6; emphasis added)

[strange faculty granted to *vivid imaginations* to *turn herself into an actor* in *a life arranged* as if in a *dream;* to *envision* desired things with *an impression so sharp* that it *borders on reality,* to *be rapt in thought,* to devour everything including the years, to marry, to *see herself* old, to attend her funeral like Charles-Quint, to *act out* for herself, finally, the *comedy* of life, and, if needed, of death. Modeste *was acting out* the *comedy* of love.]

The italicized terms overdetermine a naïve theory of representation, the system that underlies the writing of the self in the letters. In this writing, imagination has an immediate expression in representation, which is something like Barthes's figuration, the appearance of the erotic body in the text: "the text itself, a diagrammatic and not imitative structure, can be revealed in the form of a body," which attests to a figure of the text. Representation, on the other hand, for Barthes, is "*an embarrassed figuration . . .* a space of alibis (reality, morality, verisimilitude, readability, truth, etc.)"—the *other* purposes that the text may be made to serve, the reality to which it is subordinate.[15] In terms of this opposition, one can say that the first part of the novel is structured by figuration, a fragile structure of desire. Modeste's lettered love object is only the mental figuration of Canalis, not Canalis himself. It is a representation Modeste reads as naïvely as she "reads" his publicity portrait found in a store window, in which the man of letters is "sketched in a rather Byronic pose" (510), the fertile but false ground from which her love springs. Such a reading of the figuration of love in letters matches a naïve reading of the mimetic novel, one that would believe in the existence of the created world and characters just as it believes in the reality conveyed by the letter writing, one that resembles Suzanne Simonin's belief in the ability of writing to convey reality directly, in *La Religieuse.* The first part thus addresses a reader who, guided by the device of the correspondence, confirms the power of figuration *par lettres,* by letters.

With the arrival of the father, Charles Mignon, in what Balzac calls the "third act" of the drama, the plot of Modeste's novel draws to an end; it comes completely untied when Mignon informs Modeste that she has corresponded with La Brière instead of Canalis. If Love is the prime mover of the first part, that other prime mover of *La Comédie humaine,* Money, now flatly introduces its incontrovertible materiality. Exposing the correspondents' real names and stations puts into question the entire fairy tale story of the anonymous correspondence, and fantasy fades into a mundane (worldly and banal) comedy of manners, dubbed "the Heiress." Suavely addressing a sophisticated reader who enjoys the social and economic operations of the devious moral comedy of marriage, this section is realistic in that rank and wealth are the serious issues, and reasonable considerations crowd out the romantic desires of the heart. The very notion of the husband was, after all, "Reality, that hideous Harpy" (510). Indeed, the first part is not needed for the second, strictly speaking, except to bring La Brière into the picture as one of the pretenders to Modeste's hand. His presence would not otherwise be justified, or very well motivated, in the comedy of manners now playing, because he is not socially on a par with the other pretenders, Canalis and the duc d'Hérouville.

Playing out an archetypal structure that follows on the transgression of interdiction, this part of the novel puts both Modeste and Ernest to the central tests: Will her heart recognize the man she loves? Will he win her through his real valor, rather than his epistolary costume? Before the end, Modeste will make a mythic choice for the weakest of her three pretenders. In folklore and myth, the third child, the ugliest, poorest, most neglected; the third casket; the third fairy—these are always the least likely choices, yet always turn out the best and truest. Here, the two flowers of fame and glory, or at least of ancient name and rank, are the two noblemen, Canalis and Hérouville, whereas La Brière, the wallflower, is not yet noble. (He will be allowed to add Charles Mignon's former title comte de La Bastie to his name after his marriage with Modeste.) Indeed, the duc d'Hérouville seems to have little importance except to help the reader make (or accept) the choice for La Brière in the end. During much of the mundane comedy, there is nothing in Modeste's behavior to remotely suggest that she will prefer La Brière; instead, she treats him harshly, with disdain. Amusingly, nothing so clearly marks the choice she faces than the pretenders' three replies to her indirect question: Will her husband gratify her capricious desires?

—Je ne trouverai jamais . . . de mari qui supportera mes caprices avec la bonté de mon père qui ne s'est jamais démenti, avec l'indulgence de mon adorable mère.
—Ils se savent aimés, mademoiselle, dit La Brière
—Soyez sûre, mademoiselle, que votre mari connaîtra toute la valeur de son trésor, ajouta le duc.
—Vous avez plus d'esprit et de résolution qu'il n'en faut pour discipliner un mari, dit Canalis en riant. (654)

["I will never find . . . a husband who will humor my caprices with my father's goodness, which has never faltered, or with my adorable mother's indulgence."
"They know they are loved, Mademoiselle," said La Brière.
"You can be sure, Mademoiselle, that your husband will know the full value of his treasure," added the duke.
"You have more than enough wit and resolution to discipline a husband," said Canalis, laughing.]

La Brière's reply is sentimental and implies his love; the duc d'Hérouville's reveals his formal recognition of rank and his financial interest; the poet's is witty (not to say callous) and skates on the social surface of life.

The mythic reign of three thus manipulates the reader into rooting for La Brière, the underdog to the brilliant Canalis. And Balzac does not mince words to express his opinions about La Brière's value, as when he describes him as "abîmé dans les terreurs du véritable amour" [submerged among the terrors of true love] (622). Moreover, the poor secretary has the father's and therefore the Family's imprimatur. The reader is likewise manipulated into disliking Canalis by the sham of his theatrical poses and by the narrator's direct, pointed commentary: "Or, Canalis, *vous le savez,* a le cœur sec" [Now Canalis, *as you know,* is cold-hearted] (624; emphasis added). Hérouville represents the "ancienne noblesse," a third, backward-leaning temptation for Modeste. The Ancien Régime can still have some viability, and something like a dying spark is visible in the puny Hérouville. And of course the hunt, with its protocol and ritual, is a dusty remainder of that other time. Yet one realizes that the new aristocracy that Mme de La Brière-La Bastie will join will be forward looking, and indeed she will help Hérouville enter the world of industrialization not incompatible with noble sentiments, because she and her father will assist him in developing his marshy lands (see her noble refusal of the duke, 707–9).

During this comedy of marriage, representation becomes its own object: the theatrical posing of the heiress and the three suitors is representation for its own sake; it is sometimes misrepresentation; and it is devious because it is self-conscious. It is Barthes's "hampered figuration," an overt mechanism. Here is obdurate reality, the space of alibis that resists figuration and opposes pleasure, refusing the system of naïve representation of the first part. Here too, in this second half, writing stops and reading ceases. While the reader enamored of realities may enjoy the show, it is only because the beguiling correspondence has already won Balzac's wager. Now let us see how.

Love by Letters

By a semantic slippage, an attractive contrivance designed to seduce the reader, love, in the first part, occurs doubly *par lettres:* it is both in literature and in a correspondence. Modeste thinks she loves, through literature, a man of letters, Canalis. But La Brière is "l'homme *aux* lettres" [the man *of the* letters], not only the man who produces letters but also the man *created by* his letter writing. Balzac suggests we are to participate in the creation of the fiction of his self-representation: the "sentiments vraiment héroïques du pauvre secrétaire intime" [truly heroic feelings of the poor private secretary] (553), the truth of his character, are an effect of the reader's imagination, which may well make the letters "finer than they are" (553), the narrator allows. Without pausing to consider the interesting way this echoes Diderot's "Question to men of letters," I note how important this move is for the composition, for the semiotic activity. It is as if Balzac's purpose, with this warning, is to stimulate the reader's imagination, for where, if not in Balzac's writing, did that imagination arise? Have we any choice but to follow along "literarily" and literally and fashion the new figures of the letter-writers in the images they present to each other? In such a way the reader nudges love by literature, which is false, into love by correspondence, which is true. Dare we say that this slippage takes us from *l'amour par lettres* to *l'amour parle l'être*: from love by letters to love speaks the self? Modeste Mignon writes herself into existence, and reads La Brière into existence: each creates the self and creates the other, in the complementary acts of reading and writing.

We know that love by correspondence is true when we heed an important guide: an allusion to Beauty and the Beast (*La Belle et la Bête*). About midway, this apparently insignificant intertext stands for the principle governing the writing *in* the novel and *of* the novel. In a suggestive and ironic dialogue with Modeste, the faithful, devoted "dwarf" Butscha is compared, implicitly, to La Brière, and both are likened to the Beast. Butscha, who has, with the prescience of his own love for Modeste, figured out that she is enamored of her correspondent without knowing his real identity, lays a trap by asking "si l'on peut se faire aimer indépendamment de la forme, belle ou laide, et pour son âme seulement" [if one can be loved irrespective of one's beautiful or ugly appearance, for the soul alone] (570–71). He has guessed that the letter-writer is not Canalis. In reply, Modeste reminds him that "vous oubliez que la Bête se change en prince Charmant" [you are forgetting that the Beast turns into Prince Charming]. The little man, who styles himself a model lover for a woman and not coincidentally constitutes one of the innumerable partial doubles of Balzac in *La Comédie humaine,* claims that the Beast's changing into Prince Charming indicates "le phénomène de l'âme rendue visible, éteignant la forme sous sa radieuse lumière" [the phenomenon of the soul made visible, extinguishing the form with its radiant light] (572). Such a "Prince Charming effect" recalls the various materialist phenomena, such as magnetism and somnambulism, which impart concrete realization to the ineffable, to thought, to the deep inner self. As the very mechanism of the love letters, this Prince

Charming effect reveals the radiant light of La Brière's soul, blinding one to the form, the external appearance of the modest secretary. Thus, the quasivisionary father, Charles Mignon, penetrates immediately to the truth of Ernest's character when the young man protests he would marry Modeste without a dowry, "et la rendre heureuse, comme vous avez rendu [votre femme], être pour vous un vrai fils" [and make her happy, like you have made [your wife] happy, be a true son to you] (598): "Charles Mignon recula de trois pas, arrêta sur La Brière un regard qui pénétra dans les yeux du jeune homme comme un poignard dans sa gaine, et il resta silencieux en trouvant la plus entière candeur, la vérité la plus pure sur cette physionomie épanouie, dans ces yeux enchantés" [Charles Mignon stepped back three paces, fixed La Brière with a gaze that penetrated into the young man's eyes like a dagger into its scabbard, and wordlessly noted the utmost candor, the purest truth on this open physiognomy, in those enchanted eyes] (598). The Beast really is a Prince Charming; his beastliness is merely a mask, and all happy endings throw away the mask.

Thus, Balzac believes the real being lies in the hidden soul, a kind of true self both masked and revealed in the writing and reading. Yet the very choice to write the self incurs the risk of deception and self-deception, and that is the intimate matter the letter-writing device puts forth in the novel, the source of its tourniquets. What is in question is the truth or falsehood of the figuration. From the start, self-representation is immodest and thus risks giving permanent consistency to the falsehood the writers adopt. It is immodest of La Brière to pass himself off as Canalis, and yet he is a modest person; his writing masks and reveals his modesty, as Balzac reminds us frequently, as in the phrase: "Les gens véritablement modestes, comme l'est Ernest de La Brière" [Truly modest people, like Ernest de La Brière] (589). His very refusal to sign "Canalis" illustrates this precarious ontology, as if he takes on the glory of the poet only by not signing his own (or another) name—by default, as it were. The assumption of Canalis's identity is immodest, the refusal to pretend to it is modest— the same writing act achieves both. As for Modeste, her signature O. d'Este-M. is a name for the imaginary representation of herself that she creates, especially in the early letters: a noble and very rich marriageable girl. With an admirable economy, by displacing a single character, Modeste eliminates the generic "Mignon" and acquires the nobiliary particle d', the powerful name Este, and the hyphenated addition of a second name indicated only by the mysterious

M. but suggesting an alliance important enough to preserve both family names in one.[16] (By just such a mechanism will her husband become vicomte de La Bastie-La Brière.) Thus, she deploys the modesty of her given name into something much more pretentious, including an entire family history. Truly Modeste's name is rich—in imaginary possibilities! On both sides, in short, the reality of the self is modest, morally or economically, whereas the written mask is decidedly immodest—and both are available meanings in the correspondence. This is important for the happy ending because much, if not all, of this immodesty finally adheres to the true selves of both protagonists and provides the handle to which the reader's approval is attached, as we shall see.

The letters ostensibly circulate between a pseudonym and an absent name: between the not true and the not false, in semiotic terms. Modeste, who has masked her truth with her pseudonym, very easily transforms her self by letters into her true self, simply by revealing her real name in her last letter. Returning to her real name removes the negative: the not true becomes the true. In fact, in the details of her letters, she has never left the axis of truth about herself. But Ernest, who has not signed his letters, passes from an absence of name (not false)—which is possible because Modeste thinks she knows who her correspondent is—to a false name, "le faux Canalis," a periphrasis that repeatedly and maliciously designates La Brière in the second part. In other words, Ernest unmasked is not automatically truthful; he must shed the apparent falsehood he acquired in wearing Canalis's name, which is Modeste's entire complaint against him. Knowing who really wrote the letters is not yet the condition of what has been called one of the four happy marriages in *La Comédie humaine*.[17]

If Ernest's true self is antipoetic, it is precisely against the literary extreme represented by Canalis. His first letter (522–24) is an immediate corrective to the lyrical enthusiasm and the adoration of genius that gush from Modeste's initial letter, which are couched in these terms: "Oui, j'éprouve le besoin de vous exprimer l'admiration d'une pauvre fille de province, seulette dans son coin, et dont tout le bonheur est de lire vos poésies. De René, je suis venue à vous. La mélancolie conduit à la rêverie" [Yes, it is a need I feel to express to you the admiration of a poor provincial girl, alone in her retreat, and whose entire happiness consists in reading your poetry. From René, I have come to you. Melancholy leads to reverie], and so on (514). La Brière's reply to this *romanesque* language is replete with double meanings addressed to the real reader. Turning Modeste away from Canalis, he attracts her to himself—but without removing the mask:

Tous les écrivains ne sont pas des anges, ils ont des défauts. Il en est de légers, d'étour-
dis, de fats, d'ambitieux, de débauchés; et, quelque imposante que soit l'innocence,
quelque chevaleresque que soit le poète français à Paris, vous pourriez rencontrer plus
d'un ménestrel dégénéré, prêt à cultiver votre affection pour la tromper. Votre lettre
serait alors interprétée autrement que je ne l'ai fait. On y verrait une pensée que vous
n'y avez pas mise, et que, dans votre innocence, vous ne soupçonnez point.

[All writers are not angels, they have defects. Some are dissipated, thoughtless, pom-
pous, ambitious, debauched; and, however imposing innocence may be, however chivalrous the French poet may be in Paris, you could encounter more than one degenerate
minstrel, ready to cultivate your affection the better to deceive it. Your letter would
then be interpreted differently than I have. Some would see in it a thought that you did
not put in and, in your innocence, do not even suspect.]

From the outset he establishes a disdain for poets, and he does so from within,
with all the value of truth associated with the confessional, self-critical mode.
As the outside reader realizes, La Brière roundly criticizes Canalis, under cover
of being Canalis: "si vous étiez tombée sur un talent hypocrite, sur un railleur
dont les livres sont mélancoliques et dont la vie est un carnaval continuel" [if
you had chanced upon a hypocritical talent, upon a joker whose books are
melancholic and whose life is a continuous carnival]—he writes as a poet only
to de-poetize; his disinterested air and a seeming objectivity immediately estab-
lish his honesty. Thus, he wins an extraordinary freedom to continue the correspondence without having to pursue the falsehood that he is an artistic genius;
henceforth he can write as a man. As a mere man, he implies, by contrast, that
he has correctly interpreted the truly poetic thoughts of her letter.

At the same time, the letter begins to mold Modeste:

Laissez-vous apprécier par un homme digne de vous, et devenez ce que doit être toute
bonne jeune fille: une excellente femme, une vertueuse mère de famille. . . . S'il est
glorieux d'épouser une grande renommée, on s'aperçoit bientôt qu'un homme supérieur est, en tant qu'homme, semblable aux autres. Il réalise alors d'autant moins les
espérances, qu'on attend de lui des prodiges.

[Let yourself be appreciated by a man worthy of you, and become what every good
young girl must become: an excellent wife, a virtuous mother. . . . Though it may be
glorious to marry a famous reputation, one soon realizes that a superior man, as far as
being a man is concerned, is the same as the others. He then fulfills expectations all the
less in that prodigious feats are expected of him.]

In short, La Brière's first letter goes a long way toward rejecting love by literature and creating love by correspondence.

The success of La Brière's stratagem clearly depends on the reader's participation. Unlike Modeste, we do not think of the letters as composed by the author Canalis (and as mentioned there is no signature to urge that pretense upon us). Although Modeste does not yet know that truth penetrates through the mask in La Brière's letters, we do, because the omniscient narrator repeatedly assures us we have heard the true La Brière in the correspondence, "si sincère de son côté" [so sincere on his part] (590): "La Brière était trop l'homme de ses lettres, il était trop le cœur noble et pur qu'il avait laissé voir pour hésiter à la voix de l'honneur" [La Brière was too much the man of his letters, he was too much the noble and pure heart that he had given a glimpse of to hesitate at the call of honor] (590). We are already reading the letters as a portrait of La Brière, whom we are coming to know in his positive reality: honest, just, honorable, forthright, upright (a "spirit of rectitude" [525]). That is, we read the letters differently than does Modeste, who listens to Canalis "talking" in them and does not know she is hearing La Brière. Like Cyrano wooing for himself in the name of the handsomer and younger Christian (curious intertext: the man has loved his last, but the play is yet to be written), La Brière speaks for himself but avows only Canalis. At first we may be amused by the layering of voices—Balzac writing for La Brière writing for Canalis—which we see from a certain critical distance; soon, however, Balzac and Canalis disappear and we hear La Brière talking. Talking serves to create the self—*parle l'être*—and secondarily to create the self of the other in the desired image. Comparing his writing to his talking about Modeste's first letter, in the pages just before his first reply, we see that La Brière is true to himself, for La Brière does not talk like Canalis, and his talking speaks his being: "Oh! Combien j'aimerais une femme venue à moi! . . . s'écria La Brière en retenant une larme" [Oh! How I would love a woman who came to me! . . . cried La Brière, holding back a tear] (521). But Canalis: "Non, non, toute lettre anonyme est une mendiante! Et quelles exigences!" [No, no, every anonymous letter is a beggar! And such demands!] (521).

As another counterpoint, the letter Canalis sends from Le Havre to his mistress, the duchesse de Chaulieu (683–85), reveals, in the tissue of its lies and in its style diametrically opposed to La Brière's, the vain, deceitful character of the "great man." Canalis in Le Havre is far more false than "the false Canalis"—false in his preening theatricality, and false to Modeste when he is told she is not a millionaire. La Brière in using Canalis's name, in the first part, is less false than Canalis using La Brière's *love,* in the second, for that is the only reason

Canalis can come to play his part in the comedy of the heiress. The entire device of the correspondence considered as addressed to the *reader* hammers home the fact that La Brière has never ceased being true—literally, perhaps, because he was "the false Canalis," but, quite factually, simply because he is not Canalis—and he is what he is *in his writing.*

For both letter-writers, then, the narrative inscribes a transformation that passes from the representation of self by letters as *literature* to the true selves in the letters as *correspondence.* This mutation in Modeste is initiated in her writing and is aggravated with each letter until the eighth, in which she immodestly proclaims her love and admits her real name is somewhat ironic (581–84). This extravagantly bold letter rises to the height of moral immodesty, in terms of both impropriety and pride. The Modeste who has given herself in letters, whom Canalis wittily and perhaps inevitably names "cette Immodeste" (684), is the written self that survives as a promise of enduring love, a necessary ingredient of the united contraries of the ending. Her voluptuous, desiring being here named Modeste for the first time will become the self that archly and understatedly accepts La Brière's immodest, Freudian riding stick a page before the end. The ending escapes from "hampered figuration" and returns us to a powerful confirmation of the truth of figuration in the poetic speaking found in the letters, circulating signifiers of the self.

Writing the Real Self

A "Question to men of letters" this novel may be said to pose is the following: Does Modeste marry a wimpy, timid, eternally modest, possibly impotent specimen of bourgeois positivism, who lives in the shadow of a glorious man and only lives through him, preaching the morality of Family in his letters, or is he in fact the flower of the feminine romantic ideal, the perfect blending of ideal and positive, the unique heart meant for Modeste's heart, the love encountered only once in one's lifetime (in conformity with Balzac's belief)? In other words, speaking from Modeste's point of view, is the truth of the portrait in the letters or not? In the preface of the Folio edition, Anne-Marie Meininger mounts a detailed attack against La Brière and issues a peremptory challenge to those who would choose the happy ending—no doubt those "happy few" for whom "the cloudless happiness of Modeste Mignon" is evident, according to Arlette Michel.[18] Meininger laments: "The exceptional person [Modeste] that

Balzac portrays only too well cannot end up marrying, *in one of the most depressing endings of La Comédie humaine,* a sulfur-yellow vest," and so on (emphasis added).[19] It will, of course, be apparent already that my reading prefers to consider the ending happy, not depressing. It should also be apparent that the ending is happy because it unites contraries.

Reading produces "the paradisiacal coalescence of the subject with the Image" (Barthes, "Sur la lecture," 43)—but to take pen in hand is to incur the risk of reaching the wrong reader. Modeste's first letter to Canalis proves him a bad reader: "Ce poème, cette exaltation cachée, enfin le cœur de Modeste fut insouciamment tendu par un geste de fat" [This poem, this veiled exaltation, the very heart of Modeste was carelessly handed over with a fatuous shrug] (519). For the cynical Canalis, the anonymous female author of this letter joins the thirty or so others who have written to the great man of letters; the very choice to write makes her common and commonplace, either a *rouée* or an "aging Englishwoman" (the nineteenth-century stereotype of the unattractive female), or poor and out to snare a husband. Such is, for a man like Canalis, the model of the female reader's literary admiration. The self of the writing courts these dangers, perhaps unwittingly. A task for Modeste's candor, then, is to skirt these risks safely and convey the real self, to find a corresponding soul.

It is La Brière who reads the first letter as a "parfum de modestie" (522), unknowingly realizing Modeste's very name, whose innocence proclaims the letter is written by "une vraie jeune fille, sans arrière-pensée, avec enthousiasme" [a genuine young girl, without reservation, with enthusiasm] (520). As for Canalis, "comment deviner" [how can one discern], he later says pompously, "à travers les senteurs enivrantes de ces jolis papiers façonnés, de ces phrases qui portent à la tête, le cœur vrai, la jeune fille, la jeune femme chez qui l'amour prend les livrées de la flatterie et qui nous aime pour nous, qui nous apporte la félicité?" [through the intoxicating scents of this prettily designed paper, of these sentences that go to one's head, the truthful heart, the young girl, the young woman whose love takes on the colors of flattery and who loves one for one's own sake, who brings one happiness?] (595). Avoiding this risk, the poem of her heart arrives miraculously in a heart of equal candor; only the name was wrong. When the writing of Modeste's letters reaches its desiring reader, its mixture of imaginary and real composes a self that allies contraries: chaste, innocent, idealistic, but also spiritual, passionate, desiring, and voluptuous like her lips, a perfectly balanced combination of "les différentes

Modestes [qu'Ernest] avait créées en lisant ses lettres ou en y répondant" [the different Modestes [that Ernest] had created by reading her letters or answering them] (628). What Canalis had read accurately in Modeste's first letter was in fact her only misknowledge of herself: her idealization of genius, which makes her see herself as the poet's muse and companion. Modeste's fanciful, literary enthusiasm, treated with irony, would have found a proper addressee only in Canalis. This misknowledge threatens to prevent her from receiving the heart of La Brière, the antipoetic real man, and it is this defect that La Brière's letters have the task of correcting.

The writing corrects any mistaken address because it drifts. A basic quality of the letter writing in *Modeste Mignon,* drifting opens to the reader's pleasure, by a precise design that is the advantage of the very "defect" in Modeste's love letters (about which her father teases and scolds her). The correspondence circulates among people by passing through texts: Canalis writes poems that find their way to Modeste's romantic heart and elicit her letters to "Canalis"; these letters arising in her heart reach not Canalis but the heart of La Brière (and this is the point where the circuit of correspondence ceases to be the habitual closed loop), which causes La Brière to write letters that go straight to the heart of Modeste; there the letters create yet another text, so to speak, the "livre que nous commençons" [book we are starting] (552), the "novel" of their love. Thus, though the source of their novel springs from the poems by Canalis, that source lies outside the circulation of the letters; a schematic representation of this precise but drifting structure would make it obvious that the posturing Canalis and his poems are left altogether outside the circuit. Modeste's marriage to La Brière is fated, structurally, by the circulating signifier that arises in Canalis's portrait and poems *but never returns to its origin.* There is drifting on both sides of the equation between persons and texts: a signifier circulates, with a double displacement. Drifting is a structural strategy that eliminates the false, redressing the error of address emblematically represented by Canalis, for Modeste's speaking of her being was not in fact addressed to a counterfeit lover.

In the midst of the correspondence, Modeste stages a novelistic scene in the church of Le Havre (574–77), in which she assumes an incognito to observe her correspondent, but a moment's reflection shows that the episode is another case of drifting. It might have been an appropriate maneuver for Modeste if she knew she was writing to the poet's secretary, and wished to assure herself of his appearance, but she thinks she is writing to Canalis, and she has his portrait. This slippage in the narrative design engages the reader's need for explanation. Its implausibility is motivated only by the creation of the selves in the correspondence, in its many stages, of which this is a particularly succulent one. The true self of her correspondent is the portrait *par lettres* and the visible portrait she sees in the church; the mistaken address is the name attached to the portrait she bought of Canalis.

Writing not only speaks the self of the writer but also creates the self of the reader, as I have said. La Brière molds Modeste by teaching her to give up the artificiality of her literary, ideal love and to fuse the love she learned in books with the common destiny of a woman: marriage. In his third letter (531–34), La Brière recognizes in Modeste "le beau idéal de l'Art, la Fantaisie" [the beauteous ideal of Art, Fantasy] and judges her "à la fois un poète et une poésie, avant d'être une femme" [both a poet and a poem, before being a woman]. He also sees in her "un désir secret d'agrandir le cercle étroit de la vie à laquelle toute femme est condamnée, et de mettre la passion, l'amour dans le mariage" [a secret desire to widen the narrow circle of life to which every woman is condemned, and to put passion, love in a marriage], a difficult but not impossible dream. While admonishing her that "this little novel is finished," he advises: "Jetez, dans les vertus de votre sexe, l'enthousiasme passager que la littérature y fit naître" [Cast into the virtues of your sex the passing enthusiasm that literature brought forth]. That very synthesis unifies her double nature in the ending. When Modeste jettisons the mask in her last letter, she completes the transformation from her self as literature (the imaginary) to the real that her love speaks.

In addressing Modeste the letters seek to arrive at a destination as knowing as the omniscient real reader. Both the visionary father and the blind mother, good readers of the correspondence, will confirm the truth of La Brière's character. The writing effectively raises Modeste to the level of such a perspicacious reader, creating the Modeste who allies realism and romanticism, whose willful forehead no longer contradicts her voluptuous lips. The worldly comedy culminating in the hunt perfects the creation and has its fitting closure, on the next to last page, in Modeste's acceptance of La Brière's riding stick. The riding stick is suggestive; its beauty, skillful execution, and prodigious value announce and foretell La Brière's manly stature. Perhaps this is what Modeste, in all her newly blossomed knowledge of sexuality, means to suggest when with a single sentence she both informs La Brière she will marry him and describes the gift as "un bien singulier présent..." [a very singular present...] (712). The telling ellipsis invites the reader—and La Brière—to dwell on the hidden meaning, the encoded reassurance: the imaginary is real; the real includes the imaginary. The gift of the stick and its reception figure a reprise of the writing and reading that dominated the first part. Modeste's acceptance is her last act of "good reading," now entirely on the real plane. And it shows that she, like the real reader, is now able to merge naïve and devious representation, retaining the romantic and novelistic even in the context of worldly marriage. Modeste learns, in a few short hours, how to be an aristocrat; the hunt completes her education. Her success in verbal sparring with the grand ladies present, among them Eléonore de Chaulieu, Canalis's mistress for the last ten years, appears in the mythic dimensions of the novel as the ratifying test that validates the heroine. Is there not also a suggestion, with Eléonore, that passion, and no doubt sexual passion, may endure in spite of the passage of time? For if the novel has reached its best readers, they will know that the outcome of the second, mundane part is also romantic, but newly romantic; it is not the superficial and artificial "blue flowers" of a young woman's fantasies, the object of Balzac's irony, but the unheard-of persistence of the ideal dream in the reality of social life.

To arrive at the happy ending, the marriage of the ideal and the positive, the reader sees to it that Modeste and Ernest safely avoid the risks of falsehood inherent in the self-representations of the letters. It is our reading that satisfactorily answers Modeste's anguished question about Ernest: "Ses vertus, ses qualités, ses beaux sentiments ne sont-ils pas un costume épistolaire?" [His virtues, his qualities, his fine sentiments—are they not an epistolary costume?] (607). In German, Ernst approximates the English earnest: ernst = serious, im Ernst = truly, verily, faithfully—all the things the reader must believe La Brière is. The earnest, serious, and sincere Ernest will not only be a suitable mate, "le compagnon que Dieu vous a fait" [the companion God made for you] (534), in his own words, but also an heir to continue the former line of the comtes de La Bastie of the Ancien Régime, which had ended with the Revolution and the fall of the Empire. The present of the novel ties the past to the future, thus uniting Love and Money and restoring the lineage to nobility. Even the underlying archetypal structure suggests that "they lived happily ever after" and had many children.

Romantic Realism

In *La Comédie humaine,* to speak of the union of contraries is usually to evoke the cynical dénouement of the drama of a girl's marriage: a sentimental mismatch. In this rare novel, reuniting contraries instead validates both conflicting parts, the modest and the immodest, the naïve and the devious, the false and the true, poetry and reality, the literary and the positive, the novel and the mundane, the lover and the husband, Love and Money, even the old and the new aristocracies. The act of writing, which is essentially reading, culminates in a philosophy of oneness, neutralizing doubleness by retaining the best of both parts. "Ne suis-je pas un peu allemande?" [Am I not a little German?] Modeste had pleaded with her father, moments before the unliterary truth emerges. "Nous sommes, nous autres jeunes filles, entre deux systèmes: laisser voir par des minauderies à un homme que nous l'aimons, ou aller franchement à lui..." [We young women fall between two systems: to let a man see, by flirting, that we love him, or to go to him openly...] (604). To be "a little" German is to unite these deeply rooted contraries.

In this novel, Balzac shows us in his story that writing produces the real, what Barthes defined as "that which is demonstrated but not seen" (*Le Plaisir du texte,* 74). La Brière's letters compose the unnamed real self with every sentence, whereas the name Canalis designates the vain, empty reality ("that which is seen but not demonstrated"). The real is composed of fragmented practices, Barthes said, in spite of or alongside a named reality ("what is seen"). In La Brière's letters, the named reality or at least the implied reality, to which Modeste has given the name Melchior Canalis, opposes the real of La Brière; Ernest's reality, without ever being named, inhabits his every sentence, and it asserts that he loves Modeste, that he is sincere. Canalis remains poetic in the pervasively negative sense, whereas La Brière, poet "by the heart" (517), achieves a figural lyricism founded in positive reality: "Il n'y a rien de plus poétique qu'une élégie animée qui a des yeux, qui marche, et qui soupire sans rime" [There is nothing more poetic than an animated elegy that has eyes, that walks, and that sighs without rhyming] (691)—and whose name, one might add, rhymes with Modeste's. Not insignificantly, Balzac counters false with real poetry; in Canalis lie the illusions, the false representations, the versification on paper "for so much a line" (518). If, as Butscha claims, "Un poète, mademoiselle, n'est pas plus la poésie que la graine n'est la fleur" [A poet, Mademoiselle, is no more poetry than a seed is a flower] (579), it is clear that Balzac's scorn goes for the versifier, but Poetry in motion remains admirable.

Because La Brière's romantic reality is fragmented into the pieces of his prose, embedded like the jewels in the riding stick, the reader must compose it (like the mosaic of *La Comédie humaine*). Modeste as reader does just that, but with her heart and unwittingly, while her head foolishly seeks the glory of the name Canalis. Of the two real receivers of Ernest's letters, Modeste and the reader (in addition to the imaginary addressee, Mlle O. d'Este-M.), one has the task of creating the romantic realism that alone makes the marriage of the ideal and the positive possible at the end, and that is the reader. Modeste is distressed when she learns she has played *Le Jeu de l'amour et du hasard* on her side only (608), as long as she persists in seeking the poet's glory; we, on the other hand, are perhaps already conditioned by the happy outcome of Marivaux's play. (Furthermore, Canalis in his fatuous pomposity resembles no one so much as Arlequin!) Modeste's only chance of composing the real like a mosaic out of the fragmented and not obviously valuable bits depends on her succumbing to the manipulations of representation, as the reader does.

To join the fragmented, unnamed pieces of the real into a whole is to practice romantic realism. It is to see the soul of the beast hidden by the form, beautiful or ugly. It is to see how writing both masks and reveals the real. In the ending, naïve representation or figuration will endure, even in a sophisticated or devious reader. As Arlette Michel notes, Balzacian young women in general seek to associate the Ideal of passion with "the realities of life" in marriage; but "this reconciliation of the Ideal with the positive, if it is attempted naïvely, remains utopian" ("Balzac juge du féminisme," 199). Perhaps Michel did not intend it, but I see her comment as contributing to the argument in support of the utopian reading of this novel. Less naïve, the appropriately conditioned reader—conditioned by the writing of the letters—can uncover this unity in doubleness. Reuniting contraries is the reader's critical task as ultimate addressee of the letters. And I am tempted to propose that the ideal reader is essentially "female"; even La Brière has the requisite feminine qualities, heavily underscored (without his mustache, "il eût trop ressemblé peut-être à une jeune fille déguisée" [he would have looked perhaps too much like a girl in disguise] [575]). (Others have mentioned the most important real female reader, Mme Hanska.) Anyone who would read the ending as depressing reads effectively as a "male"—perhaps like Canalis. The point is not that we must choose between the depressing or the happy interpretation of the ending, but, rather, that we inevitably read with one optic or another, and if I call the happy one the female reader and the depressing one male, I understand those adjectives not as human sexes but as reading positions that the text defines. (Thus, Meininger, writing the preface of the Folio edition, reads not as a female reader, and Vandegans essentially agrees with her.)[20] The tension between the depressing and the happy interpretations of the ending can be understood in terms of the writing and its address to the reader, and I say the reader, like Modeste, is as pleased as a Princess Charming.

Modeste Mignon demonstrates how the novel—as Balzac invented it—can indulge in realism and still give full play to the romantic; the positive may flourish without destroying desire. Beyond the life of a young girl in marriage, the novel sustains a purpose for writing, in *La Comédie humaine*: to achieve a new alliance of the romantic and the realistic. And this is the deeper philosophy of Balzac's composition, which maintains that *the ideal is not contaminated by the real.* The analysis of *Ursule Mirouët* will help explain what I mean by that philosophy.

Ursule Mirouët: Genealogy and Inheritance

In this first novel of the *Scènes de la vie de Province*, written in 1841, a familiar picture of the provincial town emerges, one that is found in several other Balzac novels. Here Nemours is represented as a stifling, narrow-minded milieu in which a stupid, greedy, and powerful bourgeoisie smothers the good and the noble. As if to underscore the underlying dichotomy of Paris and the provinces, several escapes to the capital designate it as the place where one makes money (or spends it), as well as the locus of illumination and knowledge. Whereas money flows loosely in Paris, in Nemours it is as inbred as the social structure, in which noxious ignorance breeds unchecked. The peasantry are exploited and cheated by the rising bourgeois, who hold all the positions in town, while the aristocracy stubbornly retains its Ancien Régime prejudices and falls by its own impoverishments, under the determined attack of the bourgeoisie. The social picture is a standard in Balzac, as I have suggested, but two figures of semiosis particularize it: the omnipresent relations among the four families of Minoret, Levrault, Massin, and Crémière representing the pervasive extension of the bourgeoisie, on the one hand, and, on the other, the extraordinary coterie enfolding the heroine, uniquely identified by its belonging to no class and by its elite intellectuality. I characterize as genealogical the relations constructed among the four bourgeois families, whereas the classless intellectuals are connected by inheritance, particularly in the case of the two central characters, Ursule Mirouët and her tutor.

The pure and innocent Ursule is put in grave danger by the lowly evils of the triumphant bourgeoisie, as in *Pierrette* and *La Vieille fille,* but all nevertheless ends happily, with order, justice, truth, and light, thanks to spiritualism—for a major purpose of the novel is to demonstrate that spirituality triumphs over materiality. Balzac opposes these deeper themes of the novel in the same way as genealogy and inheritance, mimetic structures that these themes extend into the domain of thought. The topic is central and vital to *La Comédie humaine,* but no subject however profound is immune to those puns and word games Balzac can never resist. Consider this sterling example, in which lapidary wit puts spirituality and materiality momentarily on the same plane: "Croyez-vous aux revenants? dit Zélie au curé. —Croyez-vous aux revenus? répondit le prêtre en souriant" ["Do you believe in ghosts?" said Zélie to the priest. "Do you believe in gold?" replied the priest, smiling].[21] The play on words is brought out by a kind of ironic or dubious chiasmus: the materialistic Zélie speaks of ghosts, while the priest reminds her of money. Like so many Balzacian novels, it seems, this one is built on a series of oppositions, functioning in tandem.

The action begins in 1829 (like *Modeste Mignon*) and turns repeatedly to near and distant past times to provide necessary explanations, until a return to the present and the actual start of the drama. After a rich, enlightened life in Paris, the philosophically minded doctor Denis Minoret returned in 1815 to Nemours, where he was born, to finish his life with his ward and three chosen friends: the abbé Chaperon, justice of the peace Bongrand, and captain Jordy. Together, these four men have been raising Ursule Mirouët, Minoret's deceased wife's half-brother's child, who in 1815 was an orphan of ten months. By 1829, Minoret's nieces and nephews in Nemours are fearful of losing their inheritance to Ursule. The striking opening pages portray their alarm when the doctor attends mass for the first time in his life (his conversion is the work of Ursule, who is now fifteen years old, and of animal magnetism). When the doctor dies, Ursule does not receive the fortune he left her, because Minoret-Levrault, the nephew, steals three "inscriptions de rentes en trois pour cent, au porteur" [government stock certificates at 3 percent, to the bearer] intended for Ursule and together worth 36,000 francs of income. For good measure, Minoret-Levrault also burns the doctor's will. In the purity of her spirituality, Ursule is visited by the doctor's image in her dreams. He shows her Minoret-Levrault's crime, and the numbers of the *inscriptions de rente*. She recovers the fortune, marries Savinien de Portenduère, the aristocratic object of her heart, and moves to Paris. Minoret-Levrault is converted to an honest life, but his wife Zélie loses her mind when their son Désiré dies after an accident.

This astute narrative design thus combines an affair of succession with a story of animal magnetism: Ursule regains her stolen inheritance only because she possesses somnambulistic powers. For Balzac, this combination whereby a spiritual faculty produces a material gain is not in the least contradictory. Rather, it is central, as I will illustrate.

Minoret at eighty-three can well be called an "uncle to inherit from" (776): his nephew Minoret-Levrault, niece Mme Crémière-Crémière, and first cousin once removed Mme Massin-Levrault with their spouses expect to inherit the doctor's considerable wealth, and in fact they have virtually no other collective designation than "the heirs." Upon first arriving in Nemours, Minoret asks his nephew: "Ai-je d'autres héritiers?" [Have I other heirs?] (786), and, henceforth, whenever they are collectively mentioned, *héritiers* is the word for the Massins, Levraults, Minorets, and Crémières, almost exclusively. It is used 105 times in the 220 pages of the Pléiade edition—by far the greatest number of occurrences among the 49 novels included in an electronic concordance of *La Comédie humaine*. In addition, *héritier* occurs seven times in the singular, and the feminine, *héritière*, five times in the singular and plural forms. *Cohéritier* and *cohéritières* occur six times. The word *héritier* applies to family members; the *Petit Robert* gives: "relative designated by law to receive the succession of a dead person. . . . The *heirs* or blood heirs are distinguished from irregular *successors,* from *legatees*" (emphasis added).[22] The term *heirs* thus represents immense narrative potential or plot value, which is only heightened when Balzac, in a sociological vein, uses instead the broader terms *bourgeois* and *bourgeoise* (twenty-nine times), and *bourgeoisie* (ten times). Savinien de Portenduère, referring to the heirs, will say, "Ces bourgeois sont comme des chiens à la curée" [These bourgeois are like dogs with quarry] (925). The strength of their evil lies partly in their common purpose as *cohéritiers*: "Conspiracy or coalition, the instances of cupidity readily come together into an association of forces directed toward a single goal. In almost every novel by Balzac, around a figure who is both a victim and an object of envy, there forms a ring of greedy desires, as for instance in the novel *La Vieille Fille*."[23]

Balzac often indulged in complex genealogies, notably in *Pierrette*, *La Rabouilleuse*, and *Les Paysans*, but none is so relentless, so pervasive, so inescapable in its action as the one he created here. Thierry Bodin sketches the development of Balzac's idea of the evil in bourgeois genealogies in the case of *Les Paysans*.[24] The unfinished *Les Héritiers Boirouge* consists almost entirely of the family tree whose final version will end up in *Ursule Mirouët*, but Balzac complicated the genealogy so much that he had to abandon that novel. Madeleine Ambrière-Fargeaud writes, in notes to the novel: "*Ursule Mirouët, La Rabouilleuse*, and *Les Paysans* can be considered incarnations of *Les Héritiers Boirouge*, a recurring project, undulating and diverse, but always centered on the vast theme of division, of succession" (3: 1524). The genealogy in *Ursule Mirouët* is a mimetic figure of his semiosis. The four indigenous families of Nemours—Minoret, Massin, Levrault, and Crémière—forge the links of a "zigzag" network; they are the four "shuttles" that weave the "lacework" of a "human cloth," the pieces configuring the "domestic kaleidoscope" of the bourgeois "cousinage" (782, 783). The image of a kaleidoscope, in which the same few pieces taking different positions form many pictures or configurations, aptly figures the internal genetic crossings and the thousands of possible varieties stemming from them. Minutely, obsessively explicative, the genealogy of these families, which Balzac anchors in the time of Louis XI, is both an obstacle to reading and an excellent example of a text presuming ignorance. Its complexity would stump a genealogical scientist, Balzac writes: "Les variations de ce kaléidoscope domestique à quatre éléments se compliquaient tellement par les naissances et par les mariages, que l'arbre généalogique des bourgeois de Nemours eût embarrassé les Bénédictins de l'Almanach de Gotha eux-même" [The variations in this four-piece domestic kaleidoscope were becoming so complicated by births and marriages that the genealogical tree of the bourgeois of Nemours would have embarrassed the Benedictines of the Almanach de Gotha themselves] (782). (My own response to such complexity is to draw the family tree. See appendix B.) Ubiquitous hyphenated combinations of the four names arise under Louis XIII, and arise in Balzac's text as an astonishing exercise in excessive, unreasonable writing:

Ces quatre familles produisaient déjà des Massin-Crémière, des Levrault-Massin, des Massin-Minoret, des Minoret-Minoret, des Crémière-Levrault, des Levrault-Minoret-Massin, des Massin-Levrault, des Minoret-Massin, des Massin-Massin, des Crémière-Massin, tout cela bariolé de junior, de fils aîné, de Crémière-François, de Levrault-Jacques, de Jean-Minoret. (782)

[These four families were already producing some Massin-Crémières, Levrault-Massins, Massin-Minorets, Minoret-Minorets, Crémière-Levraults, Levrault-Minoret-Massins, Massin-Levraults, Minoret-Massins, Massin-Massins, Crémière-Massins, all variegated with juniors, the firsts, Crémière-François, Levrault-Jacques, and Jean-Minorets.]

Surely this is Balzac at his most obsessive. These connections (to which are added a fifth name, the lawyer usually called Dionis whose full name is Crémière-Dionis, and who is associated with Massin-Levrault in usury) make it impossible to apprehend a character without also interrogating his relationships; in reading for knowledge, we read multiple relations, and thus we approach impossible closure and endless language. The hyphen linking different items signals the alliances that offer "le curieux spectacle de l'irradiation de quelques familles autochtones" [the odd spectacle of the irradiation of a few autochthonous families] (782) and the "entrecroisements de races au fond des provinces" [intertwining of races in the depths of the provinces] (781). One also finds this odd spectacle in the Swiss cantons, Balzac writes (782). (Still recently, in January 1996, in Saas-Fee in the Wallis canton, one could see the surnames of about ten families, often linked by hyphens, emblazoned on every hotel, restaurant, store, or service in town.) These "hyphenated" relations become emblems of the complex narration, mimetic figures of the plot and the structure of writing. A further complication, for my reading at least, stems from a certain laxity in using the full versions of the names: Massin-Levrault is often called simply Massin; Crémière is actually Crémière-Crémière, and so on. Balzac relies heavily on the reader's assiduity in acquiring knowledge. But also, this repeated mechanism allows the name Minoret to apply equally to the two chief antagonists in the possession of the fortune: the doctor and his nephew.

A second set of relations concerns what Balzac innovatively called "cognomonisme": the connection of a person's name to his *métier*; the profession gives rise to the name. In the present case, cognomonism justifies designating the person by the profession. Thus, Minoret-Levrault is the "maître de poste," or captain of the post; Crémière is the "percepteur de Nemours," or tax collector of Nemours; and Massin is the "greffier de la justice de paix," or the clerk of the justice of the peace. And these designations are as likely to occur as the names, in Balzac's writing. The effect is to lend greater weight to the dominating forces of the bourgeois, which govern both the social and the narrative structures.

In juxtaposition to this semiotic structure of genealogy, excessive in its manifestations, Balzac places the harmonious unity of Ursule Mirouët. Several passages underscore this unity. For instance:

Bientôt la mélancolie de ses pensées insensiblement adoucie teignit en quelque sorte ses heures, et relia toutes ces choses par une indéfinissable harmonie: ce fut une exquise propreté, la plus exacte symétrie dans la disposition des meubles . . . une paix que les habitudes de la jeune fille communiquaient aux choses et qui rendit son chez-soi aimable. (930–31)

[Soon the gently stilled melancholy of her thoughts colored her hours, as it were, and brought all these things together by an undefinable harmony: it was an exquisite cleanliness, the most exact symmetry in the position of her furniture . . . a peacefulness that the young girl's habits communicated to things and that made her home lovable.]

While the spider's web of the bourgeois genealogy surrounds the doctor's succession ("ils essayèrent d'entourer moins l'oncle que la succession" [they tried to surround less the uncle than the inheritance] [790]) and nearly destroys the rightful heiress, the plot schemes to explain how the fortune comes to the central figure, Ursule Mirouët, after being lost among the collaterals. The circulation of money, never secondary or insignificant in Balzac, follows a complex structure analogous to the excessive complexities of the genealogy.

Autochthonous families thus form the bourgeoisie of Nemours, which is endogamous, materialistic, anti-intellectual, and antimusical. The heirs fail to appreciate Ursule's piano playing of Beethoven's seventh symphony ("Bête à vent" [Beet oven], says Mme Crémière, the Mrs. Malaprop of the *héritiers* [871]). They want nothing so much as to demolish Minoret's exquisite library after his death. By contrast, Minoret's chosen company explicitly excludes the bourgeoisie and is exogamous, spiritual, intellectual, and musical. Ursule's upbringing reproduces the ideals of the Enlightenment, and the members of the minute society that separates her from the town are repeatedly characterized by their luminosity and illumination (793, 794, 797). They constitute a "family of chosen minds," whose "fraternity" forms a "compact, exclusive society," an "oasis" (798) in the doctor's living room. Under the effect of the light that streams forth from Ursule, the doctor's wall of incredulity cracks and crumbles (837–38). From the opening pages, after Minoret's conversion, the mystical and the spiritual hold sway in his household, with the support of the priest. In the confrontation between the heirs and Ursule, these many structures of opposition repeatedly place Ursule outside the materialistic pathways by which a succession may pass. Hence, the transfer of money to her is made problematic by the very semiotic structures of the novel.

As if to exacerbate this repudiation of bourgeois breeding and inbreeding, the plot, not without irony, is structured to bring about the passage of the succession through illegitimacy, for Ursule's father, Joseph Mirouët, is the illegitimate though recognized half-brother of the doctor Minoret's wife. (Nicole Mozet has called the novel "a veritable apology of illegitimacy and misalliance").[25] It is useful to spell out this relationship (an *explication nécessaire,* so to speak). Minoret's wife, also named Ursule Mirouët, was the daughter of Valentin Mirouët, an organist and builder of musical instruments. (Having left Nemours in his youth, Minoret did not take a wife from among the bourgeois cousinage.) This first Ursule Mirouët died in 1793, leaving the doctor childless after several of their children died. Her father, Valentin, meanwhile, had an illegitimate son in his old age, Joseph, whose mother he did not marry in order to avoid bringing dishonor to the legitimate Ursule. Joseph Mirouët, "excessivement mauvais sujet" [an exceedingly bad fellow] (812), after an adventurous life, married Dinah Grollman in Germany, and the legitimate product of that union is the Ursule Mirouët who is the heroine of this novel, born in 1814 and costing her mother's life. Joseph Mirouët, "the natural brother-in-law" of the doctor, or the half-brother of the doctor's wife, died soon after, leaving Ursule an orphan. Thus, Balzac can describe her as Minoret's "natural niece" (843), because her father is the illegitimate brother of his wife. Note that the blood relation, which is only half a blood relation, passes through the wife, not the doctor, and that the first Ursule Mirouët was dead twenty-one years before the heroine was born. There is, strictly speaking, no blood relation between Denis Minoret and Ursule Mirouët, and the text underscores this fact by calling him her "godfather" and her "guardian," never her uncle.

Exogamy compounded by illegitimacy thus defines Ursule's distinctness from the bourgeois cousinage. In this matter the text exploits French law, which held that legitimization of bastards did not extend to the next generation: "Illegitimate descent does not continue beyond the first degree," according to notes in the Folio edition.[26] The legitimate child of an illegitimate child can make no claim on its grandfather. Ursule, second-generation offspring of illegitimacy, is a stranger to Minoret (851), "car on peut soutenir qu'il n'existe aucun lien de parenté entre Ursule et le docteur" [for one can maintain that there is no family relation between Ursule and the doctor] (843), according to Dionis the lawyer. The text insists on this absence of relationship, and indeed depends on it. (Nicole Mozet's observation is not entirely in agreement with Balzac. She writes: "Because of this fact, with respect to the laws and mores of the time, she is neither a relative nor a stranger to him, and any will in her favor would be susceptible of being the object of a lawsuit brought by the nephews and nieces awaiting their inheritance.")[27] The legal situation, however, is complicated enough to require two sets of explanations in the novel (which are yet not adequate without the extensive additional information found in the editor's notes). The explanation Dionis supplies to the heirs, supplemented by information from Goupil the clerk and Désiré, who has newly become a lawyer (843–48), favors the heirs, while justice of the peace Bongrand's detailed discussion with the doctor (850–52) seeks Ursule's interest, naturally. Yet both come to the same conclusion, the gist of which is that Minoret cannot leave his fortune to Ursule by making a will in her favor. This is not, strictly speaking, the case, however. If Minoret were Ursule's natural father, the law would prevent his leaving his entire fortune to her, for the spirit of the law is to prevent the natural parent's predilection for the illegitimate child from disinheriting the legitimate children. But, as Balzac wrote (in referring to an earlier version), "Ursule Mirouët est évidemment une étrangère pour le Dr Minoret" [Ursule Mirouët is obviously a stranger for Dr. Minoret] (1533). In fact, Minoret could write a will in Ursule's favor, just as he does write a will bequeathing 36,000 francs of income to Savinien de Potenduère. What really prevents the doctor from bequeathing his fortune directly to Ursule is quite precisely the greediness of the heirs and their very conviction that they deserve Minoret's entire fortune. So certain and predictable is this circumstance that both camps reach the same conclusion, that the doctor cannot bequeath his fortune to Ursule, and for the same reason: the heirs are sure to bring a lawsuit against Ursule, who would be, though legally in her right, too feeble to win. As Balzac wrote, "Le docteur, justement effrayé de cette perspective, renonce à laisser à sa filleule sa succession par testament" [The doctor, justly alarmed by this perspective, abandons the attempt to leave his inheritance to his godchild by testament] (1533). Instead, the text exploits this situation, which gives rise to a different kind of writing in the form of the government stock certificates to the bearer. The monetary value is thereby translated into a written form that avoids the mechanisms of legal succession.

In legal terms, then, there is no family relationship and thus no relation of genealogy between Minoret and Ursule. Instead, by a semantic turn, the doctor "inherited" her when Joseph Mirouët "légua sa fille au docteur" [bequeathed his daughter to the doctor] (813). This welcome metaphor provides an excellent example of Balzac's supplying pointed markers for our guidance. Inheritance is the indicator of desire and preference: Minoret is father, mother, friend, doctor, and godfather to Ursule (855); desire and preference characterize their relations by will and testament, whereas mindless and reiterated intermarriage produced the genealogy. One may say that interest governs the genealogy, desire the inheritance; or, in the basic terms that so frequently arise as prime movers in *La Comédie humaine,* Money on the one hand, Love on the other. As Nicole Mozet writes, "Balzac's Nemours, a utopian space to a degree, is the site of a stunning redefinition of filiation, conceived in terms of love rather than blood."[28] We learn in detail about the "disappointed paternity" of the doctor (813), who compensates for the loss of his several children by accepting "avec bonheur *le legs* que lui fit Joseph Mirouët" [with joy *the bequest* that Joseph Mirouët made him] (813; emphasis added). (Just as the heir is distinct from the legatee, the "legs," or bequest, is defined by the Petit Robert as "free disposition made by testament.") In Minoret's letter expressing his last wishes and telling Ursule where to find the stock certificates, he recalls her resemblance to the first Ursule Mirouët, his wife, which also motivates his paternal affection; and he mentions "le serment que j'ai fait à ton pauvre père de le remplacer" [the oath I made to your poor father to replace him] (915). The oath is the subtext of this text and a metaphor of inheritance. Thus, Ursule replaces the doctor's wife, the doctor replaces Ursule's father, in a perfect and closed system, which also recovers lost time by superposing past and present. Attached to this letter is a testament that gives 36,000 francs of income to Savinien de Portenduère, in case Ursule refuses to take the money herself. Indirectly, this provision shows how Ursule is defined by her refusal of greediness, her refusal to "salir par des pensées d'intérêt" [soil by thoughts of self-interest] (930) her affection for her guardian, while thoughts of interest alone characterize the greed of the heirs. Most important, I take a key word from the short testament itself to characterize the essential nature of the relations of inheritance between Minoret and Ursule: preference. The doctor's money goes to Savinien "par préférence à tous mes héritiers" [in preference to all my heirs] (917). (As a minor point contributing to the relations by inheritance, captain Jordy writes a touching will by which he bequeaths his 10,000 francs of savings to Ursule [817].)

In short, Minoret chooses to pass the succession to Ursule by a mechanism that does not fall under the legality of the relations defined by intermarriages and births. This mechanism relies on the significant instances of writing called the *inscriptions de rente au porteur.* These and the holographic will each represent sure values. The fortune Minoret leaves to his cherished pupil in the form of the government certificates to the bearer is hidden in the pages of a folio volume of the *Pandectes* in his library. Not only is it worthy of Minoret's keen sense of fairness to place these writings in a volume of the Roman civil law, which forms the basis for European law, but the wit in Balzac no doubt chose this title because it means, in Latin, *book containing everything* (*American Heritage Dictionary of the English Language*). Everything, indeed, for without the *inscriptions de rente* Ursule has a mere pittance; she is described as "sans aucune fortune" [with no fortune at all] (925). The money that has been converted to these inscriptions, or certificates, no longer has any connection to the succession or the doctor's estate, any more than Ursule has to Minoret, legally speaking. Rather, these written papers have value only for the hands that hold them. Because they are immediately related to their cash value, they can be removed from the succession both literally (as by robbery) and in terms of the financial portion they represent. This monetary writing thus becomes an emblem for the *position* of the writing in this novel. Both the nature of the writing and its location are figures for how writing achieves significance and value by its location: eventually the position of the inscriptions will become the focus of spiritualism, the value of which resides specifically in its placement in the narrative. As for the doctor's will, once it is stolen and burned it has no value of any sort. The fact that both camps continue to look for a will as if it were merely unfound indicates that it too depends on position for value. As Balzac writes, "Pour les monuments comme pour les hommes, la position fait tout" [For monuments as for men, position is all] (777).

By these mechanisms Minoret sees to it that his preferred relation will inherit most of his money. When Minoret-Levrault steals the money, and tells no one, the full value of the estate becomes moot. ("Et les valeurs?" [And the shares?] asks the priest. "Courez donc après!" [See if you can catch them!] says Bongrand [926].) Those portions of Minoret's succession that are publicly known, including his house, are divided among the three heirs, while Ursule receives nothing. Thus, the theft of the inscriptions and the will restarts the action—a *rebondissement,* or sudden revival, so well known in the theater— which then requires the other significant mechanism of the narrative, the one grounded in spirituality. Predilection characterizes the reader's desire to see the money returned to Ursule, but, true to her nature and upbringing, Ursule refuses to employ various greedy strategies proposed to her by the townsfolk. The harmful actions of the domestic coalition, centered on Minoret-Levrault's theft of the government stock certificates to the bearer, vulgar narrative expedient, counteract the reader's desire until spiritualism, a concrete and active manifestation of a penetrating influence focused by will and desire, conquers materialism and brings the money to the unitary figure of composition—Ursule. .

The Science of Spirituality

Just as somnambulism arises in a concentration of the will, the narrative's recourse to somnambulism, in which the dead doctor appears and tells Ursule where the documents are, figures the concentration of unitary thought, a compelling goal for Balzac's composition. In this we recognize the genotextual process by which money enters the system of the spiritual, in the narrative. Somnambulism is the mechanism that transfers the inscriptions from the semiotic figure of genealogy to that of inheritance. A passing mention of Geoffroy Saint-Hilaire (823) in the *explication nécessaire* that justifies the doctor's conversion to magnetism and mesmerism is no incidental reference, but rather a precious guide to the structure of the plot and its thought. Balzac is at his most fervent in his explanation of magnetism, which is anchored in its opposition to the materialism of eighteenth-century philosophy (for which "the void does not exist" [822]) and supports the unity of composition. For Balzac, what is a misrecognized or badly exploited phenomenon of nature manifest not only in the inscrutable Orient but also in Jesus Christ was in the eighteenth century "repoussé par les doubles atteintes des gens religieux et des philosophes matérialistes également alarmés" [repulsed by twin attacks from religious people and materialist philosophers both equally alarmed] (822).

Balzac compares this erroneous assessment of magnetism to the "sort qu'avait eu la vérité dans la personne de Galilée" [fate truth had had in the person of Galileo] in the sixteenth century (822). To Geoffroy Saint-Hilaire belongs the merit of the "immense progrès que font en ce moment les sciences naturelles" [immense progress that the natural sciences are now making] (823), under the idea of unity. That such a unity takes the form, in this novel, of magnetism or mesmerism, in their somnambulistic variant, stems from Balzac's profound belief in the "ancient human power" (822) that allows one person to influence another by concentrating one's will.

In *Ursule Mirouët,* the mesmeric expression of unity of composition under-lies the novel as the principle of its effects. This "science of imponderable fluids" (823) is profoundly rooted in the luminous figure of Ursule Mirouët; Balzac says it is "étroitement lié[e] par la nature de ses phénomènes à la lumière" [narrowly linked, by the nature of its phenomena, to light] (823). Music, which plays a significant role, provides another expression of mesmer-ism. Thus:

Il existe en toute musique, outre la pensée du compositeur, l'âme de l'exécutant [Ur-sule], qui, par un privilège acquis seulement à cet art, peut donner du sens et de la poésie à des phrases sans grande valeur. . . . Par sa sublime et périlleuse organisation, Ursule appartenait à cette école de génies si rares. . . . Par un jeu à la fois suave et rêveur, son âme parlait à l'âme du jeune homme [Savinien] et l'enveloppait comme d'un nuage par des idées presque visibles. (890–91)

[One finds in all music, in addition to the composer's thought, the soul of the performer [Ursule], who, by a privilege pertaining only to this art, can give meaning and poetry to phrases lacking much value. . . . By her sublime and perilous organiza-tion, Ursule belonged to this school of rarefied geniuses. . . . Through her at once suave and dreamy playing, her soul spoke to the soul of the young man [Savinien] and enveloped it, like a cloud, with nearly visible ideas.]

Music and harmonic unity, genius, and the mesmeric concentration of thought all combine to elevate the composition of the novel to the level of the sublime.

Readers such as Allan Pasco suggest it is necessary to recognize the part played by a Christian God in the symbolic or semantic structures of this novel.[29] The conversion of the deist but "unbelieving" (826, 828) doctor to Christian religion motivates his faith in his ability to protect Ursule after his death. Yet, because this protection from beyond death takes the form of som-nambulism, a science to which Balzac takes the trouble to provide its letters of patent, we should think of a God and a Christianity much secularized by these *explications nécessaires*. Significantly, it is to Chaperon the priest that Balzac gives the task of explaining Minoret's *scientific* understanding of somnambulism, as if to suggest that religion recognizes the superior ability of science to explain the occult:

Il avait reconnu la possibilité de l'existence d'un monde spirituel, d'un monde des idées. Si les idées sont une création propre à l'homme, si elles subsistent en vivant d'une vie qui leur soit propre, elles doivent avoir des formes insaisissables à nos sens extérieurs, mais perceptibles à nos sens intérieurs quand ils sont dans certaines conditions. Ainsi les idées de votre parrain peuvent vous envelopper et peut-être les avez-vous revêtues de son apparence. Puis, si Minoret a commis ces actions, elle se résolvent en idées; car toute action est le résultat de plusieurs idées. Or, si les idées se meuvent dans le monde spirituel, votre esprit a pu les apercevoir en y pénétrant. (961–62)

[He had recognized the possible existence of a spiritual world, of a world of ideas. If ideas are a creation proper to man, if they subsist by living a life that is proper to them, they must have a shape that cannot be grasped by our external senses, but which is perceptible to our internal senses in certain conditions. Thus your godfather's ideas can enclose you, and perhaps you have clothed them in his appearance. Then, if Minoret performed these actions, they would resolve into ideas; for every action is the result of several ideas. Thus, if ideas move about in the spiritual world, your mind, by entering it, was able to perceive them.]

Here Balzac offers the double guide of the converted nonbeliever, Minoret, and the intelligent, unbigoted priest, Chaperon, to make it possible for the reader to believe also—believe in somnambulism, that is. It takes very little reflection to extend this explanation to the process of composition, and to realize that Balzac grounds in a scientific vision of unity the spiritual basis of *La Comédie humaine.*

Although the powerful mesmerist, whose demonstrations in Paris convince and help convert Minoret, may well describe his power as emanating from God (827), and although his healing may well be compared to the Savior's (826), the narrative significantly elevates this power to the status of science and principle. Mozet also stresses the importance of science "behind" God (*"Ursule Mirouët ou le test du bâtard,"* 218). She also summarizes the effect of Ursule's happy ending in this fashion: "Her happiness was indispensable to the triumph of scientific truth" (225). Faith and unity are taken up by the scientific system of *La Comédie humaine,* in which they achieve Balzac's most glorious illustration:

they belong to its narrative and semiotic systems, no longer to the real world. Françoise Gaillard describes diversity as an avatar of the same, in a rich commentary on the science in the "Avant-Propos" of *La Comédie humaine*.[30] She shows that for Geoffroy Saint-Hilaire, as for Balzac, the theory is one of analogy, which postulates a principle of resemblance as well as a principle of continuity among species (64–65). Founded on analogy, the semiotic unity of the novel is figured by the transformation I have described from a system of relations based on genealogy (intermarriage) to one based on inheritance, desire, and the generosity that consistently characterize Ursule Mirouët, the ultimate figure of Balzac's exchange with his reader.[31] Analogy underlies Minoret's love for Ursule, because she is like another Ursule Mirouët, but also, paradoxically, because she is a stranger to the doctor, and love arises where there is no genealogy. Analogy as a principle of composition lies in the semiotic structures based on preference and predilection. When the descendant of exogamous and illegitimate unions marries the only eligible aristocrat in town, the happy alliance reaffirms the inheritance against the harmful posterity of the bourgeois cousinage of Nemours.

Spirituality at it appears in *Ursule Mirouët* focuses on written texts, especially on their position. This necessary connection between the spiritual and writing has been well prepared in the novel. Ursule's visionary genius specifically includes the ability to see written texts: while Savinien is at sea in the marines, Ursule sees each of his letters in a dream before receiving them, and never fails to announce their arrival by recounting her dream (900). Likewise, during the demonstration of mesmerism in Paris, what convinced the doctor of the real existence of magnetism was the mesmerized subject's ability to see Minoret's two bank notes stored between the two next to last leaves of the *Pandectes*, volume II, in Nemours (831). The position of the 500-franc notes gives them their value in the narrative of the experiments, for the precision with which the subject locates them leaves the doctor thunderstruck (832).

Connecting semiosis to mimesis, we can say that the passing of the fortune from a genealogy described as a noxious system, mindless and materialistic, to an inheritance formed by love and preference provides both the mimetic frame of the narrative and the semiotic structure of our reading. (By mimetic frame I am referring to the story represented, an illusion of reality.) The very materiality of money lends strength and consistency to the ideality of the moral plot here: When the money is lost among the collaterals, it figures error in the spiritual sense, and failure of the narrative; when it is at last returned to Ursule, it figures the reward of spirituality and recovery from error. In like fashion, we are in error until we realize the power of spirituality to unify composition. That is the message of the unity of composition: the ideal is not contaminated by the real.

The Unity of Composition

Both *Modeste Mignon* and *Ursule Mirouët*, so similar in this effect, achieve a unity that we can only describe as miraculous. It is a unity that maintains as one the realism of marriage and the romanticism of desire: Love and Money allied in perfect harmony. These novels repair the disastrous disjunction that separates these prime movers in so much of *La Comédie humaine*. On the level of the great work, in other words, the progress Balzac perceived the novel could make, by following the zoological principle of the unity of composition, emerges in contrast to the catastrophic disunity of the work and of science to this point. To be exact, this progress occurs when writing finds unity in the domain of disunity. *Le Père Goriot* did nothing so much as to illustrate the calamity, the tragedy that results when characters cannot unite love with money: calamities that make tragic victims of Victorine Taillefer, Vautrin, Mme de Beauséant, Goriot, Delphine, and Anastasie, and against which, famously, Rastignac announces his struggle. Arlette Michel aptly points out that "the trick is to maintain simultaneous antagonistic postulations, play them against each other so that the result of this confrontation is not a middle ground that would be reassuring in its stability, but a reality that is radically new, because born from a tension, from a corrected disequilibrium" ("Balzac et la rhétorique," 258). Balzac needs the noxious semiotic system of the genealogy to arrive at the happiness of inheritance; he needs the opposed structures represented by Renée and Louise to prepare the way for the unity of composition; he needs to blend hideous reality with poetry to invent a new romantic realism.

The oft-cited paean to Cuvier that Balzac included in *La Peau de chagrin*, in 1831, praises the science that the naturalist had raised to its acme. Balzac found in this science a foundation for his geology, his genealogy, and his archeology, the rich concrete matter of his created world; he felt it was cause for celebration. Cuvier was the greatest materialist scientist and hence a great creator. Starting with a mere bone, he could describe the organism:

Cuvier n'est-il pas le plus grand poète de notre siècle? . . . notre immortel natura-
liste a reconstruit des mondes avec des os blanchis, a rebâti comme Cadmus des
cités avec des dents, a repeuplé mille forêts de tous les mystères de la zoologie avec
quelques fragments de houille, a retrouvé des populations de géants dans le pied d'un
mammouth.[32]

[Isn't Cuvier the greatest poet of our century? . . . our immortal naturalist has recon-
structed whole worlds out of bleached bones, rebuilt cities, like Cadmus, from teeth,
repeopled a thousand forests with all the mysteries of zoology out of a few fragments of
coal, rediscovered populations of giants in the foot of a mammoth.]

It suffices to come upon a fossilized trace, and the trick is turned—a world
emerges: "Soudain les marbres s'animalisent, la mort se vivifie, le monde se
déroule!" [Suddenly the marble turns animal, death comes alive, the world
unfolds] (75). The novelist's task is no less: to call forth the legions of the real
world by describing a handful of them. Balzac could hardly help identifying
with Cuvier.

Had Balzac taken his distance from this science by the time he wrote *Ursule
Mirouët*, ten years later, in 1841? I think not. Rather, to Cuvier's science is *added*
the revolution wrought by Geoffroy Saint-Hilaire and adopted by the author of
La Comédie humaine, the mammoth work Balzac is just then formulating.
What Cuvier represents for Balzac is the need to accumulate facts to make the
work the most complete document possible—the work seen as a phenotext.
But Geoffroy Saint-Hilaire affirmed in the natural sciences what Balzac had
long known in his art: that no meaning is possible without a structure that
makes sense of the facts by putting them into positions where they carry
meaning by their relations to others. The *inscriptions de rente au porteur* in
Ursule Mirouët have this double value: they are simultaneously positive facts
and a structure based on a principle of analogy, in their relation both to real
money and to their location in the *Pandectes.* In the marriage plots, Cuvier
stands for the material "science" of collecting a succession—whether Canalis's
actions in regard to Modeste Mignon's wealth, or the maneuvers of Minoret's
heirs. Beyond this, the inspired science of Geoffroy Saint-Hilaire gives a foundation to the spiritual, which forges new relations based on desire, preference, generosity, and literature; then do the happy couples gain both love and
money. As Goethe reportedly enthused, upon learning of Geoffroy Saint-
Hilaire's triumph in the 1830 debates with the system of Cuvier,

L'esprit dominera et sera souverain de la matière. On jettera des regards dans les grandes lois de la création, dans le laboratoire secret de Dieu! Si nous ne connaissons que la méthode analytique, si nous ne nous occupons que de la partie matérielle, si nous ne sentons pas le souffle de l'Esprit qui donne à tout sa forme et qui, par une loi intime, empêche toute déviation, qu'est-ce donc que l'étude de la nature?[33]

[The spirit will dominate and reign over matter. We will cast our glance into the great laws of creation, into the secret laboratory of God! If we admit only the analytic method, if we concern ourselves only with the material part, if we do not feel the breath of the Spirit that gives everything its form and, by an intimate law, prevents any deviation, what then would the study of nature be?]

How could Balzac not recognize himself in this hubris? More than this, he realized the law that forms the principle of his composition, "that gives every-thing its form": with Geoffroy Saint-Hilaire's insights added to Cuvier's, the novelist not only sees into God's secret laboratory, he takes his place as head scientist in it. Applied to the novel, the law authorizes the claim to a superior realism founded in analogy, the ideal unification of material and spiritual, of realistic and romantic, of facts and connections. As Gaillard observes, "The obstinate quest for a linking principle is at the same time the admission of a belief in *linking as a principle of* reality" (68).

The "prince Charming effect" in *Modeste Mignon* is a semiotic structure, as are the relations of inheritance in *Ursule Mirouët*. These relations create money for Ursule when she would not have had any after Minoret's demise, just as she had no family of whom she was the necessary heir. The mechanism of Modeste's love letters can be compared to the mechanism of the inscriptions in *Ursule Mirouët*: both create a real relationship where nothing existed before, and both create, out of the absence of relation, the unity of desire and prefer-ence by a mechanism involving writing. By analogy with the composition of the novel, this genotextual mimetic figure shows what it means to create the composition out of whole cloth, to make it exist where nothing existed before. When the novel passes through oppositions before finding unity, oppositions give value to unity. As de Sacy writes, "Variations in the human types, provid-ing inexhaustible material for a novel, underscore the unity and the constancy of the model on which man is built" (304). Writing is a Prince Charming effect.

Five

Breaking the Book

L'auteur est toujours présent dans son texte,
qu'il soit autobiographique ou pas, mais cette
présence manque.

[The author is always present in his text,
whether autobiographical or not, but this
presence is lacking.]

— ROBBE-GRILLET

It is likely that there have been autobiographical novels since there have been novels. The two that are the subject of this chapter are autobiographical in many ways, raising interesting generic issues that are relevant to writing realism. Nevertheless I shall not attempt to define or circumscribe the genre, nor to track the novels' fidelity to real life, because that would take me too far from my purpose. But the fact that the novels are closely connected to the authors' lives puts particular constraints on the reading, constraints that the authors exploit in significant ways to write realism. Because both protagonists resemble the authors and are themselves novelists writing novels, these novels illustrate in particularly acute ways the semiotic processes I have been describing. Both put before the reader instances of writing in which the creation of realism appears in the sharpest form, inextricably conflating embedded and embedding novels and forcing the reader to enter into the strategies and modes of existence of the novel writing.

It is hardly necessary to describe the development of self-reflective fiction in the twentieth century.[1] Such fiction displays or flaunts its own mechanisms of creation, with the result that the mimetic illusion itself is constantly put into doubt and imperiled. Owing a debt to Diderot, the two novels of this chapter reprise the issues raised by the "Question to men of letters" in *La Religieuse.* The mechanisms of realistic writing become the central matter of the text. In their modernity, these novels recognize the need to distinguish the *I* of the psychological person, in spite of its connection to real life, from the *I* of the writing, because, as Barthes writes, "contrary to the usual illusion of autobiographies and traditional novels, the subject of the enunciation can never be the same as the one who acted yesterday: the *I* of the discourse can no longer be the place where a previously stored person is innocently re-created."[2] Self-reflexivity, the focus on writing, compensates for the excesses of "personal realism."

Philippe Sollers's *Femmes,* with its constant reference to the author's life and times, challenges the reader to redefine realism. Serge Doubrovsky's *Le Livre brisé* carries the confusion of real life and fiction to vertiginous new heights, in an astonishing and outrageous writing of realism in which representation brings back the real referent. In both cases, semiosis involves the reader in generic definition: novel or autobiography, imagined or real, fiction or reference to reality. Because of the foregrounding of generic questions, Sollers's novel runs rings around the model of the book à la Balzac, a model it nevertheless borrows; *Le Livre brisé* breaks it altogether.

Raw Writing: *Femmes*

Consider this passage found early in the preface to *La Guerre du goût,* a large volume of short essays on art and literature published by Sollers in 1994:

Je saisis donc cette occasion pour préciser que, contrairement à une opinion, "politiquement correcte," malveillante et, par conséquent, répandue, il n'y a eu, de ma part, aucun changement, aucune trahison, aucun reniement, aucun revirement, abandon ou relâchement subjectif, aucun "retour à," dans la publication (qui semble obséder certains), en 1983, de mon roman *Femmes.* Ce livre a fait scandale, il a provoqué des fureurs rentrées et des aigreurs durables, il a eu du "succès" (tout s'explique), il a été diffusé ou censuré par malentendus successifs, il attend toujours d'être lu. Il le sera. Le roman, pour moi, n'a jamais cessé d'être la continuation de la pensée par d'autres moyens.[3]

[Therefore I seize the occasion to explain that, contrary to a "politically correct," malevolent, and consequently widespread opinion, there was not, on my part, any change, any betrayal, any denial, any reversion, abandonment, or subjective letting go, any "return to," in the publication (which seems to obsess some people), in 1983, of my novel *Femmes.* That book caused a scandal, it provoked suppressed furor and lasting bitterness, it was "successful" (that explains everything), it was disseminated or censured by successive misunderstandings, it is still waiting to be read. It will be. The novel, for me, has never ceased to be the continuation of thought by other means.]

I do not claim to be the one to inaugurate this reading that Sollers called for eleven years after the publication of *Femmes*, and which is still needed. However, this passage is important because it shows the value of this novel for Sollers himself, and because of the last sentence in this excerpt (an allusion to a maxim on war from Clausewitz, which Sollers often cites in perverted form). The novel as a genre "thinks" and allows us to think our society. As early as 1968, Sollers had written of its importance as a commentary on society, as Roland Champagne opportunely reminds us: "The novel for Sollers is a function of a social consciousness and thus expresses reality for a culture. He once defined the novel, not so much as fiction, but as a lived, livable reality: '*Le roman est la manière dont cette société se parle,* la manière dont l'individu *doit se vivre* pour y être accepté' ([*Logiques*], 228)."[4] Sollers has never ceased to assert this purpose and intent. All his fiction since *Lois* engages the reader in the narrators' critical, cynical, and amusing observations of society's features and foibles. As for the value of *Femmes* in particular, certainly for Sollers, perhaps nothing demonstrates it so forcefully as the surprise ending of the long first sentence of the passage quoted in the previous paragraph. In the opening pages of this preface to *La Guerre du goût*, Sollers takes leave of a great many past currents of writing and thought, and this sentence seems to follow from the paragraph before it, as if continuing to take a stance ("there was not, on my part, any change," and so on). Nothing at all prepares the reader for the rabbit-out-of-a-hat—the mention of *Femmes*—at the end of the sentence. Criticism rankles, and Sollers still feels the need to set the record straight; if anyone is obsessed with the novel, surely Sollers is. The heat with which he writes here betrays above all a certainty that readers have not yet heard what *Femmes* says; it is a warning not to read it for its surface features alone, in particular the sexual affairs. Although I accept Sollers's claim and intend to heed the warning, the "continuation of thought" I am examining here concerns the novel's inscription of writing as its major theme.

Sollers writes his novels in what might be called an "autobiographical vein." An ambiguous formulation like this is necessary to describe his novelistic manner, which participates in both self-exposure and pure invention. Central to the self-description, or the apparent self-description, is the use of a first-person narrator in almost all his novels, including the earliest ones. (Although *H, Paradis,* and *Paradis II* lack conventional narrators, there is still a first-person presence, forged in the depths of the verbal din.) Embedded in the predominant present tense, narratives of events from the past typically connect to Sollers's childhood and adolescence, as seen from the narrators' present. Philippe Forest has written, "Since *H* at least, Sollers's books do portray in a very direct and repetitive manner the existence and personality of their author."[5] Sollers himself used the phrase "my disguised autobiography" in speaking about his 1997 novel, *Studio,* in an interview.[6] The 1983 *Femmes* and several other novels since then, in particular *Portrait du joueur* (1984), which Philippe Forest describes as the most directly autobiographical of his novels (*Philippe Sollers,* 273), all exploit Sollers's biography. Forest and, to lesser degrees, other writers on Sollers's novels have established the many connections. To read Forest's account of the author's life in *Philippe Sollers,* for instance, is to recognize events, places, people, opinions, and other matters found in the novels, while reading the novels affords one the pleasure of the hunt for transposed elements of Sollers's highly visible life. It is not my primary purpose here, however, nor in my analysis of Doubrovsky's novel, to inventory these connections, except indirectly and partially.

From these connections with the life of the author, the writing that occurs in *Femmes* nevertheless gains an enhanced realism. The practice I have just described of reusing real autobiographical material in a novel (which is not something to neglect nevertheless) has an even more subtle effect on the reader when it is doubled by the writing events represented in the novel. All autobiographical novels have a heightened connectivity to a particular reality, the author's life. But, when in addition the novel portrays *a novelist writing his autobiographical novel,* and some of the events he writes into his novel are those of the real author's life, we begin to lose sight of the boundaries of fiction and reality, and we may read as autobiography parts that really are fictional. A disgruntled reader once accused Simone de Beauvoir of making all her novels seem to recount her life, against her protestations to the contrary; if the attack can be said to have come from a relatively naïve reader, who was easily taken in by the fiction, nevertheless it points to an effect Beauvoir sought for, the realistic illusion that is at the root of my interest in these fictions. Most of Beauvoir's novels lie much farther from autobiography than Sollers's (although *L'Invitée* is a *roman à clés*), but a similar effect on the reader occurs in Sollers's writing: everything begins to sound autobiographical. Sollers observes, in *Carnet de nuit*: "Comme écrivain, vous avez gagné si tout le monde considère que tout ce que vous avez écrit est vrai, donc que rien n'a été écrit" [As a writer, you have won if everyone considers that everything you have written is true, and that therefore nothing was written].[7] But precisely, because writing a novel is the central topic of *Femmes*, everything is portrayed as having been written, making the distinction of "real" events from "written" ones virtually impossible, and the very categories of real and written almost indistinguishable too. This success of the writer illuminates Sollers's writing.

Writing the Novel

Femmes has some of the qualities of a *roman à thèse,* and it is certainly a *roman à clés* as well. The latter is especially important because the mechanism of fictional keys is connected with the protagonist's novel writing. Nevertheless, because the book really does concern the matter of its title, though not only in the way a casual reader might suppose, I will first look briefly at the proclaimed thesis.

The topic of women opens the book and the thesis is formulated on the first page, written in three one-line propositions: "Le monde appartient aux femmes. / C'est-à-dire à la mort. / Là-dessus, tout le monde ment" [The world belongs to women. / That is to say to death. / Everyone is lying about it].[8] Five years earlier in Amsterdam, a secret congress of women produced a program for what amounts to a worldwide feminist revolution, of which the Women's Liberation movements are merely the "vitrines officielles de l'entreprise" [official shop windows of the enterprise] (51). The Sodome Gomorrhe International Council (SGIC) established the World Organization for Men Annihilation and for a New Natality (WOMANN), of which the French section is called the Front d'Autonomie Matricielle (FAM). Not without humor, as these invented names show, Sollers begins to weave among the rest of the narrative an insistent but obscure, vaguely futuristic, and frankly apocalyptic thread outlining the narrative for women's domination in the world. A "réseau," or network, of women in Europe and America are promulgating tracts, ideas, and political action, which includes the overthrow of Judeo-Christian religion and proposes an attack on the Pope as representing the most dangerous force, the Catholic church. (The actual attempt to assassinate Pope John Paul II on

May 13, 1981, is said to have prompted the writing of this novel.)[9] The women of the network are taking over the world. A thread linking sexuality with death obsessively illustrates the second of the three statements of the thesis, "C'est-à-dire à la mort." The thrust of the thesis, the "subject of subjects" (540), associates women with death. And it is the purpose of this writing to counter the third statement—"Là-dessus, tout le monde ment"—and expose society's failure and refusal to recognize the threat. In broad outline, this is the "thought" that the novel "continues" by other means.

If I use the metaphor of weaving, and describe the thread as obscure, it is because the topic does not develop as one would expect of a thesis in a *roman à thèse*. Here and there the narrator refers to the thesis ironically, addressing the reader: "Vous pensiez que j'exagérais pour les besoins de ma cause... Comme si j'écrivais un 'roman à thèse'... Un pamphlet... Mais non... Je ne décris pas le dix millième de ce qui se passe" [You thought I was exaggerating for the sake of my cause... As if I were writing a 'roman à thèse'... A pamphlet... Not at all... I'm not describing one ten-thousandth of what is going on] (482). Sollers treats the topic with such sly intermittence, such devious energy, so consistently destructive sarcasm, such covert agency, and finally allows it so insignificant a conclusion, that the topic falls on its head and nearly dies. To be sure, the plans of the SGIC, the WOMANN, the FAM return now and again, and many pages include focused arguments on such matters as artificial insemination, test-tube babies, and Nobel Prize sperm banks. The SGIC's secret report called for "contrôle de la reproduction, inclination de ladite reproduction dans un sens favorable aux femmes, placement d'agents hautement qualifiés dans les secteurs gynécologues, recommandations sur l'éducation des enfants..." [control of reproduction, inflection of said reproduction in a direction favorable to women, placement of highly qualified agents in the gynecological sectors, recommendations about the education of children...] (52). Women plan a global takeover of power; Sollers's narrator is the one who has discovered and revealed this universal truth holding sway since there have been documents: "Le monde appartient aux femmes, il n'y a que des femmes" [The world belongs to women, there are only women] (12). Various female characters—Kate, Bernadette, Jane, and others—have a role in the revolutionary plans. But, in spite of the frequent return of this motif and the importance Sollers claims for it, through his narrator, I am convinced Sollers had an even more important message in mind when he gave his protagonist the role of revealing women's power. The profound significance of the book goes beyond these theses to the roots of meaning itself.

All the same, one may be tempted to assume that it is the narrator's insatiable appetite for women that motivates the novel at all, for its title fits nicely with a second characteristic matter of the book, which also occurs with quite chronic frequency. These are scenes of mostly sexual encounters between the narrator and several different women: Cyd, Kate, Bernadette, Flora, Ysia, Diane, the Présidente, Sonia, Louise, and his wife, Deborah, among others. Some of these scenes are frankly salacious, almost pornographic. The title is fully justified by this repetitive activity. *Femmes* leaves in the reader's mind, as part of the portrait of its epoch, its memorable portraits of the women. They are perhaps warranted by the vision of Picasso's *Les Demoiselles d'Avignon*, seen at the Museum of Modern Art (170–73), and William de Kooning's series of paintings called *Women* (189–91), which Sollers has written about elsewhere.[10] Yet to see this rather traditional thread as the central topic is also to miss the book's importance.

Primarily, then, *Femmes* is a novel about writing a novel, which is also called *Femmes,* and in this central device lies the serious matter of how meaning comes into being, in life as in fiction. Present tense verbs scroll the story as from an omnipresent, clattering typewriter, directly before our eyes. Rarely is the narration retrospective. A fully realized first-person narrator named Will speaks about the novel he is writing: "Lecteur, accroche-toi, ce livre est abrupt. [. . .] J'écris les Mémoires d'un navigateur sans précédent, le révélateur des époques... L'origine dévoilée! Le secret sondé! Le destin radiographié!" [Reader, hang on, this book is steep. [. . .] I am writing the Memoirs of an unprecedented navigator, informer of the ages... The origin unveiled! The secret sounded! Destiny X-rayed!] (11). Called repeatedly to justify the novel, the narrator describes its subjects to skeptical colleagues and friends: "Les choses de tous les jours. Le vertige d'aujourd'hui. Les hommes, les femmes. L'ennui, la réflexion, les lueurs. —Un roman réaliste? Toi? —Si tu veux. Figuratif. Émotif. Déformatif-transformatif. [. . .] J'ai deux ou trois choses à dire, comme ça, à plat, dans le mouvement" ["Ordinary things. The giddy fluctuations of our times. Men, women. Boredom, reflection, insights." "A realistic novel? You?" "I suppose. Figurative. Emotive. Deformative-transformative. [. . .] I have two or three things to say, like so, flat out, in the movement of events"] (77). The immediacy of this project has an instant, exhibitionistic effect on Cyd, the woman whose sexual passions most closely match Will's: "Ça l'excite, un écrivain" [She's excited by a writer] (78). When things have taken their most apocalyptic turn, and Will lies wounded in a hospital from a machine-gun attack that has killed Cyd, an investigator asks: "—Un roman? Sur les événements actuels? —Oh, de très loin, dis-je. Un roman philoso-phique, si vous voulez" ["A novel? On current events?" "Oh, from a real distance, I'm saying. A philosophical novel, if you will"] (583). At this late stage the description of the novel as philosophical comes as a retrospective comment inflecting our understanding of what has gone before: the reflections of the narrator on his times.

Taking stock, midway, just after one of several criticisms of his title, the narrator justifies it to himself: "*Femmes...* Un mauvais titre? Pour un jugement global sur un point du temps, de l'espace? Sur l'état social? Sur le degré de développement de l'histoire humaine? Allons donc! Excellent, au contraire..." [*Femmes...* A bad title? For a global judgment on a point in time, in space? On the state of society? On the degree of development of human history? Come on! It's excellent, on the contrary...] (315). This series of explanations studding the novel constantly reminds the reader of Will's goals and intent; he thus assumes the classic functions of the *captatio benevolentiae,* which seeks the reader's belief in his writing. His last description laconically summarizes as follows: "Oh, tu sais, l'époque... Les femmes, le terrorisme, la politique, le journalisme, l'argent... [. . .] Surtout les femmes... —Pourquoi 'les femmes'? —C'est l'axe de la démonstration" ["Oh, you know, the times... Women, terror-ism, politics, media, money... [. . .] Especially women..." "Why 'women'?" "It's the axis of demonstration"] (611).

Demonstration of what? Like minitreatises, little self-contained develop-ments cover topics distantly or closely related to the thesis but in all cases anchored in contemporary intellectual and cultural reality, generally identified with Sollers's own vast culture. These topics include the Polish coup d'état; the Revolutionary calendar; the death of Barthes, the crime of Althusser, the col-lapse of Lacan, the suicide of Nikos Poulantzas; an ingenious return of Emma Bovary to comment on the current scene; Shakespeare, Hamlet, and Hamnet, in an echo of James Joyce; many other snippets of literary interpretation; Mozart and Sade; a short disquisition on personal advertisements; an audience with the Pope. The philosophical development on a point of time and space, the cultural history of the present, the status of society—these reflections, instructions, or provocations are both the urgent matter of Will's novel, arising in his culture, and the subjects of Sollers's *Femmes.*

"Qui je suis vraiment? Peu importe. Mieux vaut rester dans l'ombre" [Who am I really? It doesn't matter. Better to stay in the shadows] (12). It is with these words that the writer of the "Memoirs of an unprecedented navigator" introduces himself, in a mixture of self-presentation and concealment that characterizes his presence in the entire work. Not until page 180 will he be called Will (by Jane, an American friend); it is the only name he will ever have, variously suggesting Shakespeare, de Kooning, and free will. The proper name makes itself scarce; the reader is obliged to use it much more often than the narrator does, who simply identifies himself by using the first-person singular pronoun. But the ingenious device Sollers created uniquely for this novel gives this manuscript a twofold origin: Will is doubled by a French writer who will correct his text, assume authorship, and publish the book in his name: "J'ai demandé simplement à l'écrivain qui signera ce livre, de discuter avec moi certains points... Pourquoi je l'ai choisi, lui? Parce qu'il était haï. [. . .] Je voulais quelqu'un d'assez connu mais de franchement détesté..." [I've simply asked the writer who will sign his name to this book to discuss certain points with me... Why did I choose him, particularly? Because people hate him. [. . .] I wanted someone quite well known but frankly detested...] (12). The topic of the writer well known but frankly detested will return like an insistent melody. Later we learn that this French writer is called S. and that Will is an American journalist who has been living for many years in Paris; he chooses to write his novel in French: "Question de tradition... Les Français, certains Français, en savent davantage, finalement, sur le théâtre que j'ai l'intention de décrire..." [A question of tradition... The French, certain French, know more, in the end, about the arena I intend to describe...] (12–13). The paradoxes here–Why choose a writer nobody likes? Why not publish the book under one's own name? Why act clandestinely? Why should an American comment on the French scene?—contribute to the air of mystery that requires the reader's active engagement with the question of the origin of the writing.

An important point for this discussion concerns the irony that pervades the doubled narration. As I have suggested, one always hears the voice of Philippe Sollers in the text of the novel, and this causes no strange reading effects as long as one thinks of the novel written by Sollers. *Femmes* is firmly anchored in the author's past and present life, his intellectual activity, his desires, interests, opinions, philosophies, and readings. These are its primary subjects, the stuff and matter that returns like leitmotifs. But when we think of the novel that Will, the American journalist, is writing, perhaps in uncertain French, there is a difficulty and a strangeness for the reader. Will's identity is unsettled. Throughout, a French man seems to be speaking, defined by his culture both as culture is broadly understood and as it is narrowly marked by friends, intellectual associations, travels, opinions, and so forth—all the ingredients of a personal culture that tag Will's story with Sollers's presence. At times Will's narrative acts as though it has forgotten he is American and describes a past that matches Sollers's—then suddenly reminds us with a biting "Sale Yankee!" [Damn Yankee!] (355). Or, when he describes for several pages his relation with Werth we are certain we are reading about Sollers's relation with Barthes: "Goût commun pour la voix, le chant, les abréviations de la poésie chinoise, les carnets, les cahiers, les stylos, la calligraphie, le piano..." [A common taste for the voice, singing, the abbreviations of Chinese poetry, notepads, notebooks, pens, calligraphy, the piano...] (155)—until a phrase brings back the American, with a jolt: "Il trouvait étrange que je sois américain et catholique" [He found it strange that I should be American and Catholic] (155). Strange indeed. The effect is to encourage us to forget Will is American for much of the time, which is necessary for the working of the novel, and which also brings him closer to his double, S. And there is a strangeness or estrangement every time Will's American quality reasserts itself, as if it is needed to push the text back away from its real author, after it has come too close. When the individual and personal background that is supposed to make Will a southerner from Savannah fails to convince, the effect of distancing reinforces the irony and serves to remind the reader of the specular play of the fiction.

Before describing the special effects that stem from this doubled origin of the represented writing, let me situate the novel with respect to a genre that has had a certain presence and history. To a large degree, *Femmes* depends on and exploits the tradition of the "novel within the novel" in France. Called "mise en abyme" by André Gide and more recently the "récit spéculaire" by Lucien Dällenbach, the novel in which a character is writing a similar novel was famously illustrated by Gide's *Les Faux-monnayeurs* in 1925. Among many other events, the character Edouard gathers material for a future novel of the same name. When he says he will put into it everything that happens in *Les Faux-monnayeurs*, the relation between what is to be written and what is already written is not indifferent: anything that occurs in Gide's novel may be put into the novel Edouard has not yet written. More classic cases, such as *Albert Savarus* by Balzac, insert a separate text into the outside text; the inserted text serves multiple reflective functions for the embedding narrative. Later novels, particularly among the French new novel, pursue and update the device with excruciating self-reflexivity. Nathalie Sarraute's *Les Fruits d'or* of 1963 places a written and published novel of that name in the center of all the characters' discussions—but the reader is never allowed to see or read any of it and knows only that it is not at all like the embedding novel. In Butor's *L'Emploi du temps,* a complicated double chronology corresponds to and represents the protagonist's double experience of living and writing. Since the new novel, there has been a veritable explosion of novels that refer to their own act of writing, whose subject is a novel being written, whose characters allude to the novel they are in. Every possibility has been tried out, in all likelihood. The self-reflective novel claims to create a novelistic art that no longer "cheats"; its pretension to imitate "reality" removes the mask, affirms itself, and becomes the foregrounded topic of the book.

Sollers's novel exploits this updated tradition in a personal vein, inflecting it to his purposes. Because of the embedded novel, the initial question is: Who is writing or, again, whose writing are we reading? The novel that Will is writing is also called *Femmes.* It is autobiographical; it concerns present events, as I have said. Most important, the *mise en abyme* forces the reader's attention on the writing of reality. But is it Will's autobiography, Will's sexual appetites, and the present events in which he has been involved? To narrate is infallibly to reveal the self. In an interesting reflection on the novel, Will describes it as "la seule mesure de la liberté. [. . .] Racontez, et tout est dévoilé. [. . .] Racontez, et vous allez vous trahir. [. . .] Et moi, et moi, et moi, et moi" [the only measure of freedom. [. . .] Narrate, and everything is revealed. [. . .] Narrate, and you will betray yourself. [. . .] And I, and I, and I, and I] (185–86). The observation applies both to the novel Will is writing and to Sollers's novel, so that there is a confusion and conflation of the embedding and embedded novels. This is partly accomplished because, as a *roman à clés,* it maintains a constant reference to the real world of Philippe Sollers through its episodic references to real people and events. Keys have been identified—many are transparent. Bernadette is Antoinette Fouque; Flora Valenzuela is Maria-Antonietta Macciocchi; Elissa is Hélène Cixous; Jean Werth is just as transparently Barthes as Laurent

Lutz is Althusser and Paul Fals is Lacan; Boris Fafner, spoofed as one of Wagner's dragon-and-giant pair whose greed and blind ferocity merit the hero's revenge, represents Jean-Edern Hallier, irascible novelist and self-promoting social gadfly and a founder of *Tel Quel* with Sollers; Robert, tall and gay, is François Wahl; in the publishing world, Les Éditions du Vestibule must lie somewhere just beyond the Seuil, while Gallimard is glorified with the appropriate sobriquet of La Banque Centrale. The effect of the *roman à clés* is to create mythical versions of real people whose lives are already public. This of course integrates those people into the fiction and enhances the connection of the fiction to reality, but it also fictionalizes the world in which they live; the novel comes from that intellectual scene, but also changes it by creating these mythologies (in the Barthesian sense).[11]

The conflation of embedded and embedding novels occurs also because the connection of Will the American with the French writer S. produces a single figure with a double origin. Their relationship is described episodically as an agreement or a contract, the details of which gradually are learned. S. comes twice a week in the mornings, takes what Will has written and returns it with corrections; they discuss strategy, debate literary technique, politics, women, punctuation (93). S. contributes documents or articles to discuss in the novel (387–89); the novel is "our work" (388). At the beginning, the narrator takes pains to demarcate his difference with S.: "aucun rapport, aucune comparaison surtout..." ["no connection, no comparison especially..."] (36). The reader will find it difficult to agree. Will explains his need for anonymity, covered by S.'s notoriety: "Une alliance technique. Puisque je ne suis pas français. Puisque je ne suis pas habitué aux subtilités du français... Déjà dans ma famille, mère, tantes, sœurs, cousines. Vous comprendrez que je veuille garder l'anonymat. Je ne veux pas les ennuyer, là-bas, ceux et celles qui restent" [A technical alliance. Since I'm not French. Since I'm not used to the subtleties of French... Already, in my family, mother, aunts, sisters, female cousins. You will understand that I wish to remain anonymous. I don't want to annoy them, down there, the ones who are still there] (36). Anonymity is supposed to protect the innocent who reveal the truth, as it were; hence, an augmentation of the truth value of the writing. In the real world, some keyed novels on contemporary topics appear without the author's name, or with a provocative code name like "Doctor X," for that very reason. Toward the end of *Femmes,* when events have taken a turn toward disaster, the narrator returns to the need for anonymity:

N'acceptez pas la mise entre parenthèses de votre nom... C'est moi, l'Anonyme, qui vous le dis solennellement ici, à travers ce livre... Voilà pourquoi les écrivains ont toujours été et seront encore de plus en plus surveillés... A qui le dites-vous! grognera S., en arrangeant ces lignes... (610)

[Do not accept having your name put between parentheses... I'm the one, I the Anonymous One, who solemnly tells you this, by means of this book... This is why writers have always been and will continue to be more and more the object of surveillance... Who're you telling! S. will grumble, while rewriting these lines...]

The named and known S. suffers under surveillance, whereas Will hides in anonymity. There is here a double game on names given and taken away. It is far too easy for the reader to doubt the existence of Will as a real person—the presumed real writer hidden behind the anonymity, according to the usual practice of the *roman à clés*. This is true within the diegetic frame and outside it; in fact, Will may be the only character who is not a key, in Sollers's novel.

In short, if we want to read as keyed novels require us to read, we must pay attention to the autobiography of S. written through the narrator's words, both as he describes S. *and in his own experiences.* Strange as it may seem, Will is living and writing S.'s autobiography. As Katherine Kurk has noted, from *Femmes* on, Sollers's novels dance on the line between fiction and reality, in the *intermédiaire*, a zone of actuality that Sollers has known since his earliest writings.[12] Moreover, in both S. and Will we read Sollers's life. The narrator is not only doubled but tripled. The relationship is analogous to the superposition of Elisor, Dagoucin, and Marguerite de Navarre in the twenty-fourth tale of the *Heptaméron*.

On an Apocalyptic Tone: *Femmes* and *Paradis*

Of course S., French writer and author of an impenetrable book called *Comédie* written without punctuation, indicates Sollers himself and his notorious avant-garde novel *Paradis*. This key provides a central figure of the writing of realism in *Femmes*. In his excellent studies of Sollers and *Tel Quel*, Philippe Forest has situated *Femmes* in relation to the contemporary *Paradis*, of which the first volume was published in 1981. Forest has claimed that, with all punctuation, capitalization, and paragraph divisions removed, sections from *Femmes* would have fit into *Paradis* without the reader's noticing any difference, and that punctuated passages from *Paradis* would not be out of place in

Femmes (*Philippe Sollers*, 266). I have experimentally confirmed this claim. The subjects of the two works are closely related. Forest writes:

> The point of departure is an observation basically no different than the one made in *Paradis*: the misunderstanding between men and women is radical and, as a result, sexuality is essentially comparable to a sort of infernal merry-go-round on which individuals are turning one behind the other, incapable of understanding each other, just barely capable of hating each other. Such is the system whose comical and fearsome logic Sollers's novels since *Lois* strive to explain. (*Philippe Sollers*, 279)

Forest was writing, initially, about *Portrait du joueur,* but the comment applies to all the novels since 1970, and particularly to *Femmes.* He postulates that *Paradis* prompted the writing of *Femmes*:

> For ten years, [Sollers] accumulated many notes that already constitute a kind of fragmentary picture of today's society. On the 13th of May 1981, the assassination attempt on Pope John Paul II acts like a mysterious switch; it serves as a sign. Sollers decides to convert this proliferating mass of notes into a novel. No doubt the reception given to the first volume of *Paradis* had something to do with this decision. (*Histoire de Tel Quel,* 590)

That reception had been almost universally negative.

Elsewhere Forest writes: "Translating the themes of *Paradis* into a 'general audience' readability, integrating them into the less disruptive structure of a classical narrative, *Femmes* thereby makes 'visible' the density of a work whose very perfection of form made it difficult to grasp for many readers" (*Philippe Sollers,* 264–65). Speaking of cards that can be shuffled, he comments that "From one work to another, the same images, the same theses, and even the same analyses or the same fragments of narrative are taken up and modulated according to the particular nature of the text in which they are inscribed" (*Philippe Sollers,* 265). In *Paradis,* the phonetic transcription "yapadom" (something like "thrarnomen"), repeated here and there like a refrain, restates what *Femmes* phrases in these words: "l'absence, en ce monde, d'hommes dignes de ce nom... Pas d'hommes! Pas un seul! Tous des fantoches, des lâches, des vantards, des veaux..." [the absence, in this world, of men worthy of the name... No men! Not a single one! All puppets, cowards, braggarts, dolts...] (141). (This is a passage of free indirect discourse by an assertive Emma Bovary who has returned to France in 1980 to comment on the novel, critique Flaubert's writing, and shed the light of her experience on the man-woman question.) In short, "Read in retrospect, *Femmes* appears as a continuation of *Paradis*. The same proliferating material (social and sexual, literary and philosophical) is treated in the two books" (*Histoire de Tel Quel,* 591).

Sollers has also used *Femmes* to explain and justify *Paradis,* in a process characteristic of his writing since 1983. Typically, he cites the negative criticism of the previous novel, in sarcastic tones of mock outrage; often he ascribes the derogatory comments to antipathetic characters (in *Femmes* these are especially Kate and Boris), and destroys the criticism by damning the critic. The writer Alfredo Malmora, representing no doubt, in heavy-handed caricature, Alberto Moravia, joins the general chorus of condemnation of *Comédie* when he describes it as "un gros livre sans le moindre signe de ponctuation... Illisible... Qui s'appelle *Comédie*... Et par-dessus le marché, [l'auteur] se prend pour Dante!..." [a thick book without the slightest punctuation mark... Illegible... Which is called *Comédie*... And on top of all that, [the author] takes himself for Dante!...] (204). Every mention of *Comédie* seems to be accompanied by the indications "without punctuation" and "illegible": "sa *Comédie* que personne ne semble pouvoir lire... Ou vouloir..." [his *Comédie* that no one seems to be able to read... Or want to...] (89). In Will's analysis,

S. absolument intransigeant sur sa recherche actuelle... Il ne se rend pas compte qu'il est dans un désert complet? Que tout le monde s'en moque? Trouve ça fou? Sans intérêt? Peut-être, mais c'est sa fierté... Être le monstre incompréhensible... Bizarre type... Prêt à crever d'orgueil sur son chef-d'œuvre inconnu... (327)

[S. absolutely intransigent about his current research... He doesn't realize he's completely out in a desert? That everybody's making fun of it? Thinks it's crazy? Uninteresting? Maybe, but that's his pride... To be the incomprehensible monster... Strange guy... Ready to die of pride for his unknown masterpiece...]

Will and S. together make a rich portrait of Sollers, and both are writing the novel *Femmes*. Only S., however, is the author of *Comédie*. Will therefore has an external perspective on S.'s book, can even play the part of the potentially good reader—because he has not yet read the book!—to balance the universal scorn it has met. Through *Comédie* treated almost as a character, and by his doubled narrator, Sollers thus defends *Paradis*.

What exactly is *Comédie* about? "Sa grosse machine, là, *Comédie,* collante, continue, biscornue... Après tout, c'est peut-être important, on ne sait jamais..." [That big machine of his, *Comédie,* gluey, continual, quirky... After all, maybe it's important, you never know...] (117). With such a hint, the reader might seek to understand. As mentions of the book accumulate, one begins to form a view of its contents. At the least, it decries the banality of everything: "Une lutte à mort est engagée entre la stéréotypie intéressée et la perception réellement personnelle. Entre la répétition étalée mortelle et la sensation interne..." [A struggle to the death has begun between self-interested stereotypes and truly personal perceptions. Between mortally spreading repetition and internal sensation...] (88). Described as S.'s "smoky modern opera" (407), it speaks of the Nazi crimes against humanity in Dantesque terms:

Cœur de l'énigme... Cœur du crime... J'entends comme un immense gémissement lancé et répercuté dans l'ombre, —les corps suppliciés, les os cassés; le tremblement de la mort sur elle-même, indifférente, acharnée... J'ai le plus souvent l'impression d'être un survivant d'une catastrophe vécue à côté de moi, sur une scène parallèle... Populations, déportations, trains, froid, neige, camps, chambres à gaz... (285)

[Core of the mystery... Core of the crime... I can hear a kind of immense wail hurling and echoing in the shadows, —the tortured bodies, the broken bones; death trembling for herself, indifferent, relentless... Most often I have the impression that I'm a survivor of a catastrophe that took place alongside me, on a parallel stage... Populations, deportations, trains, cold, snow, camps, gas chambers...]

Will wonders: "La source de sa *Comédie,* ce serait donc ça? Son obstination serait là?" [The origin of his *Comédie,* could that be it? His doggedness comes from that?] (286). Underscoring the insistence of the theme or leitmotif concerning Jews and the Occupation, as if to guide the reader to observe the same insistence in *Femmes,* this obsession, beyond its thematic interest, creates a three-dimensional specular effect. The *mise en abyme* within Will's *Femmes* of the obsessions in *Comédie* works to cast illuminating reflections on Sollers's novel *Femmes,* reflections that ultimately return also to *Paradis.*

No one understands *Comédie.* The public vaguely gathers "qu'il réclame la fin de la reproduction humaine, l'expérience enthousiaste du gouffre, un culte ironique de la Vierge Marie..." [that it is calling for an end to human reproduction, the enthusiastic experience of the void, an ironic cult of the Virgin Mary...] (348). And: "L'essentiel de son message, si j'ai bien entendu, est une violente dénonciation de l'emprise sexuelle... De l'emprise tout court..." [The essence of its message, if I understand it right, is a violent denunciation of sexual power... Of power itself...] (348). Here we are in the topic announced in the three-part thesis of *Femmes*: "Le monde appartient aux femmes. / C'est-à-dire à la mort. / Là-dessus, tout le monde ment."

Somewhere in *Comédie* is a proposition that seems almost an outline for *Femmes*. It would reverse the Gospel: instead of a message emanating from a master, to be propagated by twelve disciples in nearly identical form, "le héros mettrait au point une manière de se faire censurer de douze façons différentes par douze femmes..." [the hero would devise a means of getting himself censured in twelve different ways by twelve women...] (392).[13] Contradictory, undefinable, ungraspable, our double hero-narrator would propagate himself in his writing in a dozen different guises.

Just as Sollers produced audio and video in which he reads *Paradis,* S. has transferred his *Comédie* to aural media. The following description is pure and simple autobiography:

S. m'explique comment il a enregistré l'intégralité de sa *Comédie* en lisant lui-même à toute allure: douze heures, et ce n'est pas le premier volume [. . .]. Il se balade un peu partout, maintenant, pour lire en public le début de son second volume, toujours sans ponctuation, entouré par huit écrans de télévision... Sur six écrans un film où l'on voit rapidement Venise, S. en train de jouer au tennis, des incrustations de flashes pornos, une tête de bébé endormi, des fontaines... Sur les deux écrans qui restent, il se fait prendre en direct colorisé en train de cracher sa prose vaudou, transpirant, cataleptique... (347)

[S. explains to me how he recorded the entire *Comédie,* reading it himself at breakneck speed: twelve hours, and that's not even the first volume [. . .]. He is traveling around pretty much everywhere, now, reading the beginning of the second volume in public, still without punctuation, surrounded by eight television screens... On six screens, a film in which one rapidly sees Venice, S. playing tennis, superimposed flashes of porn, a sleeping baby's head, fountains... On the remaining two screens, he has himself filmed live and colorized while spitting out his voodoo prose, sweating, cataleptic...]

The audiocassettes of *Paradis* were advertised in *Tel Quel* in 1982 and were broadcast over various radio stations. The latter part of this passage describes *Paradis video,* an hour-long video produced by Jean-Paul Fargier with Sollers reading the first approximately fifty pages of *Paradis II*; the production appeared in several provincial cities and in the Centre Pompidou.

In short, *Femmes* tends toward autobiography because what Will describes of S.'s *Comédie* and of his own novel and their reception matches what we know about Sollers, *Paradis,* and the other writings. In this generic redefinition we find one realistic effect of writing, an effect that writing urges upon reality. *Femmes* is used to explain *Paradis*, via *Comédie*. S.'s *Comédie* is as important to Will's *Femmes* as *Paradis* is to Sollers's *Femmes*. Sollers called *Paradis* his *Mémoires* (à la Saint-Simon), written "live"; "Il n'y a plus la moindre distance entre ce qui est en train de se passer et le récit du mémorialiste" [There is no longer the slightest distance between what is actually happening and the memorialist's narration]. He adds: "*Femmes*, ce sont aussi mes *Mémoires*. J'en tire un roman, comme ça..." [*Femmes* is also my *Memoirs*. I'm making a novel out of them, like so...].[14] In the reader's mind, this equation further solidifies the bond that makes of Will and S. the two aspects of a doubled Sollers. Thematically, the always necessary reference to Dante and the subtle reminders, like slight variations on a theme, of the emptiness of the world constitute the apocalyptic tone that extends from *Comédie/Paradis* to *Femmes*.

Getting It Down on Paper

As I have said, the present tense reigns throughout and anchors the whole in the current moment. A multitude of small verbal expressions reiterate how tightly defined that present time is, as when the narrator writes: "Je viens de m'emporter un peu devant S. qui m'écoute en souriant..." [I've just gotten a little angry with S. who is listening to me, smiling...] (117). Time of writing is the moment of living; there is a conflation of composition time with event time, and this is true both for Will's writing and for Sollers's. When the Polish revolution begins and enters into the novel, the date is 1981, the very time when Sollers was writing *Femmes*: "La DATE... 1981... After Christ... Comme disent, de façon conciliante, les Anglo-Saxons... BC! AC!" [The DATE... 1981... After Christ... The way the Anglo-Saxons put it, in conciliatory fashion... BC! AC!] (256). (I suspect that the creative substitution of After Christ for Anno Domini is not Sollers's error but S.'s.) Transcribing "live" the events he is living, Will records what he sees, like a secretary or chronicler who lives to write. Events enter the novel just as they were lived, and to guarantee their authenticity they are transcribed immediately: "Et moi, là, rentré chez moi, penché sur ma table, écrivant ces phrases" [Me, here, back home, leaning over my desk, writing these sentences] (21). As Will arrives in New York, we read: "Décollage... Dix mille mètres... [. . .] New York... Il fait très beau..." [Take-off... Ten thousand meters... [. . .] New York... It's a very beautiful day...] (160).

Sixteen lines later: "J'ouvre ma machine à écrire, je tape: 'Décollage... New York... Il fait très beau...'" [I open my typewriter, I type: "Takeoff... New York... It's a very beautiful day..."]. To emphasize that this book is the one Will is writing, he notes an instantaneous record of the writing. Self-reference is immediate: In Venice, his hostess, Sonia, asks what he is writing on now. He answers Tiepolo, the painter, subject of the last few pages of Sollers's book. Then she leaves, and: "Je tape en direct le dialogue qu'on vient d'avoir..." [I take down live the dialogue we've just had...] (628). It is as if he is taking dictation from his epoch.

Having mentioned S.'s "bad reputation," Will admits to being a little anxious about S.'s reaction to his comments on this when he gets the manuscript to correct. There follows a parenthesis: "(note après coup: aucune réaction)..." [(later note: no reaction)...] (93–94). These lines bring together the time of first writing, the time of S.'s reading, and the time after S.'s reading. On page 529 of the Folio edition, when Kate asks him how many pages he has written and he replies 529, this is not at all the luck of the typography. Here is the dialogue: "'Et tu en es où?' dit-elle, glaciale./Je ne vais quand même pas lui répondre: 'En ce moment! Ici! Maintenant! Avec toi! Dans ce dialogue même!'" ["And how far along are you?" she says icily./I'm certainly not going to answer: "At this moment! Here! Now! With you! In this very dialogue!"]. The original Gallimard edition contains this dialogue on page 452, and there Will says he has written 452 pages. This is certainly the most immediately self-reflective moment of a performance of writing that will end, a page before the last of *Femmes*, with a "Bon, maintenant c'est la fin... Une des fins possibles..." [Okay, now it's the ending... One of the possible endings...] (666). In short, the punctual creation of Will's writing gives it the force to involve the reader in its inscriptions of reality.

Critical Reading

As noted, Sollers has used his recent novels to respond to criticisms (just as he took the occasion of the preface of *La Guerre du goût* to launch a totally unexpected diatribe against people's failure to read *Femmes*, published eleven years earlier). Thus, in *Le Cœur Absolu*, he creates a conversation between the narrator and another character in which real quotations from critics of *Portrait du joueur* are read and are shown up for their inanity and stupidity. A strong characteristic of the Sollers narrator persona is in fact this comical and self-righteous bitterness at not having been read correctly, yet, even by the French intellectuals who *should* know how to read his writing, those who "know more about it"—the very ones for whom Will chose to write his *Femmes*. All the narrators of the novels since *Femmes* engage in this mockery of criticism. In spite of the fact that, as Sollers affirmed in *Carnet de nuit*, the narrators are not the same character, from one novel to the next, and thus each is not the writer of the previous book, such scenes come as if from the same voice.[15] This motif does much to strengthen the autobiographical aspect of Sollers's fiction. In addition, the fact that, in *Femmes,* the novel is being written by Will (and corrected by S.) as it progresses allows Sollers to insert the criticism of the novel at the same time as it is being written, as if in anticipation of the quarrels the press will have with S. once the novel appears, and makes the double author Will and S. resemble Sollers. In short, parallel to the representation of writing as a topic, critical reading is an ingredient in writing realism in *Femmes.*

Thus, there are several scenes of criticism (similar to important reading scenes in *Le Livre brisé*) in which a character's more or less apparent goodwill (usually less) comes into play. The characters address their criticisms directly to Will, with no compunctions: His novel is rotten! It doesn't have a plot! The title is a disaster! Never mind that not one has read a single word of the manuscript: "On dit même que ton roman n'est pas fameux... —Comment ça? Personne ne l'a lu! —Si, si, Boris dit qu'il en a vu quelques pages... Que c'est du sous-Céline... Avec toutes tes obsessions contre les femmes, il paraît... Si c'est ça, tu vas te ramasser, mon vieux... [. . .] Tu vas te planter, crois-moi!" ["They're even saying your novel is not so hot..." "How come? Nobody has read it!" "Oh yes, Boris says he's seen some pages... That it's second-rate Céline... With all your obsessions against women, it seems... If that's it, my friend, you're going to fall flat on your face... [. . .] You're headed for a crash, believe me!"] (294). So speaks Kate. Here is Flora's assessment: "Robert est comme moi. Il pense que ton titre est mauvais" [Robert is like me. He thinks your title is poor] (311). As for Robert: "Et toi, toujours *Femmes*? —Oui... —Pas très bon, je trouve... Fade... Cinéma..." ["And you, still *Femmes*?" "Yes..." "Not too good, in my opinion... Dull... Put on..."] (575). Under the attack, Will sometimes doubts his efforts: "La vérité, c'est que je ne devrais pas écrire de roman. Je ne devrais surtout pas écrire, *ce* roman. [. . .] Je ne suis pas fait pour ça. Je ne dois pas" [The truth is, I shouldn't write a novel. I especially shouldn't write *this* novel. [. . .] I'm not made for it. I shouldn't] (311). This does not stop him, however.

All object to the title. The devil in person appears and, quoting Laurence Sterne to good effect, tempts Will with a more appropriate, more colorful, and certainly more apocalyptic title: *La Fin du monde*. His talk, wonderfully insinuating and corrupting, as well as clever and spirited, makes Will wonder if he should not lighten the tone (356). "Mais précisément, c'est *trop* vrai! Beaucoup trop brutal! Analyse sauvage... [. . .] Ton récit va tomber à plat. Raconte! Raconte! C'est tout" [But exactly, it's *too* real! Much too brutal! Savage analysis... [. . .] Your story is going to fall flat. Narrate! Narrate! That's all] (358). Indirectly emphasizing the apocalyptic thesis of the novel, about the power of death that women represent, the devil wants the manuscript to be more marketable. Shouldn't Will hide the keys? But he holds to his title, which the devil at last grants grudgingly: "Je t'aurai prévenu! Très mauvais pour la sortie de ton livre! Ne compte pas sur moi! N'oublie pas que je dirige les médias, les supports!..." [I'm warning you! Very bad for the publication of your book! Don't count on me! Don't forget that I'm in charge of the media, the marketing!...] (360). In this scene the devil seems to represent a part of the author—a troublesome double, perhaps—who would alter the direction of his writing. While Sollers may be suggesting that his book could be more exciting and more appealing if it stuck to intrigue and developed its characters, this is also, and especially, a devious way of reminding us of its apocalyptic message nevertheless, via the devil himself. These scenes of critical reading contribute to the realism of the writing both by re-creating a situation typical of Sollers's writing, the object of society's malevolence, and by reanchoring the fictional (even fanciful) story in Sollers's serious observations about society.

Chief among the criticisms embedded in the realism of *Femmes* is the argument that it has no plot. Sollers gives this critique to Will's wife, Deborah (or Deb), who remarks several times that he should tell a story or weave an intrigue, by having the characters meet each other: "Elle trouve que je devrais raconter des histoires, soigner l'intrigue, 'planter le décor'... [. . .] Que les personnages s'affrontent, se mesurent, qu'ils échangent des regards, des silences, des sous-entendus lourds de significations, chargés de désirs..." [She thinks I should tell stories, manage the plot, "set the scene"... [. . .] That the characters should confront each other, size each other up, exchange glances, silences, sentences full of hidden meanings, loaded with desire...] (58). In particular she suggests the women should meet each other, and when precisely that happens to her, it is one event Will has not chosen to write. Flora, in a jealous rage, descends upon Deb while he is in Florence, starting the engine that runs the classic intrigue of the adulterous love affair found out. For Will's manuscript has only one real reader, Deborah, and very likely by this time we have begun to wonder how she comes to terms with the fact that Will is consorting and cavorting with women right and left (especially Cyd, Lynn, the Présidente, and Ysia, plus several others, in addition to Flora). Flora's initiative should bring his long overdue comeuppance into play. It is interesting that this event happens literally in Will's absence, with the result that we do not see him writing this scene, which Deb reports to him by long-distance telephone.

This distancing tactic, the opposite of the "live" transcription of events, corresponds to the stance he takes on the request for more intrigue. As he mentally considers his wife's critique, his response is that he cannot imagine bringing the characters together: "J'essaie d'imaginer les scènes... Le rendez-vous entre Flora et Cyd... Cacophonie! ou entre Ysia et Kate? Même pas trois minutes d'entretien... Entre Diane et Deb? Voyons... [. . .] Franchement, non, je ne vois pas ce qu'elles auraient à se dire..." [I try to imagine the scenes... The rendezvous between Flora and Cyd... Cacophony! Or between Ysia and Kate? Not even three minutes' conversation... Between Diane and Deb? Let's see... [. . .] Frankly, no, I don't see what they would have to say to each other...] (390). He is right, it turns out: nothing whatsoever comes of the one encounter that does happen. "Pauvre Flora!... Son truc n'a pas marché... Tout le monde s'en fout... Deb la première... [. . .] L'*intrigue* ne fonctionne plus... L'*histoire* non plus..." [Poor Flora!... Her thing didn't work... Nobody cares... Starting with Deb... [. . .] *Plot* doesn't work any more... Neither does *story*...] (468). Like Sollers's novels, Will's steadfastly rejects traditional notions of intrigue (plot) and story, including the adultery plot that the French often call *histoire*.

It will fall to his eventual readers to object to the lack of plot, just as some of Sollers's readers have, and Will puts them into the book too, about 150 pages before the end: "Je vous entends d'ici... Et les personnages? Que sont devenus les personnages? Que font-ils? Où sont-ils? Nous voulons les personnages! Pas l'auteur! Les personnages! Ce qui leur arrive! [. . .] NOUS-VOU-LONS-UN-VRAI-RO-MAN!" [I can hear you from here... What about the characters? What's become of the characters? What are they doing? Where are they? We want the characters! Not the author! The characters! What happens to them! [. . .] WE-

WANT-A-RE-AL-NOV-EL!] (517). The suggestion that the characters are in a different world, or a different narrative level, than the "author" augments the consistency of his manuscript as a novel within the novel. Impatient readers may have no role left to play in the novel if the characters disappear. Will scolds them: "Insatiable lecteur! Avide lectrice!... [. . .] Ah, vous voulez absolument être dans le récit, n'est-ce pas?" [Insatiable reader! Avid reader!... [. . .] Oh, you absolutely have to be in the story, don't you?] (517). This little crisis in the composition of the manuscript reminds us how fragile writing is, and provokes the writer's anger: "Ah, vous me tuez, à la fin!... Votre malveillance systématique m'accable!... Jamais contents!... L'œil rivé aux faiblesses!... Aux longueurs!... Aux petits côtés!... Attendant farouchement que je ne sache pas comment continuer... Que je cale... Que j'abandonne..." [Oh, you're killing me, in the end!... Your systematic malevolence overwhelms me!... Never happy!... Eyes glued to the weak spots!... To the boring parts!... To the small end!... Madly expecting me not to know how to continue... To stall... To give up...] (518). In the motif of the novel about the novel, the criticism of the novel contributes to the creation before our eyes of a manuscript whose writing proceeds at the same rate as the reading, not unlike Doubrovsky's writing in *Le Livre brisé.*

Double Writers, Double Genres

The strategy of doubling Will with S. becomes particularly interesting when Will reflects on and casts light upon S.:

Je remarque, quand son nom est prononcé, une bizarre dépression de l'atmosphère... De la magnétosphère... Une sorte de trou de silence... Une fermeture accablée... Qu'a-t-il donc fait de si grave, de si répréhensible, de si radical même, que seul le silence peut le signaler? Cette quasi-unanimité dans le rejet, la dépréciation spontanée, m'intrigue. (89)

I've noticed, when his name is pronounced, a bizarre depression of the atmosphere... Of the magnetosphere... A sort of hole of silence... An oppressive stopping... What in the world did he do that's so serious, so reprehensible, so radical even, that silence is the only way to mark it? This near unanimity in rejection, in spontaneous depreciation, intrigues me.

Will produces the following analysis to explain what S. has done wrong: "L'étranger venu du dedans ou s'infiltrant au-dedans... Le traître, le dérapeur, le déviant, le mutant des fibres... Par exemple, celui qui n'épouse pas une

Française... [. . .] Une juive... Une étrangère..." [the stranger coming from within or infiltrating into the system... The traitor, the blunderer, the deviant, the mutant of fibers... For example, the one who does not marry a French woman... [. . .] Who marries a Jew... A foreigner...] (89).[16] While S.'s wife is Polish, Will's wife, Deborah, has the physical and circumstantial attributes of Julia Kristeva; their son Stephen resembles David, the child of Sollers and Kristeva. Numerous other circumstances of S.'s life or Will's are like Sollers's, such as S.'s avoidance of the army during the Algerian war and the founding of *Tel Quel.* Putting Will's analyses of S. into the novel allows Sollers to present himself as seen by a sympathetic observer who becomes quite close to him, in contrast to the criticism and hatred he endures from the largely mistaken and self-damning public—and this description applies to S., to Sollers, and eventually to Will.

Will plays the role of that extra pair of ears we each would like to have to hear what people are saying about us when we are not there. Furthermore, his observations of S. produce a rather pointed self-analysis of Sollers:

La solitude de S. qui, malgré l'hostilité sourde qui l'entoure, est quand même très célèbre dans un certain milieu, a en effet quelque chose de stupéfiant. Lui qui semble à l'aise partout, il est en réalité coupé de tout, insolite partout, sans aucune possibilité de confrérie, de refuge, de groupe. (90)

[S.'s solitude does in fact seem rather astonishing, considering that, in spite of the muted hostility that surrounds him, he is nevertheless very famous in a certain milieu. Seeming at ease everywhere, he is in reality cut off from everything, an outsider everywhere, with no possibility of confraternity, of refuge, of association.]

The analysis continues for several pages. Moreover, there are enough overt similarities between S. and Will to discredit the differences in their backgrounds, as I have already suggested. Some are subtle, like this comparison of their working habits: "S. a dû s'organiser très rigoureusement, *comme moi,* pour tenir le coup. C'est ce qui m'intéresse chez lui, cette longue et instinctive discipline de l'homme qui veut accomplir son projet" [S. has had to organize his life very rigorously, *like me,* to stick it out. That's what interests me about him, this long and instinctive discipline of the man who wants to achieve his objectives] (93; emphasis added). "Sa désinvolture me désarme parce qu'elle ressemble à la mienne. Il refuse toujours de faire la moindre autocritique. Sa fantaisie du moment avant tout. C'est ce qu'on lui reproche" [His nonchalance disarms me because it resembles mine. He always refuses to make the least self-criticism. The fantasy of the moment above all. That's what people reproach him for] (263).

Because of their shared situations, S. takes an ever larger role in Will's life: "En tout cas, il rentre de plus en plus dans mon roman... Il se fait là, dans la narration, une place bizarre, insistante..." [In any case, he's getting more and more into my novel... He's making himself a bizarre, insistent space in it, in the narration...] (286). Little by little, we realize that Will is no less hounded than S.: "Je suis trop ceci, pas assez cela... Les thèmes changent, mais l'accusation reste identique... Quelque chose, en moi, ne va pas..." [I am too much this, not enough that... The topics change, but the accusation remains identical... Something in me is no good...] (239). His situation at the journal where he works is worsening rapidly. Boris bluntly tells Will: "C'est curieux, tout de même, comme vous êtes détesté... Haï..." [It's strange, all the same, how people detest you... Hate you...] (340). Later, Will lists his faults, from the public's view: "Enthousiasme pour des choses que personne ne connaît... Goût de la contradiction... Légèreté dans les choses graves... Gravité dans les légères... Irresponsable... Insolent..." [Enthusiasm for things nobody knows... A taste for contradiction... Treating serious things lightly... Light things seriously... Irresponsible... Insolent...] (497). These phrases reproduce nearly textually the complaints people have made about Sollers, as he has himself reported. Both S. and Will, then, in their doubled autobiographies, are writing Sollers's life.

We can also take the doubled authorship as a kind of allegory of Sollers's writing. Will-and-S. reproduce, together, the practice that Sollers followed to create *Femmes*: S. leaves Will some notes; Will incorporates them into his text and gives it to S. to revise (267). S.'s notes recall those notes that Philippe Forest maintains Sollers had been taking for several years, brought together to constitute this novel. The estrangement, the strangeness, the paradoxes, and the distance created by the doubled writer within the novel would be explained in terms of the real writer's altered states. When Sollers produces a draft based on his notes, he becomes a kind of anonymous other self who is neither the observer who penned the notes nor the writer intent on bringing the writing to its final polish and perfection, but rather a kind of obsessed voyeur (and *écouteur*) who chains himself to his pen and produces a first draft. Never a day without writing a line, Sollers has said. S. believes there is "une vie toute spé-

ciale pour celui qui est appelé à écrire réellement le dessous des événements...
Une vie qui n'a rien à voir avec la vie... Une vie de la mort qui écrit..." [a very
special life for the one who is called upon really to write the underside of
events... A life that has nothing to do with life... A life of death writing...] (113).
Something like that life of death, that anonymous other self, that obsessed
voyeur is represented by the figment of the writer who occasionally answers to
the name Will, the writing self. Finally, Sollers in his incarnation as S. revises
and polishes and sees the work to publication.

Two genres are involved in this autobiographical fiction, just as there are
two writers. I am not, however, trying to suggest that, of the two writers of the
manuscript of *Femmes,* one creates autobiography and the other fiction. By
doubling the writers, Sollers achieves a very special kind of writing of realism,
as if he is writing his autobiography without being its author. A good example
of the devious effects Sollers created can be found in the following passage, in
which Will is writing about himself:

[Aragon] avait lu un article de moi sur le surréalisme, il voulait me voir... J'avais vingt-
deux ans... S. a eu la même expérience quand il a été propulsé, à vingt ans, comme un
jeune écrivain d'avenir simultanément par Mauriac et Aragon... Il n'aime pas trop
parler de cette époque... Il en a honte... Comme il a honte du petit roman qu'il a publié
à ce moment-là et qu'il a tout fait pour retirer de la circulation... Alors que, moi, je le
trouve très supérieur à tous les débutants d'aujourd'hui... Un style, une souplesse...
Stendhal... (327)

[[Aragon] had read an article of mine on surrealism, he wanted to meet me... I was
twenty-two... S. had the same experience when, at twenty, he was rocketed up simultaneously by Mauriac and Aragon as a young writer with a future... He doesn't much like
to talk about that period... He's ashamed of it... As he is ashamed of the little novel
that he published then and that he did his best to remove from circulation... Whereas,
me, I find it much superior to all the young novelists today... A style, a suppleness...
Stendhal...]

Will's encounter with Aragon can only be fictional, part of the novel he is writing (about himself, just like Sollers). S.'s, however, resembles Sollers's enough
for it to fall into autobiography—but again, it is Sollers's autobiography. *Le
Défi,* a short narrative, was praised by Mauriac in 1957, and Aragon, at the
opposite end of the ideological spectrum, hailed *Une Curieuse solitude* (1958),
Sollers's first novel. It is also true that Sollers tried to disavow the novel. When
we know this, it becomes quite comical to read what amounts to self-praise

(but color it with irony . . .) when Will applauds that first novel concisely but immoderately. The advantages of doubling the writer! Sollers observes, in *Carnet de nuit*, "Ton personnage de roman existe quand tu aimerais avoir son point de vue sur le roman en question. Le livre est réussi quand tu as envie d'y ajouter ce qui s'y trouve" [The character in your novel exists when you would like to have his opinion about the novel in question. The novel is a success when you would like to add to it what is in it] (133).

The Novel as Creator of Truth

Fals, the character who represents Lacan, quotes a philosopher (actually Lacan himself): "Je dis toujours la vérité. Pas toute, parce que toute la dire, on n'y arrive pas... Les mots y manquent. C'est même par cet impossible que la vérité tient au réel" [I always tell the truth. Not the whole truth, because saying it all can't be done... Words fail it. In fact it is by means of this impossibility that the truth gains something of reality] (102). Will, disagreeing, replies: "Le roman, et lui seul, dit la vérité... Toute la vérité... Autre chose que la vérité, et pourtant rien que la vérité... Les mots ne lui manquent pas... Au contraire... C'est pourquoi on préfère le tenir pour irréel alors qu'il est le réel lui-même... Le système nerveux des réalités..." [The novel, and only the novel, tells the truth... The whole truth... Something other than the truth, and yet nothing but the truth... Words do not fail the novel... On the contrary... That is why people prefer to consider it unreal, whereas it is the real itself... The nervous system of realities...] (102). The assertion is extremely vigorous; it recalls similar tenets found in Balzac, especially in certain prefaces, and implied in Diderot's fiction. Sollers, through his writer-protagonist, holds that fiction arrives at the truth precisely because words do not fail it—it abounds, it flourishes with words. The writing in a novel possesses a wealth of language that philosophy no doubt lacks, but Will is asserting even more. Giving another turn to the screw, he situates the real in that writing, and suggests that its "fictionality" arises in the plethora of writing that we have equated, for centuries, suspiciously, with the unreal, as in the *Heptaméron*. Simultaneously, nevertheless, belief in the represented reality has continued to motivate our reading of fictions. The paradox is that the novel writes something *other than* truth and yet *only* truth: this is writing realism.

Will's retort to Fals takes place both in Sollers's *Femmes* and in the manuscript that Will is writing with S.'s help. It therefore casts both the novel and the manuscript in the light of the real. Normally, when a character who is a novelist portrayed as writing a novel claims it tells reality, within the diegetic frame of the novel, that reality is defined in terms of the second world created by the novel in which the character exists, like Edouard in *Les Faux-monnayeurs*. What is rarer is Sollers's use of the novelist character and his writing to make the reality claim about *Femmes* and the real world he would have it influence (rather than lodging that claim outside the book, in interviews, articles, and so forth). Again, this effect stems from the autobiographical vein in which it is written. Will qualifies this connection between novel and real world as a kind of magic: "Ce qui est intéressant, dans la vie, c'est quand elle se met à ressembler au roman qu'on est en train d'écrire... Magie? Oui. A partir du moment où on commence un livre, le paysage bouge... Ballet insidieux... Les personnages réels, là, se déplacent..." [What is interesting, in life, is when it starts to resemble the novel you are in the process of writing... Magic? Yes. From the moment you start a book, the landscape moves... Insidious ballet... The real people in it move about...] (272). Writing changes the landscape; the *roman à clés* can reveal the movements of the real characters; fiction doubles the self: "[Sonia] me regarde quand même avec curiosité... Roman magique... On est ailleurs en étant là, on est peut-être celui qui est vraiment là..." [[Sonia] is looking at me curiously, all the same... Magic novel... Being somewhere else while being here; we might be the ones who are really here...] (612). Possibly the written self is more truly present than the real self. The magic affects both writer and readers:

Destinée invraisemblable des acteurs d'une époque. Comme s'ils étaient liés par le fil d'un roman en train de s'écrire. Un roman auquel personne ne croirait si c'était un roman. Et moi là-dedans? Finalement, je me suis trouvé là par hasard... Ou par une nécessité qui veut précisément que j'écrive ce livre.

[Implausible destiny of the people active during a particular period. As if they were connected by the thread of a novel just being written. A novel no one would believe in if it were a novel. And what about me? As it turned out, I found myself here by chance... Or precisely by a necessity that requires that I write this book.]

"This book" is both the book that brings these characters together in their time and the book Will is writing. Life resembles a novel as much as the novel resembles life.

The narrator protests that the novelist has rights, as does fiction: "Du moment qu'il n'y a pas les noms propres? Est-ce qu'on ne peut pas raconter ce qu'on veut?" [Given that there are no proper names? Can't one tell what one wants to?]. But on reflection he continues, mentally, that the novel does not have the right to imagine everything, lest it divulge the "secret," which I take to be the following:

Bien sûr que le roman est la chose la plus dangereuse... Le risque n'est pas d'ailleurs d'appeler "les êtres et les choses" par leurs noms, mais bien de les faire exister sous d'autres noms plus vrais que les vrais... La magie du roman est de traiter la magie elle-même... La magie noire des doubles, de l'empoisonné travail invisible de substitution permanente qui fait que la vie est vécue par d'autres personnages que ceux qui se croient en vie... Le roman est démoniaque... Le roman est le diable du diable; le diable au service de la vérité... (324)

[Of course the novel is the most dangerous thing... The risk is, moreover, not in calling "people and things" by their names, but rather making them exist under other names more real than the real ones... The magic of the novel is to deal with magic itself... The black magic of doubles, of the poisoned invisible work of permanent substitution, which causes life to be lived by characters other than those who think they are living... The novel is demoniacal... The novel is the devil of the devil, the devil in the service of truth...]

The strong language of this very important passage describes the illusion of reality that novelistic writing can create, the poisoned work of language that substitutes words for things. Those other words are then more true than the things, and this is the black magic of doubles. In acutely self-reflective fashion, the magic of the novel is its ability to put into play the magic of illusion. This passage thus sustains my observation that the deep topic of the novel *Femmes* is the fundamental operation the novel accomplishes: the illusion of truth, representation itself, the reality of which is all the greater for the writing of it. This is what makes the novel dangerous, or demoniacal.

Events prove this thesis. Will realizes: "C'est vrai que, depuis que j'ai commencé ce livre, je sens autour de moi une sérieuse odeur de police. [. . .] Ecrivez, écrivez, tant que vous n'aurez pas cette sensation nette, absolument pas inventée, vous saurez que vous n'écrivez rien... Rien d'intéressant, en tout cas..." [It's true that, since I began this book, I smell a serious aroma of the police around me. [. . .] Write, go ahead and write, as long as you don't have this clear sensation, which is absolutely not invented, you will know that you are writing

nothing... Nothing interesting, in any case...] (422–23).[17] The "clear sensation" relates writing to reality, and the anxiety about the "police" comes from
the transpositions of real people and events in the book and an earlier discussion with the devil about hiding the keys (357). But police also materialize
unmetaphorically. The only truly dramatic event in *Femmes,* one that qualifies
for intrigue in both the French senses, brings into play the relation of writing
life and life itself, as well as the police. Just as Cyd is about to tell Will (very
likely) that she is pregnant (presumably by the usual means), a machine-gun
attack kills her and wounds Will, as they sit at a café. Cyd was not only the
most intimate of Will's lovers, she was also the most important of the women
(in that second sense according to which *Femmes* is a story about love affairs
with several women). Over the course of the novel, Will's relationships have
evolved, and some women have become closer to him and others farther; a
child forging permanent ties would have the potential to stamp a seal of
approval on the relation of Will with Cyd. Furthermore, because Will also
simultaneously writes this relationship, it acquires a semiotic value: Cyd has
come to be the most important woman *for his writing.* In other words, her
symbolic importance in the mimetic frame doubles her role in the semiosis.

As a result, Cyd's death poses problems for the continuation of the narrative.
Seventy pages before the end, Will discusses with S. how to proceed, after this
unplanned event. The problem is, first, that the dramatic event is too dramatic
to be believable: "no one will believe us" (596). In spite of Will's smart rejoinder
that one need only consult the list of victims, S. sees Cyd's death as implausible.
He continues: "Cet attentat écrit va paraître bidon dans le livre... Inventé de
toutes pièces! Venant à point! Trop à point!" [This written attack is going to
look phony in the book... Made up of whole cloth! Just at the right moment!
Too right!]. Diderot struggled with that very conundrum: how to maintain
plausibility without being unfaithful to reality. Then there is a further problem, more sinister: "Mais nous n'avons plus la pauvre Cyd... Ou bien, nous
l'avons autrement... De toute façon, vous auriez fait quoi lorsqu'elle vous aurait
dit qu'elle était enceinte?" [But we no longer have poor Cyd... Or rather,
we have her in other ways... Anyway, what would you have done when she told
you she was pregnant?] (596–97). Because life affected how the novel was
being written, Cyd's death changes the direction of the novel. (Similarly, in
Doubrovsky's *Le Livre brisé,* Ilse's death will completely alter Serge's book.)
A few lines later: "—Le roman est dangereux, dis-je gravement" [The novel

is dangerous, I say gravely]. Life has to be lived in a certain way to make the novel go: "—Nous ne mettons pas Lynn à la place?" [Don't we put Lynn in her place?] asks Will, referring to a sexual partner he shared with Cyd. S. responds: "—Surtout pas!... Côté aventures, je vous vois un peu seul pendant quelque temps... Enfin, à vous de voir... Si le roman est la vie elle-même, comme le pense le désespoir intuitif des nations, avouez que nous sommes au cœur du fonctionnement..." [Not at all!... When it comes to adventures, I see you being a little lonely for some time... Well, you decide... If the novel is life itself, as the intuitive despair of nations has it, you have to admit we are in the heart of the mechanism...] (597–98).

The reader can only agree. It seems the character Will has to be alone—that is, womanless—in his "real" life just to make his novel work. He has to live his life a certain way, because the novel is an account of the present. The heart of the matter is in this nexus of life and novel. Cyd's death causes this significant moment of taking into account. But not only does her mimetic death—her death as a character in the represented account—influence the course of the writing, one may also reverse the proposition. Then her "death" in the semiosis results in her death in the mimesis. Sollers had to write her out of the story. Why? With this maneuver, the female character with the most consistency, the warmest, richest, most human, most sensually realized woman of the book turns again into a mere figure of paper, a device invented by the novelist Will rather than a person of flesh and blood with whom Will created a child. This representation of a loss of the realistic illusion then reflects upon the highly autobiographical novel *Femmes* by Sollers. This is what I call a tourniquet: it shows the power of other words to take the place of realities, and hence the dangerous magic of writing.

There is a reason that Will (and Sollers) rejects ordinary plot making. Definitively, the plot of *Femmes* is the story of fiction writing. This is how Will responds to the criticism that "tout de même, il faudrait une histoire" [all the same, you ought to have a story] (391): "L'intrigue? L'histoire? Mais c'est l'Intrigue! Mais c'est l'Histoire! Transposables, indéfiniment, dans tous les espaces et dans tous les temps! De l'illusion! De la désillusion! Et de l'illusion de nouveau! Et de la désillusion encore!" [The plot? The story? But it is the Plot! But it is the Story! Transposable indefinitely into all spaces and all times! Illusion! Disillusion! And illusion again! And disillusion once more!] (391). It is not a story about characters; it is a story about story, intrigue, illusion, all the things a novel is before it is about something. As Jean Ricardou wrote about a *nouveau roman,* it is less "*the writing of an adventure than the adventure of a writing,*" a telling formula that Doubrovsky will adopt and modify to define autofiction. Barthes, without mentioning Ricardou, wrote something quite similar in November 1966: nothing happens, from the point of view of the real, but "'what happens' is language all by itself, the adventure of language."[18] No subject is more universal, arising in all times and all spaces, nor more rich in intrigue and stories, than the magical creation of illusion.

Beyond the representation of a writing, beyond the *mise en abyme* or the *récit spéculaire, Femmes* is important because of how skillfully and obsessively it puts before us the proposition that fiction writing is the best way to describe reality, and possibly to effect a change in it. It represents raw writing, seen at the moment of its creation, not yet taken up into a rational, signifying structure, which can only follow on the end of the writing.

The Death of Autobiography: *Le Livre brisé*

> L'écrivain, de ses maux, dragons qu'il a
> choyés, ou d'une allégresse, doit s'instituer, au
> texte, le spirituel histrion.
>
> [With his ills, the dragons he has coddled, or
> with a jauntiness, the writer should to the text
> constitute himself the histrionic wit.]
>
> — MALLARMÉ

Serge Doubrovsky coined the term *autofiction* to describe a genre that blends autobiography and fiction. This is how he defines it, in writing about his 1977 novel *Fils*:

Fiction, d'événements et de faits strictement réels; si l'on veut, *autofiction,* d'avoir confié le langage d'une aventure à l'aventure du langage.[19]

[A fiction, of strictly real events and facts; as it were, *autofiction,* from having confided the language of an adventure to the adventure of language.]

(The last phrase reprises Ricardou's opposition of "*the writing of an adventure*" to "*the adventure of a writing.*") In what amounts to a serial autobiography, Doubrovsky has written a series of creative works that together narrate his life.

Le Livre brisé, winner of the Médicis prize in 1989, follows upon *La Dispersion* (1969), *Fils* (1977), *Un Amour de soi* (1982), and *La Vie l'instant* (1985), and precedes *L'Après-vivre* (1994) and *Laissé pour conte* (1999). All are published as novels, although *La Vie l'instant* consists of several distinct narratives, more like a collection of short stories than a novel. Writing in 1991, Doubrovsky re-affirmed his adherence to the genre he created, and the role of his life in it:

En tant qu'écrivain, j'ai été amené, au cours des ans, à composer une série d'ouvrages directement et nommément inspirés par ma propre vie, et que pourtant j'ai toujours intitulés "romans." Pour désigner cette pratique, qui ne m'est pas particulière, mais est le fait de beaucoup d'écrivains contemporains, j'ai proposé, par opposition à l'auto-biographie classique, le vocable d' "autofiction," lequel semble avoir été adopté désor-mais par un large consensus universitaire.[20]

[As a writer, I have been led to compose, through the years, a series of works directly and specifically inspired by my own life, which I have nevertheless always called "novels." To refer to this practice, which is not unique to me, but is the case with many contemporary writers, I have proposed, in opposition to the classical autobiography, the term "autofiction," which seems to have been adopted now by a broad academic consensus.]

The term has in fact been adopted and as often adapted to a variety of narrative practices blending fiction and reality.

Reviews of *Le Livre brisé* called it a "monster book," for reasons that will become apparent. It deserved the Médicis prize, and I consider it Doubrovsky's best creative writing. The book is both novel and autobiography: it recounts the author's life and is centered on the protagonist called Serge Doubrovsky who is also writing a novel about his life. *Le Livre brisé* carries the self-reflexivity of *Femmes* a considerable step further by giving the protagonist exactly the same name and persona as the author (even his social security number). By comparison, in several of his novels since 1983, Sollers inserts his name, or rather names, including his family name of Joyaux, in diverse guises and dis-guises, like an artist signing his work (or sometimes like the sneaky appearance of Alfred Hitchcock in his films), but none of his protagonists is actually called Philippe Sollers. Alert readers are not duped, but the lack of an overt claim to be writing his own life, under his own name, so to speak, is what distinguishes Sollers's writing from Doubrovsky's. A reviewer for *Le Monde* did not hesitate to call *Le Livre brisé* an "autobiographical madness," and the same description can apply to the novel Serge the protagonist is writing.[21] To complete the representation of the writing, somewhat like *Femmes*, Doubrovsky's novel also represents reading, in compelling passages in which Serge and his wife, Ilse, discuss what he has already written and determine how the writing will continue. In addition to this relentless and inescapable self-reflexivity, Le *Livre brisé* is insistently and consistently referential: it represents the reality of the author's life so acutely, so much more dramatically than Doubrovsky's other autobiographical texts, that it explodes the very model of the *roman à clés*. In short, one can confidently say that the story Serge writes is Doubrovsky's story. So numerous are its tourniquets involving writing, reading, representation, reference, and reflection that they call for a self-aware reader, who may nevertheless stumble: one can hardly do justice to the head-spinning complexity of the book.

Le Livre brisé offers a stunning example of what Ross Chambers has called, in an article I have already cited apropos of *Les Liaisons dangereuses*, "the accidental in narrative plots," which figures "the mediated quality of narrative communication itself."[22] It is symptomatic of its scandalous complexity, arising from the writing itself, that one can never be certain whether the proper name Serge Doubrovsky refers to the character who writes the embedded novel, the character who acts in the embedded or in the embedding novel, or the actual living author. One is urged to believe that this complex persona differs little, if at all, from the author, perhaps recalling the first-person character of lyric love poetry, but the text represents not only the author's reality in his life and the writing character's reality in his writing but also something else, more nebulous and tenuous: the author's existence as textuality. Doubrovsky himself has put it, rather muddily, as follows: "Le récit de vie, suscitant l'intérêt accordé à la référentialité, sera remanié, retravaillé, en vue d'inspirer l'attirance ressentie pour le romanesque" [The life narrative, arousing the interest accorded to referentiality, will be revised, reworked, with a view to inspiring the attraction one feels for the novelistic].[23] Doubrovsky not only exploits the reader's inherent interest in referentiality, he makes it the source of the novelistic effects of his writing; the referentiality is manipulated to produce these effects, which have the attraction of fiction. What Jeanine Parisier Plottel has called "veritable truth"—life—is null, shapeless, void, fragmentary, varied, untidy, haphazard, characterized by randomness and chance.[24] The "life narrative," however magically, refers to the "veritable truth," but gives it shape: this is the action of semiosis. What then of its truth value? About *Fils*, Doubrovsky wrote: "Un curieux tourniquet s'instaure alors: fausse fiction, qui est histoire d'une vraie vie, le texte, de par le mouvement de son écriture, se déloge instantanément du registre patenté du réel" [A peculiar tourniquet is then established: a false fiction, true story of a life, the text by the movement of its writing dislodges itself instantly from the patented register of the real] ("Autobiographie/Vérité/ Psychanalyse," 90). Such tourniquets abound and are the unavoidable effect of Doubrovsky's genre of autofiction.

From these tangled threads I form the fabric of my reading of the writing of realism in *Le Livre brisé*.

Writing the Narrative

I have said that *Le Livre brisé* both recounts events in the author's life and portrays his persona writing a book about those events. These two narrations share a present time frame. In the present of the writing, we see the writing character Serge Doubrovsky produce the narrative; inserted into this present is the present of the narrative, beginning when the acting character Serge Doubrovsky is almost fifty-seven. There are thus two series of times that begin together in the text and develop in parallel toward the future; the present of the narrative starts on the morning of Wednesday, May 8, 1985, the present of the writing some weeks after that (according to my best hypothesis), and both times apparently stop in May 1988. (These happen to be the same dates during which the author wrote *Le Livre brisé*, if we can trust an indication just following the end of the text, but I am not directly concerned with this third parallel time here, although it is the only strictly verifiable time.) In the first part, "Absences," the narrative records the events of a single, "classical" twenty-four-hour day in the present, events that frame episodes from many different moments in the past (the past of the narrative). A modern book with a classical backbone, its "three unities" allow insertions of vast numbers of other times, places, and actions. Doubrovsky's *Fils* was the perfect example of this classical model, "exploded" much like a technical diagram, in a Racinian version underscored by the insistent subtext, *Phèdre*.

In a carefully constructed chronology, the present of the narrative depicts Serge alone in Paris while his Austrian-born wife, Ilse, travels to England on business. May 8, 1985, is the fortieth anniversary of Victory Day; Serge watches the celebration on television and visits the Place de l'Étoile. Toward evening he prepares his course on Sartre's *Les Mots,* reads and reflects, talks to his wife on the phone, has dinner, drinks too much wine, and goes to bed. The next morning he struggles to overcome his hangover and tries to write his auto-biography. Such is the skeletal framework of the present of the narrative, through the three hundred pages of the first part. Events from the past enter this framework and flesh it out because Serge recalls them, or tries to—episodes dating from before his birth and extending to the evening of May 7. Far outnumbering present events, those of the past concern his family's sequestra-tion during the Occupation; his love affairs with several women; his first marriage to Claudia and their two daughters, Cathy and Renée; his visits to Sartre in 1966 and 1979; and his teaching and writing in Paris and New York.

Recounted in an extremely vivid present tense, all this tells Serge Dou-brovsky's life, much of it quite familiar to readers of the other autofictions. Recurring characters contribute to the intertextualizing of Serge Doubrovsky's textualized life, forging a three-dimensional world like a personal *Comédie humaine.* The autobiography (to the extent that it is autobiography, which is very much in question) is serial, as I have claimed; spread over several volumes, it constitutes a larger Book of the author's life, of which this volume is, I think, the most important.

The moments of reading and criticism that anchor the present of the *writing* eventually determine just which past episodes enter the narrative, changing its direction. After Serge has written the first two chapters, which the reader has just read, he asks Ilse what she thinks, and this first of several scenes depicting her criticism is recorded at the start of the third chapter, "Roman conjugal." Because Ilse complains that he writes too much about other women, he begins to tell the story of their marriage, starting with their first encounter in spring 1978, when Ilse was twenty-seven and Serge almost fifty. The writing and the events it recounts thus change in response to reading. As Serge reluctantly accepts his wife's arguments, Ilse's story becomes increasingly central to the narrative of the "conjugal novel," while interspersed chapters centered on Serge continue the narration of the past within the May 8 to 9 present. Thus, throughout "Absences," starting with the third chapter, the narrative design is regularly intermittent: two distinct series link chapters 1, 2, 4, 6, 8, 10, and 12, on the one hand, whose subject is Serge and his search for mastery and the Sartrian reading; and chapters 3, 5, 7, 9, 11, and 13, on the other hand, Ilse's story. The linked chapters take up their narratives exactly where they left off, two chapters earlier, making the alternation between the two series readily apparent. Throughout "Absences," then, these alternating chapters on Serge and on Ilse underscore the tension between an "original" and an evolving design: Serge begins a book of his life, but she breaks in and demands that he write hers. Here already she has broken his book, forcing a different design; but she will cause a much more dramatic and final break.

All is not well in the Doubrovsky marriage. The couple fight repeatedly; they "divorce" over dinner and make up over breakfast, for they do love one another, passionately, and that too is recorded. Both are skilled in the colorful art of the French insult, and they can call on both English and German when that fails. Unflinching in his portrayal of the faults in the marriage, Serge also exposes his own failings (Renée Kingcaid, in her review of the book, spoke of the "characteristically unsentimental appraisal of his autobiographical narrator").[25] Ilse's complaints against Serge return again and again to her desire to have a child and his refusal. Marie Miguet-Ollagnier has pointed out the Sartrian repugnance at play here: "The first rule of this ethic, which cruelly separated Serge and Ilse during their conjugal life, is the one that emerges both from *La Nausée* and *Les Mots;* it is the rejection of fecundity."[26] Ilse and Serge also fight about the writing of the book: "Comme s'il n'y avait point assez de conflits dans notre existence, la relater en crée d'autres" [As if there were not enough conflicts in our existence, recounting it creates others].[27]

The second scene in which Ilse criticizes Serge's writing occurs at the start of the ninth chapter, "Au coin du bois." Having read the account of their early years together and several chapters about Serge's reflections on his existence, Ilse objects that the book does not seem to have a point. Where is it going? What is its design? Evoking Proust, and like Will in *Femmes,* Serge claims one will not know until he has written the end. But, like Ilse, the first-time reader does begin to wonder how the central themes are to be linked into a whole—or even if there is a whole. We suspect that Doubrovsky began his book with neither its end nor its title in mind. Two chapters later, having read the book to this point, Ilse insists that her story will not be complete unless Serge writes about her five abortions and miscarriages. These are recounted in sorry detail in the eleventh chapter, "Avortements." Another arresting sequence centered on Serge intervenes, then "Beuveries," the final chapter in the first part, again represents, for the fourth time, a present of the writing and reading. The intervening sequence, "L'Autobiographie de Tartempion" of chapter 12, depicts a self-absorbed Serge who sits down to write his existential autobiography (on the morning of May 9, 1985) as a remedy for his brokenness and *ennui;* it is his last chance to wrench the book back from Ilse: "*J'écris ma vie, donc j'ai été*" [*I'm writing my life, therefore I have been*] (255). Instead of achieving the mastery it desires, the attempt records the ultimate failure of writing about the self; not only does Tartempion ("Joe Blow") have no right to an autobiography, he is "un adulte désemparé, face à un enfant introuvable" [a dispossessed adult, confronting an unlocatable child] (277), for neither the adult writer nor the subject child is recoverable. Doubrovsky will similarly critique Sartre's *Les Mots* for its failure to recover truth: "D'emprunter une forme romanesque, le discours autobiographique s'interdit d'être le lieu d'une évidence, d'une transparence du vrai" [Because it borrows a novelistic form, the autobiographical discourse forbids itself the ability to be the space of an evidence, of a transparency of truth] ("Sartre," 19–20). At the start of "Beuveries," Ilse criticizes "Avortements" and again insists on his telling the truth about her, however harsh it may be. It is here that a narrative tornado strikes, violently laying bare a secret torment in the Doubrovsky marriage: since her 1980 abortion, Ilse has become an alcoholic. His pen enflamed by anger, Serge cruelly records Ilse's memorable and traumatic drunks, at a breathless, *furiant* tempo in the iterative present, with wrenching emotional intensity. The chapter is the keystone of the edifice.

The stunning "Beuveries" abruptly closes the first part, for the present of the writing allows into the narrative an utterly unplanned continuation. This is the beginning of the second part, "Disparition":

Un livre, comme une vie, se brise. Ma vie, mon livre sont cassés net.

Ilse est morte brusquement.

Je suis soudain frappé au cœur.

Ma femme de chair, mon personnage de roman, mon inspiratrice, ma lectrice, mon guide, mon juge. Ma compagne d'existence et d'écriture m'a quitté.

En pleine force de l'âge. En pleine force de notre amour. Au dernier chapitre de notre livre.

Un livre que nous avions fait à deux. (311)

[A book, like a life, can break. My life, my book are rudely broken.

Ilse has died, abruptly.

I am struck of a sudden in the heart.

My wife of flesh, my fictional character, my inspiration, my reader, my guide, my judge. The companion of my existence and writing has left me.

In the prime of life. At the height of our love. In the last chapter of our book.

A book we two had made together.]

Doubrovsky's grief is unspeakable. In what Hélène Jaccomard has called "raw autobiography," his anguished self-probing and tortured interrogation of Ilse's life, begun within days of her death, seek to discover why she died.[28] Writing in *L'Après-vivre,* Doubrovsky records the instant of his return to the writing:

D'un seul coup, le titre s'impose. *Brisé,* que pourrait-il être d'autre. Ce n'est plus une question. C'est un ordre, un impératif. Je dois le finir. . . . Un matin, je ne me souviens pas exactement quand, vers la fin décembre 87, j'ai été droit à ma machine. J'ai pris trois feuillets. Sur le premier, j'ai écrit le titre, *le Livre brisé.* Sur le second, le sous-titre de la première partie, *Absences.* Maintenant, il me reste à rédiger la dernière partie, *Disparition.*[29]

[All at once, the title is obvious. *Broken,* what else could it be. It is no longer a question. It is an order, an imperative. I have to finish it. . . . One morning, I don't remember exactly when, near the end of December 1987, I went straight to my typewriter. I took three sheets. On the first, I wrote the title, *le Livre brisé.* On the second, the subtitle of the first part, *Absences.* Now, the last part remained to be written, *Disparition.*]

In "Disparition," for more than a hundred pages, Serge struggles to write in spite of his suffering, portraying himself in the present of the writing dating from December 19, 1987, and narrating Ilse's death alone in a Paris apartment while he awaited her return to New York, the call on November 25 to the Paris police who found her body, and the funeral in poignant, heartbreaking detail. He questions in anguish: Did she kill herself? Who is at fault? Movingly and lovingly, he completes Ilse's story by recounting her persistent misfortunes, depressions, and suicide attempts, a "black series." Except for these past events, the reflections about the book and the narrative of the death and funeral occupy nearly simultaneous times; the narration catches up with the writing. Here too we learn that Serge had planned to begin writing, on the very day of the phone call from Paris, the next to last chapter, "Suicides," a continuation and intensification of the lugubrious series of "Avortements" and "Beuveries"; but he had been superstitiously unable to start it because for four days his calls to Ilse in Paris had gone unanswered (327–28). The series of suicides are told episodically in "Disparition." After Ilse's return to New York in early December 1987, he had intended to write the final chapter, suggestively titled "Hymne."

Had Serge's narrative realized such a hymn, it would have brought closure to the Book, completing the narrative design and supplying the missing "point." The scheme was Sartrian, the insistent models being *Les Mots* and *La Nausée.* Alain Buisine has underscored the depth and breadth of Doubrovsky's appropriation of *Les Mots:* "For in many ways *Le Livre brisé* functions like a double of the Sartrian imaginary. . . . *Le Livre brisé* never ceases readily to reflect *Les Mots,* to develop into its echo chamber."[30] Had she not died, Ilse might have brought a resolution to the excruciating *nausée* the chapters centered on Serge describe. It is because Serge suffers from a broken existence that he writes about his "gaping cogito" (32), his degradation, failures, and nothingness. The book was already broken in that sense: "En ce qui me concerne, d'emblée et à travers tout le livre, la brisure obsédante est le *trou*. Deux 'trous de mémoire' (que je garantis ici totalement véridiques) ouvrent le récit" [As far as I am concerned, from the start and throughout the book, the obsessive break is the *hole*. Two "memory holes" (which I here guarantee absolutely true) open the narration], Doubrovsky has since written ("Textes en main," 211). He hopes to recover his lost self, in the first part, by writing: "Lorsque je suis complètement perdu . . . il y a un endroit où je suis sûr de me trouver: le matin, à ma machine" [When I am completely lost . . . there is one place where I am sure to find myself: in the morning, at my typewriter] (253). Writing gives him a self. The purpose of such a book was to allow both Serge Doubrovskys, the subject and the writer, to fathom the meaning of their existence. Doubrovsky envies Sartre's mastery in *Les Mots,* his "do-it-yourself cremation" followed by his resurrection (105) in the text of the exhumed reality of his life. Following this model, Serge's writing would consume the impurities of his marriage and prepare a rebirth. For in spite of their arguments and "divorces," Serge's life is profoundly rooted in Ilse's; it is thanks to her that "mon existence brisée se ressoude" [my broken existence is soldered together] (244); or, in one of several creative rewritings of the familiar formula, "*elle pense à moi, donc je suis*" [she's *thinking of me, therefore I am*] (153). Like Roquentin envying the "guy" who wrote the song "Some of these days," Serge wants to be "le type qui a écrit *la Nausée*" [the guy who wrote *la Nausée*] (150). While in that novel everything ends with singing, the book that became *Le Livre brisé* was to finish with a similar salvation through art, a hymn

pour célébrer notre hymen je l'écrirai quand elle sera à mes côtés de retour à New York   pour resserrer notre vie refermer mon livre   absent vide d'elle au début ma conclusion sera malgré nos tourments nos tortures ENSEMBLE NOTRE PLENITUDE *Hymne*   à la joie de vivre quand elle revient de son voyage reparaît en chair et en verbe ressuscite   bouclera la boucle   son retour comblera mon *Trou de mémoire* ME COM-BLERA   l'un vers l'autre un tourbillon d'élans devra emporter le dernier chapitre. (327)

[to celebrate our marriage [*hymen*] I will write it when she is at my side back in New York   to firm up our life close my book   absent emptied of her at the beginning my conclusion will be in spite of our torments our tortures TOGETHER OUR FULL-NESS   *Hymn*   to the joy of living when she returns from her trip reappears in flesh and word resuscitates   buckles the buckle   her return will fill my *Memory Hole*   FULFILL ME   one toward the other a bounding surge should carry off the last chapter.]

A model for mastery, the hymn was to recover lost memory and self and resurrect the marriage, crowning the "whole" that Ilse had found lacking. It would have capped the *Livre*, as Mallarmé said of the hymn in *Quant au livre*: "the hymn, harmony and joy, like a pure ensemble grouped in some fulminating circumstance, of relations among all."[31] The Sartrian model of the Book, which was to be broken, owes much to this Mallarméan sublime. Thus designed, it would have contained the matter of Serge's life, in a Rousseauian attempt to confess and excuse the failures of his marriage and to recount its ultimate reconciliation, its survival. Instead, as Ilse's body smolders to ash, his dislocated self evaporates with hers: "Quarante ans de rescapé soudain se volatilisent, j'ai rejoint mon destin au crématoire" [Forty years of being a survivor suddenly volatilize, I've rejoined my destiny at the crematorium] (384)—the death he escaped during the Occupation—while the only "hymn," Mozart's piano concerto in G major, played at the cremation, brings to the closure of Serge's life with Ilse a Proustian finale (358).

Such is the design that is broken by Ilse's death from the effects of alcoholism shortly before her thirty-sixth birthday. The start of "Disparition" nearly renounces writing: "Je ne peux pas. Cela ne fait pas même un mois. . . . Comment voulez-vous que je raconte" [I cannot. It hasn't even been a month. . . . How do you expect me to tell it] (312). The brutal Real, the mimetic signified, returning in spite of the semiosis, threatens to stop the play of the signifier, of the expanded letter, which is the signature of Doubrovsky's style. "A la limite, je devrais cesser d'écrire. Puisque notre livre, comme la vie d'Ilse, comme la mienne, est brisé, le laisser inachevé. Le silence n'est pas seulement la pudeur, il est la parole même de la mort" [By rights, I should stop writing. Since our book, like Ilse's life, like mine, is broken, leave it unfinished. Silence is not only being decent, discreet, it is the very speaking of death] (316). Yet the luminous pages of "Disparition" piteously enfold Ilse's life even as they recount her death, finally to end on the silence of the signifier. They leave the reader's mind full of a groaning signified: Serge's represented brokenness is no longer curable by writing, his thoughts of suicide are unresolved. "[P]eux plus continuer, je lève les yeux, trop mal, plus de mots, cesse de tripoter ma machine, lorsque j'arrive à ce point si bas, peux plus écrire, que crier, total silence . . . le flot de tes paroles se tait, le flux de mes mots s'est tari" [Can't continue, I look up, hurts too much, no more words, stop monkeying with my typewriter, when I reach this point, so low, can't write anymore, only cry out, total silence . . . the flood of your speaking falls silent, the flow of my words has dried up] (416).

Where his words stop, the final text carries on: a complete quotation of Hugo's twelve-line poem "Demain, dès l'aube," a text of grief written in stone, an ultimate memorial. Like *Erlkönig*, Ilse's favorite poem and an emblem of her never-born son (399–400), Hugo's simple lyric mourns his lost fatherhood: "Toi, *Erlkönig*, tu as Goethe, moi Hugo" [You, *Erlkönig*, you have Goethe, me I have Hugo] (416). The poem encapsulates the Book. Recounting a day's itinerary from dawn to sunset, from le Havre to the grave of his daughter at Villequier, it mirrors the intended Book's fixing of a life into a single classical day. Giving up his pen to another, greater writer, one whose existence, unlike Tartempion's, is worthy of autobiography, a larger-than-life spiritual father and master of the word, Serge thus inscribes his inability to write on. The poem bathes in silence, "the very speaking of death" ("Je marcherai les yeux fixés sur mes pensées, / Sans rien voir au-dehors, sans entendre aucun bruit" [I will walk with my eyes fixed on my thoughts, / Seeing nothing outside, hearing nary a sound]) and memorializes the future ("Et quand j'arriverai, je mettrai sur ta tombe / Un bouquet de houx vert et de bruyère en fleur" [And when I arrive I will put on your grave / A bouquet of green holly and flowering briar]). Its compelling, relentless denial of vision makes a metaphor of the writer's suicide, discreetly suggested ("Vois-tu, je sais que tu m'attends"; "Je ne puis demeurer loin de toi plus longtemps" [You see, I know you are waiting for me; I cannot remain far from you any longer]).

Classical or Modern?

Ma vie ratée sera une réussite littéraire.

[My failed life will be a literary success.]

— *Un Amour de soi*

Such a description of the book only sketches its complexity. Serge writes to capture his self, obsessively repeating the desperate gesture that would deliver him from a torturing, originating signified: his failure to fight against those who made him a victim during the war—not just Nazis, but also the Pétain forces and those French individuals who deported Jews from France. The self-reflecting text, mirrored in Serge's extraordinary reading of Sartre, portrays the profound *ennui,* the debilitating nausea that cripples his writing, a hopeless, illusory struggle to master the failure that dominates his past. As the living, present story of Ilse's life with Serge takes over every other chapter, this obsessive purpose of the writing is broken; the book tends toward circumstantial testimonial. Yet the personal dramas of Serge's split, Jewish existence and Ilse's tormented life also have analogs on a larger historical scale that transcends the individual or couple. A tacit "point" of the book is to reconcile France and the Germanic world, as Serge peaceably reflects during the funeral: "Comme un mur, un rempart qui s'écroule, une longue haine qui s'effondre, s'efface. LA GUERRE EST FINIE. . . . Soudain, le monde germanique et moi, nous sommes en paix" [Like a wall, a rampart that crumbles, a long hatred that collapses, vanishes. THE WAR IS OVER. . . . Suddenly, the Germanic world and I, we are at peace] (399). The novel is also a memorial for the war. In what follows, however, I am concerned primarily with how the text comes to the reader—and this, indeed, is an insistent theme, similar to *Femmes*: the story and intrigue of the writing. The bearing and definition of the text are in question.

Why does the reader accept to be convinced that death broke the Book *by accident?* In spite of its disruptive and unsettled brokenness, the book has a certain organic structural integrity that it would be naïve to ignore. This is the quality I call classical. In spite of the attacks on conventional narrativity—such as an innovative use of punctuation, disruptions of chronology, and self-reflexivity—the reader may choose to read *Le Livre brisé* by emphasizing what contributes to a conventional narrative design. Such a reading would, for instance, find preparations for Ilse's death in the first part; they exist in sufficient number to be noticeable, even on a first reading. Yet to read for order and structure would be to fall under the spell of the book's expressed nostalgia for a classical whole. Early in the second part, Serge writes: "Je n'avais qu'à écrire un roman, comme tout le monde. Un roman, on est maître de le terminer à sa guise, d'inventer, envers et contre tous, si l'on veut, un heureux dénouement. Je rêvais, au long récit de nos tribulations, une fin joyeuse" [All I had to do was write a novel, like everybody else. A novel, you're the master, you can end it the way you like, you can invent, against all comers, if you want, a happy ending. I was dreaming of a joyful end to the long recital of our tribulations] (317). An ordinary novel would have allowed the happy ending in spite of real accidents.

In *La Vie l'instant,* a series of autobiographical narratives, Doubrovsky wrote quite revealingly:

Très vrai, quand j'ai une histoire, aussitôt, je brode. C'est ma nature, dans ma trame, les fils qui nous tissent, je ne peux pas supporter de les couper. Je préfère les enchevêtrer, m'y entortiller. Je n'étais pas fait pour être une Parque. Clotho, Lachésis, peut-être, celle qui tient la quenouille, celle qui tourne le fuseau, d'accord. Mais Atropos, jamais, pas celle qui tranche.[32]

[Quite true, when I have a story, right away I embroider it. That's my nature, in my fabric, the threads that weave us, I cannot bear to cut them. I prefer to intertwine them, get myself tangled in them. I was not made to be a Fate. Clotho, Lachesis, maybe, the one who holds the spindle, the one who turns the shuttle, agreed. But Atropos, never, not the one who cuts.]

With great tragic irony, Atropos is exactly what he becomes four years later in *Le Livre brisé,* the very opposite of his nature as a story maker and the contrary of the book's design. Yet even without the break caused by Ilse's death, the classical structure that was to conclude with "Hymne," the account of conflicts ending in reunion, reconciliation, and the possibilities of a fresh beginning, would have required a serious restructuring of the established chronologies, real or represented, of life or novel. The present of the narrative, May 8–9, 1985, would have had to be abandoned or updated. The account of reconciliation would have required Ilse's arrival in New York, the "promised land" (315), at the end of 1987, as the couple had planned. The reader, encouraged by the book's open invitation to read and criticize, may well ask an embarrassing question: Would their life have realized this hymn? In other words, like Will having to live his life differently in order to make his novel plausible, one feels that Serge and Ilse would have to achieve a harmonic union for Serge to write it. But this conundrum only underscores the difficulty of assigning the book to a generic definition: novel or autobiography. If there is no happy ending, it is because Serge Doubrovsky did not write a novel "like everybody else," and not even like Sartre.

In inscribing the Sartrian models into *Le Livre brisé,* Doubrovsky articulates the unresolved struggle between this desire for mastery and the infinite play of signifiance. *Signifiance* (not significance) is the active engagement of the signifier in the text, as the French gerund form *signifiant* suggests. As Serge

prepares his course on Sartre in the present of the narrative, we read a tangen-
tial, oblique commentary on *Le Livre brisé*; we are offered an optic or a grid
through which to read the book, as a *récit* of a life, whether fictional or actual.
The ending of a novel may be pure invention: "Une histoire, quand on la
raconte, il faut créer un suspense. Pour qu'on lui prête attention, on doit
entretenir l'attente, tenir le lecteur en haleine. Qu'est-ce qui va donc se passer.
Comment ça va se terminer" [To tell a story, one has to create suspense. So that
people will pay attention to it, one must prolong the anticipation, keep the
reader breathless. What is actually going to happen. How is it going to end]
(75). As Serge cites Sartre: "En réalité c'est par la fin qu'on a commencé. Elle est
là, invisible et présente" [In reality, one starts with the ending. It is there,
invisible and present] (75). According to that model, the author would exercise
control over the narrative; he would know from the beginning how it is to end.
But Sartre, in *La Nausée,* also rejects the assumption that one can recount a true
story; both novel and autobiography may appear to narrate a life, but the mere
fact of narrating makes them phony, "truqués." Already Balzac had raised this
issue in *Modeste Mignon* when he spun his narrative around the threat of
falsehood in La Brière's written self. Although Sartre conveniently "forgets"
this lesson when he writes *Les Mots,* Doubrovsky, seeking mastery, relearns it
painfully. He posits a rule, self-evident for an ordinary autobiography, which
Serge describes as Cartesian (106): "Lorsqu'on relate son existence, la suite, par
définition, on la connaît" [When you're recounting your existence, you know,
by definition, how it continues] (75–76). Because Serge does not know the
ending, and does not yet know his ignorance, including this rule in the very
text of the novel shatters the notion of the continuation. Instead, as Serge
already knows, "Même en voulant dire vrai, on écrit faux. On lit faux" [Even if
you mean to speak true, you write false. You read false] (76). The play of
signifiers keeps the consciousness of phony writing and reading just beneath
the surface of *Le Livre brisé,* and the certainty of *definition* is lost. "Lit faux"
becomes "folie"—false reading is a madness.

The question is: Just where does the fakery lie? In "L'Initiative aux maux,"
published nine years before *Le Livre brisé* in his collection of essays, *Parcours
critique,* Doubrovsky contended that the classical writer most often lies about
finalities, disguising them as motivation: "ce qui apparaît au lecteur comme
causalité (tel personnage fait tel geste *parce qu*'il éprouve tel sentiment) est, en
fait, une *finalité* déguisée (il éprouve tel sentiment *pour que* l'histoire puisse se

poursuivre et se conclure ainsi)" [what appears to the reader as *causality* (such a person makes such a gesture *because* he has such a feeling) is, in reality, a disguised *finality* (he has such a feeling *so that* the story may continue and conclude in this fashion)].[33] Diderot made a similar point. Opposing life to dramatic writing, he wrote that real life events are "a chaining of effects whose causes are unknown to us," whereas dramatic works forge visible links among events.[34] Foreshadowing Ilse's death, in the first part, may signal a device of good fiction, for the real author Serge Doubrovsky, or tragic irony for Serge the writer. Ilse drinks because she is unhappy, and she is unhappy because she does not have a child, according to a simplified causality. But in the broken book, does she drink because she is to die in the next few pages? It is an effect of the writing that the reading remains undecided about motivations and finalities.

Like the effect of Cyd's death on Will's writing in *Femmes,* the demoniacal power of writing asserts itself here to create a radical uncertainty in the reader about the mimetic illusion. A short argument opens "Beuveries," about whether Serge can tell the truth about Ilse and himself: "Mais, enfin, pas la vérité joliment attifée, élégamment allusive, enrubannée de bons mots: la vérité sans fard, sans slip, sans cache-sexe?" [But, I mean, not the truth prettily packaged, elegantly allusive, beribboned with clever sayings: the truth without makeup, without underwear, without a G-string?] (281). Did this discussion really occur, or did Serge make it up so that the story could continue? Did the real Serge Doubrovsky know when he wrote "Beuveries" that his wife-character Ilse was going to die in the next sequence? It is characteristic of this self-reflexivity that the very subject of the argument is this text's ability to proceed. Whether or not the discussion is a real argument between Ilse and Serge, it exists to inscribe in the text of the novel a way to avoid falseness. If *Le Livre brisé* presented itself as a classical novel, the opportune placement of "Beuveries" just before Ilse's death might seem contrived to provide a finality brilliantly disguised as causality, allowing the story to continue and to conclude as it does. Instead, having engaged a self-reflective system that opened the book to the effects of reading, the writer lost mastery.

Doubrovsky astutely analyzes Sartre's "maîtrise" in *Les Mots* as he describes Poulou killing and resuscitating Daisy (149). Like Sartre, Serge can kill off a character; nothing stops him. What he cannot do is bring her back to life as Sartre could, not just because the real Ilse died, but because he engaged a semiotic system that depends on the mimesis of fictional truth; the system required him to write her death, in a logical suite. He lost the liberty the novelist has to resuscitate at will.[35] And the same holds true for his creation of a self. We do not know if he narrates her alcoholic binges so that the story can continue and conclude as it does, or because he describes Ilse urging him to be complete and truthful in telling her story. A modern novel, Doubrovsky writes, is "ceaselessly *open*":

Aucune "fin" ne peut régler une production qui avance au gré des jeux signifiants; dans la mesure où la signifiance est une "infinité différenciée, dont la combinatoire illimitée ne trouve jamais de borne" (J. Kristeva), le procédé de l'écriture institue un processus indéfiniment actif, dont la maîtrise, en soi, échappe au scripteur. ("L'Initiative aux maux," 190)

[No "ending" can regulate a production that moves forward at the whim of the signifying interplay; to the extent that signifiance is a "differentiated infinity, whose limitless permutation never finds a boundary" (J. Kristeva), the procedure of writing institutes a ceaselessly active process, the mastery of which, in and of itself, escapes the scriptor.]

Or, as Doubrovsky later wrote about Sartre: "L'auteur dût-il y croire cent fois, un 'roman' reste un discours problématique, que la maîtrise d'aucun sens préalable ne saurait gouverner" [Even if the author believes in it hundred-fold, a "novel" remains a problematic discourse, which no mastery of a prior meaning can govern] ("Sartre," 20). Much more potently than any other book, *Le Livre brisé* advances "at the whim of the signifying interplay": no other book so excruciatingly flaunts its own inability to disguise a causality as a finality.

Serge began the Book of his broken life only to discover that it was really broken, by the very writing of the book. The text convinces the reader that he could not have planned to write his wife's death: he did not plot it—it plotted itself. According to Jaccomard, "In an unpublished interview, on November 15, 1992, Serge Doubrovsky insists on the fact that the structure of *Le Livre brisé* is not a fiction and that he did not rewrite his text afterward to accentuate its shock value" (272). The classical exists in the book, as I suspect it does in Serge Doubrovsky himself, only as a nostalgia, the representation of a loss; it is annihilated by the modern. Against the ineluctable linkages of tragedy the accidental stands out in its monstrous contingency.

Mimesis or Semiosis?

La véritable autobiographie est comme l'idée cartésienne: claire et distincte. Pourvu, bien sûr, qu'on possède le bon instrument critique, qu'on applique la bonne grille. (106)

[The authentic autobiography is like the Cartesian idea: clear and distinct. Provided, of course, that you possess the appropriate critical instrument, that you apply the right grid.]

Le bon instrument qui permet aux lecteurs de lire en eux-mêmes, c'est la littérature. (159)

[Literature is the good instrument that allows readers to interpret themselves.]

In the text that portrays the writing of the text, in *Le Livre brisé*, the chapter "Beuveries" comes into the book because Ilse criticizes the narrative, defiantly contending that the story of her life with Serge is incomplete and a fraud. Serge claims to be reluctant to carry autofiction so far as to make her uncontrolled drinking public, and he had apparently planned to tell the story of their marriage without it. A constant motif is what he has called "the sadomasochistic implications of the autobiographical project" ("L'Initiative aux maux," 198). Or, as he writes in *Le Livre brisé*: "Elle veut que je nous expose. Épouse-suicide, femme-kamikaze. Que je nous fasse hara-kiri, ça qu'elle demande" [She wants me to expose us. Suicide-spouse, kamikaze-wife. I should commit our mutual hara-kiri, that's what she wants] (51); and "L'autobiographie est un genre posthume" [Autobiography is a posthumous genre] (311). This reticence that Serge expresses rather more often than necessary, in *Le Livre brisé*, resembles Doubrovsky's stance after Ilse's death. "There is no returning from such an exploration into dereliction," he would tell a Montreal journalist in March 1990 (the context shows that he is referring to his character Serge, and the "exploration into dereliction" is his book). "And still today, I find I regret not having done all there was to do to save my wife from her despair and especially from her vice. . . . I could not imagine that fatal outcome at that time, but I think sooner or later she would have succumbed because of it."[36] It is Ilse who insists he write the chapter, turning the narrative into the book of *her* life, and his existential "pour-moi" into a "pour-elle." Hence the very expressive dedication: "Pour Ilse. Par Ilse. SON LIVRE" [For Ilse. By Ilse. HER BOOK]. When in the second part

Serge records Ilse's comments on "Beuveries," they are now necessarily represented as in the past—during their last overseas telephone conversation before
her death. He can no longer represent her in lively dialogues about her reading
in the present of the writing. As a result, he cannot change the writing in
response to the criticism, the way he had previously done according to the
system the book had established. Her death not only turned the Book away
from the planned harmony and reconciliation, it forced an unplanned, one
hundred page ending in which the function of the writing (as opposed to the
narrative) is to understand why the book is ending this way. While the narrative searches for the cause of Ilse's death and the measure of Serge's guilt, the
text now asks *if his writing took her life.*

Probably Ilse Doubrovsky knew she risked death when she drank the final
bottle of vodka: doctors had told her so, and she had promised to be sober. But
Serge cannot avoid examining his own guilt in cruel detail. Although the
anguished search for answers eventually concludes that Ilse did not kill herself
intentionally, the tortured self-examination in "Disparition" comes finally,
suspensefully, to a stunning and chilling hypothesis: *had he not written the book
she would not have died.* Had he not sent her the chapter "Beuveries" in Paris,
she would not have bought the vodka to drown her depression. Had she not
insisted on his writing about her, on changing the course of the continuing
book, on giving her imprimatur to the writing before he proceeded, she might
not have died.

With this hypothesis comes the most self-reflective tourniquet in the book,
the source of its unique reading effects. Here the narrative folds back on itself.
Not only does the book change course because it includes Ilse's criticism, it is
this altered writing that ultimately produces the break in the narrative. *Le Livre
brisé* exacerbates this tourniquet of what Kingcaid called "mimetic deferral"
(described as the dominant reading mode in *Un Amour de soi*), because the
reference to the reality of Ilse's death is fictionalized not by any identifiable
intertext, as in the earlier novel, but by *the very text of this novel.*[37] Ilse's death is
not just recounted in the text but is also produced by the very writing, and this
too is portrayed in the writing. As Doubrovsky has himself written: "Pour
l'autobiographe, comme pour n'importe quel écrivain, rien, pas même sa
propre vie, n'existe *avant* son texte; mais la vie de son texte, c'est sa vie *dans* son
texte" [For the autobiographer, as for any writer at all, nothing, not even his
own life, exists *before* his text; but the life of his text is his life *in* his text]

("L'Initiative aux maux," 188). Life as told in the text is what gives life to the text: "Disparition" could not have existed without "Beuveries." By every rule that we know about telling a story, Serge could not have recounted Ilse's death from alcoholism without having written an account of her excessive drinking, for the events in the story that caused her to die would not have been understandable without the chapter "Beuveries." Yet the very choice to include the untold, hellish series of drunks breaks the mold of the novel. "Beuveries" participates in both structures of time, the time of writing and the time of the narrative, and is at least doubly motivated. The book could not have been a broken book without this chapter. Again the reader poses awkward questions: Did the real Serge Doubrovsky cause the real Ilse's death by writing "Beuveries"? Did the writing character Serge portray his acting character as causing Ilse's death? It is the nature of the tourniquet to make it impossible to know whether we are reading the real portrayal of an imagined reality or the imagined portrayal of a real reality.

This conflict between the representation of a referential reality and self-reflective writing puts semiosis in a position of exact contrary to classical mimesis, understood now as a relation between writing and event—something like the naïve representation we saw in *La Religieuse,* for instance. Representation, or realistic writing, the tools of narrative fiction, have called forth a real referent (in this case, a life), so that the signified enacts the real referent, not just an illusion of reality. Semiosis, on the other hand, is the play of the signifier recording the process of signification. A simple way to understand semiosis is to say that a sense comes into being because certain words are chosen, which are themselves evoked by other words. As Riffaterre writes, semiosis "is therefore opposed to referentiality, the assumed relationship between a sign and nonverbal objects taken to be reality."[38] Semiosis is a subject throughout *Le Livre brisé* because of its presentation of writing and reading; it concerns not what the writing tells, but how it tells it (and potentially why). It speaks the relation between text and writing. As such, it is unlimited, because it is concerned with the signifying effects of its own signifiers. Or, as Barthes writes, "Texts then attempt to constitute a *semiosis,* that is, a putting into play of *signifiance.*"[39] What is not simple is the relation, in *Le Livre brisé,* of semiosis to representation. The drifting relations among life, text, and writing are suggested in a passage of Mallarmé's poetic prose, from *Quant au livre:* "The book, total expansion of the letter, must from it take, directly, a mobility and, spacious, by correspondences, initiate a game, I know not, which confirms the fiction" (380). Because the spacious book, a total expansion of the letter, necessarily owes its vitality to the mobility of the letter, the play of its correspondences (found on many levels, beginning with Doubrovsky's fluid, allusive style) fosters a play of signifiers that confirms the fiction.

Those who wonder, like Ilse, what the point of the book is have two conflicting, almost irreconcilable ways of reading the writer's understanding of Ilse's death, according to classical mimesis or semiosis.[40] Like Rousseau's *Confessions,* one of the autobiographical models of *Le Livre brisé,* the narrative and the writing sit uneasily between their double functions, to *accuse* and to *excuse*.[41] The very writing of *Le Livre brisé* engages excuse and accusation: "C'est vrai, depuis qu'on raconte sa vie, de Rousseau à Sartre, en montrant, on démontre. Plaidoyer ou réquisitoire" [It's true: since people have been telling their lives, from Rousseau to Sartre, to indicate is to vindicate. Defense or indictment] (176). The reference to Rousseau is particularly telling because Doubrovsky's refusal to have a child by Ilse contributes to the "suite" of her abortions, depression, drinking, and suicide attempts, while Rousseau's hope to excuse himself, by accusing himself of abandoning his children, compels him to write *Les Confessions.* Serge is only fifty when he first refuses to let Ilse have a child, but he claims he does not want children because he is approaching sixty. This is his age only in the present of the writing, not in the time of the narrative. He has thus used the system of time in the very writing of the book to justify his actions, as Ilse does not fail to point out to him. With the advantage of having read Rousseau, Doubrovsky knows how slippery any writing project is: "Évidemment le moment que l'on décrit, le moment où l'on écrit sont séparés par une pente savonneuse, on glisse sans le savoir de l'un à l'autre. Il y a souvent fusion. Confusion. . . . De toute façon, quand on se raconte, même quand on s'accuse, c'est toujours, en fin de compte, pour s'excuser" [Evidently the moment you're describing, the moment you're writing are separated by a soapy incline, you slip from the one into the other without knowing it. There is often fusion. Confusion. . . . In any case, when you recount yourself, even when you accuse yourself, it is always, when all is said and done, to excuse] (280). To the extent that the writer has mastery over the direction of his book (classical mimesis), he accuses himself, the better to confess; but the writing drifts into excuse. The drift of the writing and acting characters and the real author produces an ambiguous category, the mimesis of a semiosis, representing a textualized Serge Doubrovsky writing the book and including the striking semiosis that breaks the book.[42]

When Ilse demands a faithful account of her life with Serge, she rejects and sometimes rectifies his fictionalized narratives, which allow him to excuse himself; she would take the fiction out of the story and return his writing to truth. If "Beuveries" followed "Avortements," according to the writing, it is only because it is required:

obligé, il y a la suite, "Beuveries," notre entente, notre pacte, l'autobiographie, faut que ça soit vrai, total, ou pas l'écrire, si on raconte sa vie, pas de cache-cache . . . si c'est son vœu, je fonce, j'enfonce le clou, "Beuveries" la crucifie, pourtant les chapitres, à mesure que je les termine, elle qui les demande. (390)

[have to, there's the continuation, "Beuveries," our agreement, our pact, autobiography, must be true, total, or shouldn't write it, if I recount my life, no hide-and-seek . . . if it's her wish, I push on, I push in the nail, "Beuveries" crucifies her, yet the chapters, at the rate I finish them, she's the one who asks for them.]

Mimesis follows the laws of the signified, requiring a coherent story, a "suite," obeying the pact between writer and reader to tell all, like Rousseau. But engaging the mimetic system inevitably engages semiosis, the relation between writing and text. Then: "L'enchaînement des épisodes, suite et fin, le récit ne nous appartient plus" [The linking of episodes, continuation and ending, the narrative no longer belongs to us] (317). The true, total autobiography, for Ilse, is alive: "Elle s'était lancé ce défi allègre et douloureux: que nous entrions ensemble, vivants, dans l'écriture" [Jaunty and woeful this is the challenge she had thrown down: that together we enter, living, into writing] (311). What she did not know was that one enters writing at the cost of losing the pure relation to life as it is lived; semiosis interposes its spirited histrionics and blinds that relationship. Ilse becomes more and more angry at the book. Furious, she accuses Serge of lying, and at the same time insists he tell of her failings. Her response to his writing is masochistic: "Devant cette œuvre de mots, faite largement de sa chair, elle éprouvait fierté et angoisse" [In the face of this work of words, made largely from her flesh, she felt pride and anguish] (312). The sadomasochism of autobiography is nowhere so evident as in the "the very grain of the writing" ("L'Initiative aux maux," 198).

With the breaking of the classical design, the role of semiosis in Ilse's death forces itself on the reader, when the text in the last part concerns itself insistently with its own process of signification, seeking to know *how* to write, and *whether* to write:

Début novembre, lui expédie ma séquence, conséquence, mi-novembre, se remet à boire, quand on parle boisson, la déprime, pour noyer la déprime, elle boit, le chapitre "Beuveries" l'a liquidée, mon encre l'a empoisonnée, jeu de la vérité parfois mortel . . . la pire frappe, pas celle des mains, celle des mots . . . UN CRIME, lui envoie "Beuveries" aussi sec, comme ça, pour avoir son impression, sa réaction, comme le reste, mais justement, ÇA N'ÉTAIT PAS COMME LE RESTE. (391)

[Beginning of November, mail her my sequence, consequence, mid-November, takes up drinking again, when I say drink, down in the dumps, to drown the dumps, she drinks, the "Beuveries" chapter liquidated her, my ink poisoned her, game of truth sometimes mortal, the worst blow, not from the hands, the punch of words . . . A CRIME, send her "Beuveries" flat out, just like that, to get her impression, her reaction, like the rest, but that's just it, IT WASN'T LIKE THE REST.]

Unlike the rest, this chapter was not an innocuous continuation of the "suite." If the narrative represents Serge accusing himself, the writing about the writing (the semiosis) produces the excuse, because it allows him to include in the novel itself the message "*she asked for it.*" Failing to write a novel like everybody else, producing instead a poisoned, contaminated, mixed writing, Doubrovsky accentuates his difference from his avowed models. The accusation slips along the soapy incline between event and writing and turns into an excuse.

Excuse, and the deception it implies, is familiar to alcoholics. Ilse turned to drinking first to deaden physical pain, then to console herself, finally to "cure" her depressions. The last bottle owed its deadly potency to the others (one does not seek consolation in vodka unless one has already done so more than once before); *and it was lethal because it exceeded the limits.* Drinking to excess, writing the unspeakable—these are parallel.[43] Serge's obsessive relation to writing mirrors Ilse's drinking: "Mais enfin pourquoi bois-tu ainsi? [he asks;] je ne sais pas . . . ça m'arrive par à-coups   alors c'est irrésistible" [But really, why do you drink like that? [he asks;] I don't know . . . it comes in spurts   then it's irresistible] (303). Serge first turned to writing for consolation and cure, but like Ilse he let himself be carried off by an irresistible semiotic force, lethal because it outstripped the others. When "Beuveries" wrote beyond the limit, "Disparition" ineluctably recorded that excessive writing. It matters little that Serge had warned Ilse of the dangers of excess both in her drinking (level of the narrative) and in his writing about it (level of the writing), thus finding excuses. He lost control over his text when he let her read it *and put her reading in the book,* with the consequences we have seen, for making the book into a record of its writing exceeded all the bounds of mimetic pretension. The real Serge Doubrovsky did not write *Le Livre brisé* to exculpate himself from guilt for his real wife's death. Writing flourishes its insidious beauty and takes us beyond reference.

Novel or Autobiography?

Un bouquin, quand on le relit, est comme le passé lorsqu'on le revit: une vaste caisse de résonance. (119)

[A book, when you reread it, is like the past when you relive it: a vast, resonating chamber.]

How simple it would be to say that Serge Doubrovsky has recounted the death of his wife! Simple and accurate, as people who know him are eager to confirm. Called a novel on the cover and title page, *Le Livre brisé* nevertheless does tell the author's life. (Did Doubrovsky's publisher require him to use the designation "roman," as Marie Miguet-Ollagnier speculates ["La Saveur Sartre," 141]?) Had it pursued its planned design ending with "Hymne," we might have been content to let the multivalence of the term *autofiction* describe its ambiguous status: a fiction of strictly true events, like the other novels. With its representation of the drinking bouts in "Beuveries" (which is not like the rest) and the consequent death of Ilse, *Le Livre brisé* ceases to be a novel like the others or even an autofiction. Philippe Lejeune, compelled to believe author and character are the same, confessed to having first read *Fils* as "an autobiography that employed new methods," but concluded: "Doubrovsky is clearly of the novelists' race and not of the autobiographers'."[44] In *Le Livre brisé* such a conclusion is by no means obvious. The book is neither a mere fiction nor a simple account of Ilse Doubrovsky's death, even if that is what the book does tell. Just what we are reading depends on how we attempt to assign it to a generic definition as novel or autobiography, and this is the task the book confers on us. It may be that the designation "novel" no longer indicates "fiction"; instead of wrenching the text into the definition of a novel as fiction, perhaps the effect is to redefine novel. In any case, the relation between novel and autobiography lies in the hands of the reader, for the text is a productivity in the Kristevian sense, "the very theatre of a production where the producer and reader of the text meet."[45] The book represents the active producing of a product and it produces or reproduces an interplay between the producing and the product. *Le Livre brisé* demonstrates, but without finality, that one can tell about oneself without establishing generic boundaries. In *L'Après-vivre* this takes the following form: "Avec de petits faits vrais, je me suis recomposé comme un personnage de roman" [Using small factual realities, I recomposed myself like a character in a novel] (327). The "law of the genre"—when one recounts oneself, one thinks necessarily of oneself (219)—includes both this monstrous egotism and the semiotic display of manipulative excuse (280). The reader's ineluctable participation in the demonstration lends a poignant, belated interpretation to Ilse's demand that the book have a "point," for this address to the reader suggests a point that Ilse did not live to read.

Ilse's presence as both character and reader, and Doubrovsky's passing of control to her—his permitting her to enter the book and even to "write" a few passages—undermines the text's authority. As reader, Ilse often asserts a version of the truth different from what Doubrovsky has written: "J'ai beau m'abriter derrière mes fictions, elle cherche les réalités, la petite bête" [It's no good retreating behind my fiction, she's looking for the realities, the worm in the apple] (60). Thus, she supplies a model for reading by verification and rectification—one that is finicky and attentive to detail: "Si tu ne racontes pas les choses comme elles se sont passées, je te fais un procès!" [If you don't tell things the way they happened, I'll sue you!] (221). This device allows the reader to think of the text as an autobiography, however inaccurate Ilse may think it is. We may be tempted to follow her guide. There is a passage apparently written by Ilse, telling of her first encounter with Serge's daughter Cathy, from her point of view (125–26 and 131–33). Like Doubrovsky interviewing Sartre, we could ask him to verify our strong suspicion that Ilse Doubrovsky actually wrote this. The reference to the real world, in which there is a living man called Serge Doubrovsky and verifiable events, dates, locations, and proper names, thus threatens the book's status as novel. (We might borrow the phrase "factor of verifiability" from Steven Ungar to describe this quality of the writing.)[46] The text makes us want to know if what Serge recounts really happened; if it were a novel like any other, we would never suffer such cruel doubt. And this very procedure sabotages the reader's ability to read critically.

Yet, like many authors, Doubrovsky found it difficult to leave so much authority in the hands of the reader. In "Textes en main," published in 1993, he explained that Ilse could not write the way he portrayed her writing; it was he who composed the passage by Ilse, expressing her sentiments and resentments, "comme on ferait pour un personnage de roman" [as one would for a character in a novel] (215). We can observe Doubrovsky's stylistic virtuosity, but also note that the explanation lies outside his writing. Within the writing, the tension remains between the "made up" and the verifiable, and the manipulative effect on the reader is to make us read as autobiography what is no longer factual. A similar effect occurs in Sollers's *Femmes*.

For instance: When, in the present time of Serge's writing, did Ilse die? This question is not the same as asking: When, during Doubrovsky's writing of *Le Livre brisé*, did Ilse Epplé Doubrovsky die?—a date that we know from reading the autofiction (which gives strictly real facts). Yet the very fact that the question has to be posed defines the uniqueness of the book's generic definition. In the time of Serge's writing that the novel portrays, over the course of the chapters in "Absences," Ilse dies after "Beuveries." How much of the book Doubrovsky had actually written when his wife died can only be found out from evidence external to the book itself—by asking its author, in particular. Aliette Armel quotes Doubrovsky as saying, in an interview: "The process described in the book exactly reprises the circumstances of its elaboration."[47] No doubt every novel has such externally knowable facts that can be found out, and that bring greater understanding to our interpretations, but in this case the book both gives and takes away: it prompts the urgent desire to know if writing *Le Livre brisé* really did cause Ilse's death, and it takes away our ability to have faith in any answer.

If we do not ignore the book's self-reflection, its generic ambiguity, and its manipulation of the reader, we must accept that what we know about the book is in the book itself. Writing realism makes this knowledge for us, and we cannot escape it. Although inscribed in the text, the model of verification is only a temptation that the writer leads us to discard, just as a written life raises only false hopes that it can capture the real person:

Le roman, bien joli, bien agréable, mais il ne produit que des songes, il ne crée que des vapeurs. . . . Mais une vie romancée, même la sienne, devient une vie imaginaire. Ça ne veut pas dire qu'elle soit fausse: elle n'existe que dans l'imagination. Si je me transforme en Julien Sorel, j'existe comme lui. Je veux exister COMME MOI. Ressaisir enfin ma VRAIE vie. (254)

[The novel, very pretty, very pleasant, but it produces only dreams, it creates only vapors. . . . But a novelized, romanticized life, even one's own, becomes an imaginary life. This does not mean that it is false, but it exists only in the imagination. If I transform myself into Julien Sorel, I exist as he does. I want to exist AS MYSELF. Recapture at last my REAL life.]

Serge protests insistently that writing cannot adhere strictly to the letter of truth: "L'écriture n'éclaire pas la tache aveugle, elle se produit à partir d'elle" [Writing does not illuminate the blind spot, it is from there that it emerges] (160). "Mistakes" are not just the record of a bad memory or the willful reinvention of a self-image; when a life is written, mistakes happen because of the writing. Ilse's reading thus stands for mimetic nostalgia, for the lost premise, the never-attained ideal. Although Diderot could both maintain naïve representation and foreground the writing act, Doubrovsky can no longer do this. As Doubrovsky wrote about Sartre's "autobiography," "le statut référentiel du récit autobiographique nous échappe" [the referential status of the autobiographical narrative escapes us] ("Sartre," 21). Ilse becomes the metaphor for the failure of writing ever to achieve mastery over event. The metaphor breaks the mastery of the Book on the Sartrian model (developed in the chapter "Maîtrise"). So powerful is this lesson, however, that with another turn of the spiral its effect is to increase the truth value of the writing: we are so convinced by the demonstration that writing cannot achieve mastery over event that we discard the rectification model of reading and attend to writing. This is a key moment, marking a revolution. Breaking the Sartrian design of the Mallarméan Book enhances the truth of the fiction; it moves the novel closer to autobiography and the autobiography closer to novel. Doubrovsky recognized this "virtue" or power of writing autofiction in a recent interview: "Tout est fragmentaire, déconnecté et ne se reconnecte que par la vertu de l'écriture" [Everything is fragmentary and disconnected and is only reconnected by virtue of writing].[48] Ilse's death, the one thing that she as reader cannot criticize, verify, rectify, or revise, finalizes these lost certainties; it is the death of the possibility of the reader's verifying, forcing us to accept the text as semiosis and not just classical mimesis, parallel to the writer's loss of a harmonic closure.

When the book proves that writing can kill, it is not merely saying it, but enacting it: the book *performs* its semiosis. Life brings striking changes to the writing, but this is not unique, in fiction. When the writing changes the life, however, semiosis realizes an unheard-of power: "Writing always includes the moment of dispossession in favor of the arbitrary power play of the signifier and from the point of view of the subject, this can only be experienced as a dismemberment, a beheading or a castration" (de Man, "Excuses," 296). For the writer, this is the ultimate *ennui*. Allowing the book to be taken over by the process of its writing, the subject guarantees his loss. As Barthes wrote, " 'Signifiance' is a process, in the course of which the 'subject' of the text, escaping the logic of the ego-cogito and engaging other logics (that of the signifier and that of contradiction), struggles with meaning and is deconstructed ('is lost')" ("Theory of the Text," 38). The last representation of this loss occurs when the writer gives up his pen to another writing, the Hugo poem. The two modes of the book, the referential truth of Serge's "crime" and the unreliable verbal excuse, stand in constant conflict, which would be resolved only if the book came down squarely on the side of "novel" instead of "autobiography." Perhaps this is why, despite whatever critical assessments Doubrovsky has made of the relation between truth and writing, he resolutely publishes all his autofictions as "novels." As de Man claims, the text "shelters itself from accusation by the performance of its radical fictionality" ("Excuses," 294). We may reconcile the biographical referent as textuality with the aesthetic pretension of the book only if we read it as novel. According to de Man: "Not the fiction itself is to blame for the consequences but its falsely referential reading" ("Excuses," 293). Doubrovsky wrote about *Fils,* "Par fiction, il faut entendre, à ras de sens, une 'histoire' qui, quelle que soit l'accumulation des références et leur exactitude, n'a jamais 'eu lieu' dans la 'réalité,' dont le seul lieu réel est le discours où elle se déploie" [By "fiction," we need to understand, in the rawest sense, a "story" that, whatever accumulation there may be of references and whatever their exactness, has never "taken place" in "reality," whose only real place is the discourse in which it unfolds] ("Autobiographie/Vérité/Psychanalyse," 93). The novel transforms the unveiling of truth into fiction.

But *Le Livre brisé* is split the way the defensive, neurotic self is, in Lacanian psychology. Novel and autobiography are the Paris and New York of the book's generic self, joined but separated by the Atlantic Ocean (193), although Serge and Doubrovsky do the heroic impossible to convince us they are one. The generic term *novel* is thus a defense against the profound loss of self, but the defense teeters ceaselessly on the brink of failure. For we read the book as autobiography as well, and this too is given us: "Telle est l'astuce. Si le lecteur a bien voulu me suivre, si j'ai réussi un peu, rien qu'un peu, à éveiller son intérêt pour mon personnage, je lui refilerai ma personne. . . . En dévorant le roman, il avalera l'autobiographie" [Here's the ploy. If the reader has consented to follow me, if I have succeeded a little, only a little, in awakening his interest in my character, I will slip him my person. . . . In devouring the novel, he will swallow the autobiography] (256). If autobiography can perform an imaginary life, is it possible that Doubrovsky has realized the supreme tourniquet that relegates the only real to novel—a real that no longer has a certain connection to referentiality, a real of phantasm? As Lejeune wrote of *Fils*, "it is the generic indication that is ambiguous" (66). Barthes's ambiguous text, *Roland Barthes*, comes to this excruciatingly self-reflective observation about the impossible project of writing about himself writing: "I do not seek to *restore* myself (as one says of a monument). . . . I do without imitation (description) and put my confidence in nomination. Is it not true that, *in the field of the subject, there is no referent*? The (biographical, textual) fact abolishes itself in the signifier, because it *coincides* immediately with it."[49] There is no referent of the self other than the written self: he lives in his text *because he writes*. As Doubrovsky himself repeated in an interview, "Moi, je veux jouer sans masque autre que l'écriture qui est la recréation du réel dans le langage" [As for me, I want to act without a mask other than writing, which is the re-creation of the real in language] ("Entretien avec Serge Doubrovsky"). We know what he has written: nothing exists *before* the text; rather, the life of his text is *his life in the text*—semiosis.

This axiom has a moral consequence, which Doubrovsky has encapsulated in a minute and subtle opposition: "En aucune façon les jeux du signifiant ne libèrent du signifié: ils libèrent le signifié" [By no means does the play of signifiers liberate from the signified; it liberates the signified] ("L'Initiative aux maux," 183). It is not that the play on the signifier lets us escape from a meaning we might or should tell into a world where only signifiers circulate, unattended and unsecured by a meaning—and perhaps therefore amoral. Instead, the game opens the door to the meanings imprisoned in the signifiers. However eye-catching and engrossing signifiance and semiosis may be, the writer cannot escape the signified; the play of signifiance only liberates the signified from the dominance and control of the writer. An unleashed signified remains when the signifiers fall silent: the "universal signified" of death (Chambers, "Reading," 418). That is the dangerous magic of realism; Sollers would be in total agreement with the ethic Doubrovsky expresses here. Doubrovsky's stunning example of signified death proves that the writer does not have mastery over what his signifiers signify, precisely because the text allows itself to liberate a verifiable reality. The real referent both is and is not present. One need hardly emphasize that the reader will never have mastery either, that aporia is our only possible reaction. Yet we think we are reading the truth—indeed, we *know* we are. For Serge Doubrovsky, the novel is the only real and the best avenue to truth, and autobiography is its inevitable product. He has said it repeatedly, as in a recent interview: "My pact with the reader means that I must tell the truth—the modalities of the telling are my business—but the events in themselves must be biographically accurate."[50] Writing the truth means self-exposure, and that includes, especially, the exposure of the self's writing. Generously, Doubrovsky lends us the good instrument that permits us to validate the morality of his project, inherent in the writing: the grid of literature.

Writing or Living

Ultimately, the book exists in an ineffable "both-and land" where the two forms of writing that are text and existence are indistinguishable in their common relation to reading. It is the final stance to which Doubrovsky has come, as he writes in *L'Après-vivre:* "Pour moi, il n'y a plus de frontière entre le vécu et l'écrit" [For me, there is no longer a boundary between the lived and the written] (21). Writing is a "truquage," a fakery, when it seeks to recapture a preexisting referential reality, to master signification. Writing about *writing that referentiality* can only be honest, and this is the important discovery Doubrovsky helps us make.[51] For "l'écrivain n'a pas le droit de se taire" [the writer does not have the right to keep silent] (311), no more than the reader has the right not to speak her reading. Not only does writing (and reading) answer an immediate need—"Si je veux te recréer, je dois écrire" [If I want to re-create you, I have to write] (415)—it is the most profound reality for the writer; the only truth is to continue to write. Those who, like the *Figaro* reviewer, haughtily decry the immorality of making a book—hence profit—out of Ilse's sad death completely miss the integrity required to write on in spite of the real world's certain condemnation.[52] Such people are not reading at all.

Doubrovsky dared to turn existence into textuality, the biographical referent abolishing itself in the realm of the signifier and unleashing a nonimaginary signified, the brutal Real of Ilse's death.[53] Did writing make Ilse die, or is the writing merely the mimetic record of her death? Does writing kill only in the writing, or did it actually happen that way? These aporias are never re-solved. The book is split for the reading too, and thus is ungrammatical in its productivity. We are never certain which text we are reading, the empirical event or the fictional discourse, but we constantly wish to know. We are pushed to an excessive, obsessive reading. To read this novel is to accept our forcible entry into its defensive performance; Serge Doubrovsky unquestionably exists as himself in this book, but we as readers are transformed into exemplars of Serge Doubrovsky. Radu Turcanu demonstrates, in a brilliant psychoanalytical reading, how the self signifies itself in the writing, through the appropriation of the reader: "Hidden among the letters and simulated by his (auto)fictions, this writer first loses his real consistency to find himself afterwards, as a subject of his written text, in the reply that comes to him from an always ideal reader, always implied in the act of writing."[54] Jacqueline Piatier, writing in *Le Monde*, affirms similarly: "It's enough to take your breath away, but not to take away the irresistible attraction that, from page to page, propels you to read. You are no longer yourself, you are this Serge Doubrovsky who is fighting with him-self."[55] If we let the book work its manipulative magic on us, we may well wish to be "the guy who wrote *Le Livre brisé*," and that is its dangerous attraction. The text insidiously plays on our irresistible dependence on the "drug" we turn to for consolation, the last and most lethal in a series: our habit of mimetic reading, our belief in the mimetic illusion. Refusing to read as we always do, with the credulity required to believe that signs signify, would be our only escape from the death our literary "alcoholism" causes. Alain Buisine says of Doubrovsky's writing: "See how it makes us drunk when we read it. . . . Drunkenness of the writing in which the writer immerses himself to escape the final drowning" ("Serge Doubrovsky," 165).

Real lives resonate in this vast echo chamber of a book, but so do its writing and what we bring to it in our reading. The book portrayed a broken Serge Doubrovsky, but once broken the broken book became a monumental memo-rial to Ilse Doubrovsky; Ilse compelled the writing that turned *Le Livre brisé* into an act of mourning. Doubrovsky's book is the apotheosis of Ilse's life in his: "Il faut bien que je le crie, avant même qu'on t'incinère tu t'es déjà tout entière évaporée, évanouie, de toi que j'aime rien ne subsiste, qu'en moi, là tu renais, tu te retrouves" [I cannot help but shout it out, even before they incinerate you, you have already evaporated, vanished entirely, of you whom I love there subsists nothing, except in me, there you are reborn, you are recovered] (373). Crushed between writing and not living, the text chose writing. Dignity and grandeur resound in the bearing of the book; to mishear them is to refuse to read.

The Postmodern Ethic

There is some risk of misunderstanding in my treating Sollers and Doubrovsky together in one chapter. It must be recognized that their fundamental projects are different. One can even find evidence of a disregard between these two important, living novelists. In *Le Livre brisé,* when Ilse protests that Sollers portrays his wife in *Femmes* and *Portrait du joueur,* and demands as much from Serge, we are treated to the following acerbic comments by Serge:

Quant à Sollers, il mentionne sa femme entre autres, perdue parmi d'autres, dans quelle position il fait royalement l'amour avec... Des audaces prudentes. L'essentiel, ce que ça veut dire, pour un homme, de vivre avec une femme qui en sait plus que lui, qui est plus intelligente que lui, là-dessus motus. Des postures provocatrices, il est toujours aisé d'en prendre. Dire la vérité sur sa vie vraie, la quotidienne, la réelle... Difficile, peut-être impossible. (50)

[As for Sollers, he mentions his wife among others, lost among the others, in what position he royally makes love with her... Prudent audacities. The essential thing, what it means, for a man, to live with a wife who knows the score better than he, who is more intelligent than he, on this he's mum. Provocative postures are always easy to take. To tell the truth about one's true life, daily life, real life... Difficult, maybe impossible.]

(A curious observation is that Doubrovsky uses ellipses for punctuation here, which are not at all characteristic of *Le Livre brisé*—as if he is momentarily influenced by Sollers.) In Sollers's terms, Doubrovsky would be one of those who have not really read him, yet, who have not discovered the significance of his novels, so that in some ways, this opinion reflects a worse light on Doubrovsky than on Sollers. The insight that makes this paragraph worth quoting nevertheless lies in the last three sentences, which imply that Doubrovsky's project, to say the truth about real, daily life, is more difficult than Sollers's "provocative postures" about society's ills. An essential difference in their projects lies in this evocation of the small, personal, but all the more real life of the self, the real matter of Serge Doubrovsky's autofictions, even in this unique volume for and by Ilse. Sollers's obsessive vision turns by preference to the larger, the social and the external; Doubrovsky's glance peers into the cruel unconscious. Doubrovsky's project is frankly egotistic and narcissistic; Sollers claims to raise the consciousness of his readership. (I have not yet seen, in Sollers's voluminous writing, any comment on Doubrovsky's novels.)

Sollers has never claimed to be writing autofiction, although he might have, particularly as the genre has been adopted and revised by others.[56] In an unpublished interview, Sollers told me he does not seek the generic designation autofiction because he considers it too restrictive and subjective and paradoxically lacking the sanction of the real. His ambition is to carry on his social critique in a realm beyond the stories of the self, in which he takes the part of the ethnographer.[57] What Sollers might have borrowed from Doubrovsky's definition of autofiction is the consigning of the language of an adventure to the adventure of language, rather than the claim to recount "strictly real" events. This distinction needs a certain qualification, however: although Sollers has not made so strong a claim about the *autobiographical* truth of his novels, being much more discreet, indeed secretive, he has always claimed to use the novel to tell the truth about what is wrong with *society*. In that sense his fictions are deeply anchored in real life, and, to the extent that the observer of this life is Sollers himself, they are autofictions. Both writers draw heavily on their own lives and documentary evidence including letters, and refer directly or slyly to their other novels. (Interestingly, French readers have not hesitated to read Sollers's autobiography into his fictions, quoting the novels to narrate events in his life and rarely pausing to untangle differences.) Most important, Sollers and Doubrovsky both foreground the protagonist in his position as a writer, an effect achieved partly through the massive use of the present tense by both authors and through the relentless play of the signifier. Doubrovsky, however, less often represents his character at the moment he is writing: we do not see him at his typewriter—the office door is shut—and there is usually a time lag between events and his writing of them. When his manuscript is mentioned, it is usually being thrown back into his face by his angry wife. This is less "raw writing" than partly digested—taken up by the many reasons why Serge writes, to which we will come shortly.

The transcription of life events in Doubrovsky and Sollers could be described as analogous to the "Cuvier" tendency in Balzac, the effort to record or re-create life's realities in toto, both in the personal (especially Doubrovsky) and in the human arena beyond the individual (especially Sollers). The narrator of those events is the one who poses as secretary and historian. The

"Geoffroy Saint-Hilaire" tendency—the one that would forge links, invent the (master) narratives, compose—finds an analogy in Doubrovsky in the complex generic features that make his writing auto*fiction* and not auto*biography*. But it is only an analogy. Links, mastery, and unity are merely semiotic; they occur in the unheard-of effort to embroider the story. Or, as Turcanu observes, the "scriptural engine" (81) of his autofiction hides rather than unveils the reality of lived existence and simultaneously remodels it into a greater reality over which the writer no longer has control (82). With excruciating pain, the writer realizes that this greater reality arises from and depends on semiosis. For Sollers, links, composition, and narrative are clearly those of fiction, but all its devices are put to the task of giving semiosis the power to write reality.

Like Sollers, Doubrovsky draws a wealth of meaning from verbal play of all sorts—the adventure of language—and on this score a wealth of stimulating comparisons can be made. Relations between sound and sense occur in both writers: a sonority, a homonym, an assonance, a rhyme, all the better for being turned slightly awry. Approximate quotations, distorted or revised to explode with new, richer meaning, are exploited by both writers and characterize the arrogance and mastery of their styles. Use of slang and popular speech, often with creative, unusual twists, produces vigorous, humorous effects in both Sollers and Doubrovsky, and, for both, humor often has sinister undertones. Rhythmic effects have been mentioned most in comments on Sollers's writing, but they are present in Doubrovsky's as well, with the difference that they are perhaps less harmonious and more unruly. Starting with *Femmes*, Sollers has for the most part abandoned the Joycian, poetic play with the integrity of the word characteristic of his earlier novels, a unique use of language that *Lois* (1972) illustrates particularly well.

Buisine has an excellent description of Doubrovsky's style: "extreme feverishness"; "short independent clauses and so many nominal phrases"; "his obstinate rejection of coordinating phrases and subordinates"; "a desire for cutting up, for unlinking"; "his staccato, his striking phrases so often reinforced by the assonance of word play"; "this machine-gun fire of short sentences"; and so on. ("Serge Doubrovsky," 164). Buisine uses the appropriate metaphor of drunkenness, which I have already quoted: "Drunkenness of the writing in which the writer immerses himself to escape the final drowning" (165). Doubrovsky himself has called attention to the effects of his writing in *Fils*, speaking of "la bivalence des calembours" [the bivalence of the puns] and the "[écriture] glissant en un mouvement perpétuel dans les frayages du double sens" [[writ-ing] that slides in a perpetual movement among the pathways of the double meaning] ("Autobiographie/Vérité/Psychanalyse," 90). Without intending to describe this rich style in the detail it deserves, I would only call attention to its role in foregrounding semiosis. Always double meanings are obtained: a repre-sentational meaning, to which the reader attaches considerable effort and finds interest rewarded, and a semiotic meaning, which reflects on the writing proj-ect, renders it self-conscious, and profoundly affects it.

Buisine also notes that for the writer today, "to write an autobiography is simultaneously to reflect on what an autobiography is in terms of a literary and existential process" and that "the novelistic gesture cannot be dissociated from the critical gesture" (162). As a result, never pretending to ignore or deny what has come before, never refusing it in the name of its modernity, such writing is essentially postmodern. "The absolute new, modernity in and of itself, no longer exists. In these conditions writing is also a constant exploration, an incessant reactivation of the annals of literary memory" (163). Sollers's ap-proach to the postmodern ethic ranges toward the outside of his personal memory, to social memories, collective mythologies of which he poses as record keeper. Umberto Eco writes that the postmodern has come beyond the de-struction of the past practiced by the avant-garde: "The postmodern reply to the modern consists of recognizing that the past, since it cannot really be destroyed, because its destruction leads to silence, must be revisited: but with irony, not innocently."[58] Irony and a definite vigilance against innocence char-acterize all of Sollers's fictional writing. In the postmodern the definition of self wavers and subtly redefines itself as subject; in parallel, the illusion of reality becomes acutely self-conscious, is no longer given. Sollers illustrates the uncer-tainty of self-definition in this declining twentieth century by doubling his narrator-protagonist and foregrounding the process that creates the illusion of reality.

In such a climate, why does Will write? Why does Serge write? Philippe Sollers, "the absolutely isolated," in Roland Barthes's enduring description, is an eschatological writer, who must take the risk of revealing the answer to his enigma from the start. There is, Barthes writes, "a certain ethic of the writer, which obliges him immediately to risk the enigma of his work."[59] Sollers writes not for the present, which does not understand him (whether or not this is true, it is the stance he takes), and certainly not for the past, although all his material lies deeply anchored in it. He speaks to a time beyond the present: "Literature is his voice, which, by a 'paradisiacal' reversal, superbly reprises all the voices in the world, and blends them into a sort of song that cannot be heard unless, to listen to it, one is carried . . . very far away, ahead, beyond schools of thought, avant-gardes, newspapers, and conversations" (8–9). A distracted listening is required, to hear Sollers. Will the outsider represents this voice crying not in the desert but in a strangely edenic space in which writing is fulfillment, in spite of the hatred it accumulates on its author's head. The discovery of what Will called the magic of writing is what makes him write, and write ineluctably about that very power to reveal the fundamentally false scene of the world, for those who will read with their eyes and ears open. Jean-Louis Houdebine describes Sollers's absolute fidelity to this knowledge that the "theater" is "faked," that the "community lie" rules the world, and that there is a "hole in the being" and a "hole in time" that only writing can fill (348).

Serge writes—has always written—literally every day to fill the holes of his broken self, to "find" himself, at his typewriter; Doubrovsky's narrator persona is always writing a book. But when Ilse's absence turned into her disappearance, semiosis took Serge at his word: Now he no longer can represent himself as choosing writing, to fill the "memory holes," the gaps in his existential self; the writing has chosen him, and has a life of its own. The gaps are elsewhere; he is no longer the center of his book. If Sollers chooses to prefer language over the body, Doubrovsky finds the choice made for him, irrevocably.

Finally, one essential fact does compel reading Serge Doubrovsky's *Le Livre brisé* in conjunction with Philippe Sollers's *Femmes*: Doubrovsky has realized with *Le Livre brisé* the diabolical dangers of the novel that Will and S. spoke of repeatedly. Whereas Sollers has almost made a career of warning that the novel should be taken seriously, a message he has repeated in many different ways, Doubrovsky with one book proved it, beyond Sollers's wildest dreams.

Six

The Magic of Realism

All fiction instructs how it is fiction, in more or less apparent ways. Even those texts that do not allude directly to the processes by which they were created leave openings or traces through which we can glimpse the semes of writing. As Julia Kristeva observes, "Parallel to those scientific studies devoted to the organization of literary texts, *literature itself* practices *research into the laws of its own organization.* The modern novel becomes a disarticulation of the constants and rules of the traditional narrative, an exploration of the language of the narrative, that brings its procedures out into the open only to break them apart" (emphasis added).[1] Clearly, the self-conscious genres of the twentieth century leave little room for conjecture about the writing that created them, but the fact that a Balzac novel does not flaunt its semiosis at every moment does not prevent our reading how it writes its realism, as we have seen. In our critical climate, the notion of the "traditional narrative" is largely a convenient fiction. As a genre, the novel explores the language of narrative and exposes this exploration for the reader to comprehend.

I. METAFICTION AND FICTION

The first of six themes of this conclusion is that metafiction is an integral part of fiction. Fiction is metafiction. Judith Spencer has made this point central to her reading of the deconstructive modalities of *Les Liaisons dangereuses.* Comparing the French term *récit* (narration) to *representation*, she considers that both words have a double meaning as both the act of producing and the product: "If 'representation' implies both the image and the process by which the image is realized, 'narration' includes both the narration of events and the way we arrive at the narration. Fiction 'supposes' metafiction."[2] The word *representation* refers simultaneously to the action of representing and to the result of this action; in like manner, *narration* means both the action of narrating and the product of that action. In our very language about mimetic fictions, then, a double purpose is evident: mimetic fictions are both the process and the result. Inherent in the writing of a fictional narrative is information about how that narrative comes to the reader. Fictions display their writing of realism.[3] This link between process and result is foregrounded in Doubrovsky's *Le Livre brisé* and in Sollers's *Femmes*. The "system" of the *Heptaméron* puts into play from the start the two phenomena of fiction and writing about fiction (or speaking about it), but it also displays this link in the more subversive form of supplementarity. Balzac's mimetic figures of semiosis rhetorically constitute both production and product. All these examples of metadiscourse show how the novel "works" in creating the realistic illusion, in a variety of styles and manners of writing realism.

The idea that a novel can work out its own conditions of existence did not begin with structuralism. In "Le Roman comme recherche," Michel Butor commented on the difference between the writing of objective reality and the writing of realism. Although his essay remains strongly marked by the moment in which it was written, in the late 1950s, the distinction he defines is useful: "Whereas the truthful narrative always has the support, the resource of external evidence, the novel must suffice to call forth what it speaks about. That is why it is the phenomenological domain par excellence, the place par excellence where we can study how reality appears to us or can appear to us; that is why the novel is the laboratory of narrative."[4] Opposing the *récit,* or truthful narrative, to the novel, Butor here limits the word *récit* to the nonfictional account, what I would call the narrative of a true event. The truthful narrative is defined by the fact that it can call on the resources of reality external to it. Clearly, however, Butor's purpose is to promote the novel—the true narrative of an event—to a level somewhere above the *récit*: the novel is "the phenomenological domain par excellence," contrary to what one might expect. Better than the true story, which relies on external evidence, the novel can teach us how reality can be made to appear to us, and thus furnishes the laboratory for true narrative. This is not the place to trace the historical ramifications of Butor's idea, but, in broad strokes, one can say that the novel's ability to represent phenomenological reality has forged a blending of genres since the 1970s, so that the verifiable truthful narrative (the *récit*) has come closer to the novel, and vice versa. By tracing a trajectory whose end lies in the autofiction of Doubrovsky's *Le Livre brisé*, a "fiction of strictly true events," I am suggesting that all fictions carry within them the germ of this ability to narrate true events.

2. THE LABORATORY OF WRITING REALISM

The metaphor of a laboratory in which the process is tried out is particularly appropriate. In this laboratory, semiosis is at work making realism: only the elements that the novel contains combine to produce our phenomenological reality. But a novel's success in writing realism does not depend on success in resembling reality. On the contrary, necessarily failing to reproduce reality, mimesis succeeds only in leading the reader into falsehood, to the extent that one defines falsehood as that which does not arise in external evidence as verified or verifiable. Thus, a corollary of this theme might be phrased as follows: mimesis may lie, but semiosis does not. There are enormous consequences of this statement, which underlies my conclusions.

I have proposed the term *naïve realism* in contrast to the devious and self-reflective strategies of the author who shows his hand, as Diderot does. Naïve realism particularly characterizes both Suzanne Simonin's writing and Modeste Mignon's. Suzanne herself, in many ways, is not naïve. On the contrary, a case can be made for the nun's amazing sophistication in manipulating people, men and women alike: Ursule the nun who sympathizes with her plight, the second mother superior, Don Morel, even her own mother. But if I speak of the naïve realism of her writing, it is to describe the relation of her writing to her self. It is also the relation of Modeste Mignon to her own writing and to the writing of the false Canalis. In a different way, *Les Liaisons dangereuses* is also founded on naïve realism. For the original writers of the letters, there is a belief in the ideality of the letters: a narrow correspondence between the signifier and the signified, which Derrida described by recalling Lacan's notion of the "point de capiton," the concentrated quantity of real to which signifiers attach. According to Derrida, the "point de capiton" "hooks the signifier to the signified."[5] As a construct, naïve realism may be very useful in an ironic time determined by the languages of criticism—a time that is precisely not naïve—to explain the immediate relation of writing to the creation of a realistic reality. Diderot's time resembles ours, in this matter. We may usefully contrast both times with the period known as French classicism. The verisimilitude that is found in the seventeenth-century historical novella and in the *histoire galante,* or the romance, bears little resemblance to such realism; it is highly codified, and it is realistic only in the sense that it does not break the rules of the genre. Examples of narratives existing in the regime of verisimilitude are the well-known *Désordres de l'amour* (1675) by Villedieu, or the early eighteenth-century collection of interconnected short novels *Les Illustres Françoises,* by Robert Challe. In these works, narration is produced to embellish rather than to render a truthful image. By contrast, Modeste Mignon and Suzanne Simonin use language as if it were transparent, the faithful rendition of an image they create, and most of the correspondents in *Les Liaisons dangereuses* hold such an idea of writing as an ideal. It is, of course, an ideal constantly contaminated and broken, and that is in many ways exactly what Laclos's novel is about. And it is the purpose of the semiosis in all these novels to indicate that such realism is false: the mimesis lies.

Opposed to naïve realism, the term *supplementarity* has served to identify and describe a practice of writing that seeks to create realism by indirect routes (in this, my usage broadens the description Derrida gave in *Of Grammatology*). We saw it at work in Marguerite de Navarre's *Heptaméron* and, differently, in Balzac's *Ursule Mirouët.* When the mimesis of experience is the primary focus and method of narration, there is a risk of "nuysance," or harm—that was the message of the *Heptaméron.* It is the problem of mimesis as lying. There is no question that the material aspect of mimesis has a function, in both of these works. It represents the desired reality: love in the *Heptaméron,* money in *Ursule Mirouët.* But it is the inscription of the semiosis that turns the risk of harm to profit; harm becomes our profit when we attend to semiosis. The semiotic relationship of writing to event is supplementary: both a substitute and an enhancement of event and experience. We saw supplementarity at work in the form of a third term: neither truth nor lie, but something that avoids the truth/lie paradigm. We also saw it at work in the rare form of spirituality, in *Ursule Mirouët,* where it gives presence to immaterial objects, which is exactly what writing does.

The structure of the *Heptaméron* immediately puts mimesis into a semiotic frame, which takes charge of the mimetic narrative. Diderot's play with the preface in *La Religieuse* describes semiosis as devious while the nun's narrative is an example of naïve self-representation. It is the task of the semiotic action to make the reader "listen" badly, in order to hear well. Disruptions to hearing, in *Les Liaisons dangereuses,* make the ideal consolations of naïve representation impossible. Mimetic writing fails to correspond to and change reality and, like *La Religieuse,* makes the reader hear well only at the price of losing the direct imitation of "reality." In Balzac's novels, mimetic figures of semiosis constitute the laboratory of writing realism. The facts and the structures in which the facts make sense together make up the vast signifying network that creates realism. All of the self-consciousness of the two recent novels by Philippe Sollers and Serge Doubrovsky plays on this theme opposing the falsehood of mimesis to the necessary truth of semiosis. Autofiction is neither wholly true nor false; it is real and true, not false and not fiction, reversing two of the four terms in play in the *Heptaméron.* With their protagonists drawn in their self-image and writing books in the image of the authors' books, both Sollers and Doubrovsky flaunt the opposition of naïve representation or classical mimesis to self-conscious writing. As such, they reinstate a concept of mimesis that Derrida considered "a quite classical interpretation of *mimesis*: a turn toward truth, greater truth in the fictive representation than in reality, increased fidelity, 'superior realism'" (496). Doubrovsky caps the process, opposing semiosis to this classical concept of mimesis, thus breaking the book.

These processes require the reader's presence, especially when the text attempts to break with referential reality:

One can break entirely with realistic *writing* as soon as one no longer refers, in any manner, to any sort of relation of the content with external reality, when only the totality of the signifiers, their internal relations in the text, constitute a field of reading. Yet, at the same time, it is apparent that every text has a certain readability, and, in addition, the reader, in trying to decipher the text, succeeds, on the condition of conferring a meaning on it: in appropriating it for himself, he interprets the text, and does so in terms of reality. Thus the most unrealistic, or anti-realistic, writing, the most devious or the most critical of the real is recuperated at the moment it is *read,* therefore as an object of reading, or rather: in the course of the process of communication which transforms writing into *the written.*[6]

The explanation is ponderous, but it does give singular importance to the reader.

3. THE READER'S ROLE IN WRITING REALISM

Representational works of fiction are "props" in a game of make-believe which the reader plays, according to Kendall Walton.[7] In the twenty-fourth tale of the *Heptaméron,* the supplementary relation of the mirror and the epistle to the narrative models the relation of the reader to the text: just as the mirror and the epistle write a reality for Elisor, the text of the *Heptaméron* writes realism for the reader. Elisor achieves his reality by going beyond the mimetic—the simple but risky business of speaking his love for the queen of Castille—to semiosis, by engaging the logic of the supplement. Elisor is, as it were, writing fiction; he is dwelling on semiotic features. Hearing and mishearing, "entendement" and "malentendu," are opposed in *Les Liaisons dangereuses*. What is misheard for the characters, in their naïve belief in the ability of writing to record and to change reality, is understood by the reader, by the ultimate readers of the characters' writing. Suzanne's writing in *La Religieuse* is split between the two poles of the naïve and the devious. Because she falls between them, she has to be disposed of. Reading *La Religieuse* is naïve and devious as well; that is, the novel calls for a devious reading, which nevertheless does not forget its naïve reading. This is the difficult position the reader must occupy. The naïve and uncomplicated relation of writing to reality contrasts with the devious, obstacle-strewn course of Diderot's writing. Diderot "improves on" Laclos by carrying the cacophony of the crisscrossing letters in *Les Liaisons dangereuses* into the extreme of its many tourniquets of reality and illusion.

Balzac implies a reader conversant with and interested in the myriad facts he creates to describe society, but guides the interpretation by making of his imitation of reality the figure of his semiosis. This is quite clear in the case of *Mémoires de deux jeunes mariées*; only the reader operates the union of contraries, by alternately occupying the position of reader of Renée's letters and of Louise's letters, and the epistolary form serves to force this role on the reader. The novel is unique among all the titles of *La Comédie humaine* in the notable absence of the strong Balzacian narrator (or one of his deputies), the one who guides the reader determinedly through the facts he would expose and the explanations that serve his descriptions. With such a vacancy, the letter writing alone guides the reader to make sense. Modeste Mignon writes her romantic self into existence, and La Brière creates her reality by reading her letters. Both are writing realism as if they had no other purpose in life. Because the correspondence is anonymous, neither has a clear picture of the other; the referent of their writing is separated from the writing and largely unavailable. Across the relations among the signifiers, through the processes of writing, new senses emerge, disconnected from the original referents. As for *Ursule Mirouët,* the dual reality Balzac forges, in Nemours, forges also the structure of the novel: both materialistic and spiritualistic, doubly dependent on structures of genealogy and inheritance. Sollers's *Femmes* and Doubrovsky's *Le Livre brisé* are but two excellent illustrations of the prevailing modern ethos that disallows any innocent, naïve, or disengaged reading.

Philippe Hamon has described the text as a "reading machine": "the literary text, always stemming from a preceding fiction (the rewriting of an intertext), is also, before being a reference, or representation, a 'reading machine' that the reader will manipulate, which will manipulate the reader as well."[8] It is appropriate to think of the semiotic activity of the text as comparable to a machine, whose primary function is to manipulate the reader in myriad ways so that the reader forges realism. The process comes to life as it passes through the reader.

4. TRUTH AND FALSEHOOD IN WRITING REALISM

The fourth theme follows logically from the considerations discussed until now. We have seen that the text, the laboratory of our reality, can exploit our reading of it to write realism. Most mimetic fictions purport to write realism by claiming to portray a faithful image of a reality that has the potential of verifiability. In their metafiction, they affirm that they tell the truth, in one way or another—whether truth writing occurs as an imitation of a known reality, a construction parallel to reality, a transcription of reality, or any other form of representation that claims not to distort. The methods and ways of representation are innumerable, but the underlying common thread is the evocation of a realism that does not lie. That is the process operating in the text, irrespective of verifiable facts external to it. And yet all these processes are inherently deceptive. Clément Rosset goes so far as to claim that it is impossible to capture reality in words. As soon as one attempts to fix reality, one is blinded, and the attempt "is therefore transformed into the pure and simple suppression of the brilliance one tried to capture, which is replaced by a decor and a false light."[9] What has indeed been captured by words is no longer what one proposed to represent. If, in the classical sense of mimesis, one attempts to capture a real reality in writing, a Stendhalian mirror, perhaps, then that attempt is doomed by the very nature of the "mirror"—the writing, which produces a reality different than the original real referent of the writing. If, on the other hand, with the irony and sophistication of modern writing, one relinquishes the claim to make words correspond to reality—as I claim for all mimetic writing as we see it—then the lesson we may retain about reality is that only writing is real.

Should it be troubling that unreal people and events can bring about such a process in the reader? Have we not entered a new age of anxiety? Perhaps that is why fiction moves toward a more and more overt expression of the problem of fakery, of phoniness, eventually flaunting the ability of writing to fool the reader. Exposing the flaws serves to conjure the problem. That is why I have described writing realism as ironic in our time. In the modern attitude, displaying the deception in the mimetic illusion has become a theme of literature on a par with the familiar themes of its contents, like love or money. The two contemporary writers in my corpus have an acute awareness of this anxiety.

Sollers, in his novels especially, tends to describe real-life things as "theater" instead of reality. There is a kind of switch: all reality is theater, but the novel flourishes insidious reality. Nietzsche "authorized" this attitude for Sollers; in *La Guerre du goût,* Sollers wrote: "As for me, I would never have been able to write *Paradis, Femmes, Portrait du Joueur, Le Cœur absolu, Les Folies Françaises, Le Lys d'Or, La Fête à Venise, Le Secret,* if I had not felt soaring near me, permanently, the disengaged, active, cruel and indulgent hand of Nietzsche."[10] Truth is nothing but a construct, according to Nietzsche's authority. Sollers quotes Nietzsche to reply to the accusation of writing about known people in his *romans à clés,* using them to make latent public calamities visible, to prompt thinking. In *Théorie des exceptions,* Sollers puts it in terms of a moral error: The world has not given enough thought to its lack of thinking about itself; society does not trouble to engage in the kind of thoughtful analysis that alone may foster its betterment. Sollers has long maintained this position and claims he does not have time to cease thinking about it, because he feels it is a point that has yet to be taught to the world: "The more time passes, the more there are strong pressures to force me to speak of other things, of thought that does not think about itself, of so-called reality when everything is theater."[11] Writing realism is ironic in Sollers because of this twist by which reality is false (mere theater), but writing, in his novels, is true.

Doubrovsky has an apparently opposite tendency to assert the reality of everything he writes. In one form or another, he has given strong meaning to Balzac's "All is true." In interviews, critical articles, conference papers, and colloquia on his work, he insists that his autofictions are factual. Statements he has made about his books affirm the reality of the stories, a reality on which he "embroiders" to produce the autofiction: "It is a transformation starting with the material of my own life—what I call, by a slightly barbaric term, its textualization."[12] People who know Doubrovsky also are eager to confirm the truth of the novels. Doubrovsky is aware of the danger of creating reality, having claimed, for instance, to kill off a woman with each novel, and yet he forges ahead, always turning his truth into writing. The writer of *Le Livre brisé* hammers home this theme: autobiography is a posthumous genre. I have tried to show that the price paid to achieve this neurotic realism is excessive and that Doubrovsky is well aware of it.

A consequence of the claim to tell truth through a fiction is thus a neurotic split. Only writing justifies it. Will-and-S., the doubled narrator and writer of *Femmes,* give embodied form to narration split between truth and lie. They are melded in their product, the ongoing manuscript of *Femmes.* Of Doubrovsky, Hélène Jaccomard points out the "dialogue of the deaf" among the diverse instances of the self in *Le Livre brisé.*[13] I called Serge's neurotic split the Atlantic Ocean, which both separates and connects the parts, the material fragments of his existence. For Doubrovsky, writing brings the parts together: "J'écris ma vie, donc j'ai été" [I am writing my life, therefore I have been], he wrote in *Le Livre brisé.* Writing serves as the intermediary between divergent options. Again, truth lies in the semiosis, whatever the reality or truth of the things represented.

However, as we have seen, the problem of the faked and the phony is not raised only by these two living novelists. For Marguerite de Navarre's characters, the question is crucial to all their understanding of the stories told, and vital to their debates on love, human behavior, right and wrong. So troubled is the ethical status of fiction, already in the sixteenth century, that Elisor, Dagoucin, and Marguerite de Navarre all resort to supplementarity as a way to write reality, for their audience (or readers). Writing, for the narrators of the *Heptaméron,* is the mediated choice. Both Laclos and Diderot put into complex play representation and semiosis as a way of having their cake and eating it too: both being aware that fictions are necessarily inventions and simultaneously proclaiming their ability to serve a moral purpose as an indicator of truth. In my reading, they do this by establishing truth on the level of the writing.

Balzac's "conscience" is no doubt the clearest. This master of realism never wavered from his belief that all the dramas in his fictions are true. That was their very purpose—to tell the truth, a truth that had not yet been exposed in all its complexity. For Balzac the distinction between "true" and "real" must perhaps be maintained most rigorously. He is not blinded by the brilliance of the created "real," which is more true than real reality, nor is he troubled by the "problem" of fakery or phoniness; everything points to his assumption—his certainty—that writing is true.

In this regard it is interesting to consider how the novels I have studied claim to reprise these questions of truth in writing as some variant on a 1674 discussion of verisimilitude and truth, found among René Rapin's *Les Réflexions sur la poétique de ce temps et sur les ouvrages des poètes anciens et modernes.* However distant from most of the works in my corpus, this classical text may have said it all: the written truth is better than the truth itself. Consider this passage:

Aside from the fact that verisimilitude serves to lend credence to the most fabulous that poetry can bring forth, it also serves to give to the things the poet says a greater air of perfection than truth itself could give, even though verisimilitude is only its copy. For truth only makes things as they are, and verisimilitude makes them as they should be. Truth is almost always defective, by the mixture of the conditions that compose it. Nothing is born in this world that does not shrink from the perfection of its idea at birth.[14]

So fragile, so ephemeral is the perfection of the idea that truth cannot exist for one moment in the world without losing some of its verity; truth in the world is always defective. Interestingly, Doubrovsky could have adopted this principle entirely. Only writing overcomes the defects—Diderot's nun thought so, and so did the authors of the correspondence in *Les Liaisons dangereuses,* to their downfall. Balzac's writing explicitly aims to remedy the inability to render truth except through writing, as he claimed many times in prefaces and proved much more often in the novels and short stories of *La Comédie humaine.* Even his language mirrors Rapin's: "Truth would often not be plausible, just as literary truth could never be the truth of nature," he wrote in the preface to *Le Cabinet des Antiques,* imitating Boileau's "Truth can sometimes not be plausible."[15] Although not stated in so many words, the concept that writing overcomes the inability to express the truth in the world underlies the entire project of the *Heptaméron,* as the work's prologue suggests.

5. THE MAGIC OF REALISM, THE DANGER OF WRITING

Philippe Sollers continues to give the most insistent play to the theory of fiction's connections to truth and falsehood; it is he who formulated the concept expressed in my fifth theme. In *Femmes,* Will writes that words take the place of things: "La magie du roman est de traiter la magie elle-même... La magie noire des doubles, de l'empoisonné travail invisible de substitution permanente qui fait que la vie est vécue par d'autres personnages que ceux qui se croient en vie..." [The novel's magic is to deal with magic itself... The black magic of doubles, of the poisoned invisible work of permanent substitution which causes life to be lived by characters other than those who think they are living...].[16] A life created in words substitutes for the unreflected relation to reality: "those who think they are living." While Sollers states this theme, in many different variants and in different kinds of writing (fiction and essay, notably), all the books I have treated in this study demonstrate it. What is not always explicit in chapters 2, 3 and 4 becomes so in chapter 5: it is Sollers who proclaims that writing realism is dangerous, and Doubrovsky who proves it. What exactly is this magic—and is it appropriate to use a term so charged with an aura of superstition, with "medieval" and unscientific connotations?

Marie-Laure Ryan has written:

When texts are read self-referentially by postmodern theory, they are usually interpreted as reflecting on their own textuality and as blocking participation in the mimesis. The self-referential text is supposed to decenter and destabilize any notion of a textual actual world. Along these lines, the function of virtual narration would be to reveal the artificiality of the text, to break the referential illusion, to expose the constructed nature of the fictional world, and to encourage the reader to take an active role in constructing this world.[17]

Because all of this applies to modern or, more exactly, postmodern narratives, the question is raised: Has the mimetic illusion disappeared in the postmodern era? It will have been clear from the beginning of this study that I do not think so; moreover, I believe that the two postmodern authors I have chosen especially do not think so. Texts reflecting on their own textuality are indeed characteristic of postmodernism and, as I have often shown, of earlier texts as well, but this reflection does not block "participation in the mimesis." That the mimetic illusion persists is an article of faith not only for a Balzac but also for a

Doubrovsky. But it persists after having taken a turn of the spiral, on a higher, more self-conscious level; it persists after a turn through self-referentiality; it persists even as we acknowledge the fictional construct and our own role in it as readers. This is true for all the texts of this study, and many more, without a doubt, because we are reading them in our postmodern time. We are involved in a redefinition of the mimetic illusion. This redefinition I am calling *the magic of realism*.

Paradoxically, so far from being "medieval" or unscientific, the magic of realism is the postmodern definition of the mimetic illusion. I suggest this holds true for all our readings, of all literatures. When our consciousness is raised, to use an old phrase from the beginning of the feminist revolution, which must be counted as one of the starts of the postmodern era, what we call the mimetic illusion no longer functions in that naïve way we saw, for instance, in the writing of Suzanne Simonin and Modeste Mignon.

Among the features of the magic of realism is the self-reflection characteristic of modern and postmodern writing, which has found its way into reading. Our reading can no longer be innocent or naïve. Even first readings, so important for apprehending the initial effect of the writing on the reading, and by their essence unrepeatable, no longer can proceed with the innocence that makes us willingly submit to the deceit of the mimetic illusion, as I wrote in chapter 1. First readings too are self-conscious, now that modern and postmodern narratives have so forcefully demonstrated the danger and the black magic they foment. After the French new novel, things have changed. While that movement of the 1950s and 1960s laid to waste the standard, unquestioned features of narrative, other novels at that time and since pretended to ignore the revolution. Yet something changed. It is not that novels can no longer be written with identifiable characters, comprehensible events, an accurate chronology. Sollers's own itinerary as a novelist included a decisive moment—and a very self-conscious one—in which what looked like a return to classical narrativity again became possible. *Femmes* is the novel that marked the moment when Sollers appeared to seek a wider audience through a more classical style, but it is a classical style made new by self-consciousness. Sollers spoke of this postmodern evolution in the belligerent tone that characterizes most of the preface to *La Guerre du goût*: "Il est remarquable que *Femmes* n'ait pas été perçu comme un livre 'd'avant-garde,' de la même façon que *Drame* ou *Paradis*" [It is remarkable that *Femmes* was not perceived as an "avant-garde" book, in the same way as *Drame* or *Paradis*] (12–13). A good reading of *Femmes* would, on the contrary, see that what looks like its conventional narrativity demands nevertheless a self-reflective reading.

The same itinerary is ours as readers: it is our reading that is newly self-conscious. The very writing of modernist prose has reformed our reading habits, disallowing utter naïveté yet building on our nostalgic memory of it, which is strong enough to engage our participation in its constructs. We are like adults at a magic show: we know the performer is not a magician (in the medieval sense, that is, like Merlin), and we know something about the tricks used to deceive—sleight of hand, boxes with false bottoms, doors that look open when they are closed, and so on. Nevertheless, we can see that children at the show might in fact believe the magician is creating magic. Instead of sharing their belief, we may enjoy watching their pleasure, and at the same time, we tell ourselves that the magical illusion is magnificent and marvel at the skill displayed—which still confounds us. In short, we know the magician achieves illusions by devices and procedures that we cannot ourselves produce, which we admire, but at the same time we delight in the result, for something of the child has persisted in us. We are then simultaneously enjoying the illusion and how it is produced—at once the process and its result. We have reached a new turn of the spiral, somewhere where Diderot had long ago placed the happy few to whom he addressed his most devious conundrums. Because the mimetic illusion persists and yet we also see how it is produced, our relation to the text of realism is, in our period, one of aporia: doubt stemming from this paradox. Our uncertainty as to the role of mimesis in our lives now goes to the root of the mimetic illusion. An illusion should no longer be an illusion if we can say what produces it, and yet we hold to the illusion, just as we participate in the magic show. What permits this paradox is the power of literary language: writing, which now needs to be reconsidered.

6. THE ETHICS OF WRITING

The ethical aspect of writing realism lies in the writing rather than the realism. If we think of represented events, questions of ethics will be judged as they are in life, and in some cases this could be uncomfortable. I have claimed that the reviewers who blamed Serge Doubrovsky for his wife's death were not reading at all; in fact, they were fantasizing a story that the book certainly permits. But because nothing is simple, one could say that *Le Livre brisé* requires the reader to fantasize this represented story—in the devious manner of its semiosis. It is a story to be rejected, if we follow the guide of the book's semiosis, which leads us to the truthful real of Doubrovsky's writing. It is this truthful real that we cannot condemn.

Ross Chambers, in a remarkable article, "The Etcetera Principle," describes the role of writing or, more accurately, discourse in creating the "facts." The theory of writing he implies speaks to the very root of our culture: "Plotting depends fundamentally on giving priority to the time of narrating over the time of the narrated. . . . It is the function of the texts called the *Odyssey* and *La Recherche* to make these bare narrative facts [that Ulysses made it back to Ithaca, that Marcel became a writer] worth attending to and to do so through their mode of telling. The intervention of a narrating instance, and hence of a relation to a narratee, makes discourse-time primary."[18] This primacy of the "time of narrating," or in my term the *writing,* is what makes the events told worth attending to. And it is what makes the telling of the events ethical. James Reid writes that "art is . . . the means by which language goes beyond its prescriptiveness, its lying, and indirectly expresses, describes, reality's unique-ness. . . . Through art, language overcomes its lies and becomes a discourse of knowledge."[19]

The process I have shown working to create the realistic illusion in all the novels and stories discussed in the previous chapters lies at the root of our culture, perhaps even of culture taken abstractly. Alone among all human comportments, writing is that astonishing monster that is at once itself and something else. Because representation is not (or no longer) a reference to a preexisting reality outside the writing, only the writing is real, which means it is the only place where the sign and meaning coincide (where, as Barthes wrote, grammatical distinctions are abolished). When the story being told is a story about the writing of the story, then it can only be real. As Riffaterre writes near the end of *Fictional Truth,* "Fictional truth obtains when the mode of the diegesis shifts from the narrative to the poetic. This is the ultimate avatar of the referential illusion that replaces in literature the reference to reality with a reference to language."[20] Or, as Paul de Man has put it, "Rhetoric radically suspends logic and opens up vertiginous possibilities of referential aberration," such that this figural potential of language equates with literature itself.[21] This may well be the final lesson of Balzac's strategic use of writing in *Modeste*

Mignon, where the "novel" Modeste and Ernest write in their correspondence forges new referents more real for them than all the known reality around them, including their own prior selves. Writing allows them to "live happily ever after" or, in other terms, be true to themselves, because they know how the illusion—the mimesis—came into being in their writing.

To the notion of the ethical I give in particular the definition of the anti-ideological: writing cannot fall into error because it does not seek to impose an ideology. The analyses of the previous chapters sustain the claim that the anti-ideological lies in writing, in semiosis, or in what Barthes called *signifiance,* the activity of the signifier. Writing realism takes realism out of the realm of the ideological. Instead of showing something about the "real world," about which, necessarily, an opinion is made or a position taken, as in the old view of realism, writing realism shows us something about the *writing,* which cannot be seen in anything but realism. It shows us writing engaged at the very core of real experience. Writing is the only real referent that the reader can confidently know while reading. This is because something ineffable happens when language takes events in charge, something different from the events themselves (however fictive they may be). De Man reminds us that a literary text "simultaneously asserts and denies the authority of its own rhetorical mode" (17); this is something like knowing the illusion and believing it too, what I have called the magic of realism. Another "scene" is going on in language, according to Kristeva:

Other authors have noticed that *writing,* as *trace* or tracing (what is called, according to a recent terminology, a *gramme*), unveils inside language a "scene" that the sign and its signified cannot see: a scene that, instead of instituting a "resemblance" the way the sign does, is on the contrary the very mechanism of "difference." In writing, in fact, there is tracing but not representation, and this tracing—this trace—has furnished the basis of a new theoretical science that has been called *grammatology.* (23)

The sign that is the very mechanism of difference refers us to the semiotic level of activity of the text, where the writing of realism takes place, unseen by the signified to which the sign points. This semiotic activity disconnects from the messy business of reality. Kristeva claims that writing does not contain representation, but I would understand this to mean that no other reality is present in the writing. Representation as a construction of the reading, which I described in chapter 1, is the very mechanism that functions to disconnect literary writing from an ideological representation; this mechanism is the magic of realism. In writing realism, in contrast to a representation that would institute a resemblance to reality, there occurs the "difference," the magic, the second scene (something much less than a system), the signifiance.

This study began with mimesis, the illusion of reality, and it ends in the conviction that writing realism leads to the necessary paradox of literary writing: we believe it, and yet we know it is fiction. This can only be described as an aporia. We end in deconstruction as the necessary description of literary language. The instances of writing in the novels studied here guide the reader to a comprehension of the textual means by which the illusion is produced while simultaneously producing it. A probing reading of any work of fiction might arrive at such a conclusion; in fact, if it does not, that is only because it has not probed far enough. But deconstruction does not mean that one can make a text say whatever one wishes. Instead, it is the acknowledgment that meaning has thickened, has acquired more layers than one reading can show, and that criticism or critical reading is not something one adds to a text but a feature of the writing itself.

A vocal element of society has misunderstood poststructuralism as an invitation to immorality. But writing is at the root of culture. To write is to engage a system that has developed over centuries, in a form all of whose differences are mere variants of the same, the rooted expression of our desire to know.

Appendix A

Giving Voice, Taking Place in the *Heptaméron*

Tale	Page	Giver	Receiver	Text
1	10	Hircan	Simontault	puisque vous avez commencé la parolle, c'est raison que nous commandez
2	18	Simontault	Oisille	je donne ma **voix** à madame Oisille
3	22	Oisille	Saffredent	parquoy je vous donne ma **voix** pour dire la tierce Nouvelle
4	27	Saffredent	Ennasuite	je vous donne ma **voix** à dire la quatriesme Nouvelle
5	34	Ennasuite	Geburon	je vous donne ma **voix** à dire la cinquiesme Nouvelle
6	38	Geburon	Nomerfide	parquoy je luy donne ma **voix**
7	40	Nomerfide	Hircan	je vous laisse mon ***ranc*** pour nous racompter la septiesme histoire
8	43	Hircan	Longarine	je vous donne ma **voix** pour dire la huictiesme Nouvelle
9	49	Longarine	Dagoucin	je vous donne ma **voix** pour nous en racompter quelque belle
10	54	Dagoucin	Parlamente	que vous la nous veullez dire pour la fin de ceste Journée
11	87	Parlamente	Nomerfide	je donne ma **voix** à la plus jeune
12	89	Nomerfide	Dagoucin	je donne ma **voix** à Dagoucin
13	97	Dagoucin	Parlamente	regardons à qui Dagoucin donnera sa **voix**. Je la donne à Parlamente
14	109	Parlamente	Simontault	donnez vostre **voix** à quelcun. Je la donne très volontiers à Symontault
15	115	Simontault	Longarine	regardons à qui Simontault donnera sa **voix**. Je la donne à Longarine
16	128	Longarine	Geburon	je prie Longarine de donner sa **voix** à quelcun
17	134	Geburon	Oisille	je vous suplie que vous prenez ma ***place*** et que vous le dictes ⁴
18	137	Oisille	Hircan	parquoy je vous donne ma **voix**
19	142	Hircan	Ennasuite	je vous donne ma ***place*** pour la dire
20	152	Ennasuite	Saffredent	prenez ma ***place*** et nous racomptez
21	157	Saffredent	Parlamente	à qui il donnoit sa **voix** . . . je dois donner ma **voix** à Parlamente
22	175	Parlamente	Geburon	à qui Parlamente donnera sa **voix** . . . Je la donne à Geburon
23	186	Geburon	Oisille	voyons à qui Geburon donnera sa **voix** . . . luy donna sa **voix**
24	193	Oisille	Dagoucin	pria madame Oisille de donner sa **voix** à quelqu'un. Je la donne à Dagoucin
25	202	Dagoucin	Longarine	donnez vostre **voix** à quelcune. Je la donne à Longarine
26	207	Longarine	Saffredent	à fin que Longarine donne sa **voix** à quelcun. Je la donne à Saffredent

Tale	Page	Giver	Receiver	Text
27	221	Saffredent	Ennasuite	je donne ma **voix** à Ennasuitte
28	223	Ennasuite	Simontault	car je vous donne ma **voix**
29	226	Simontault	Nomerfide	je donne ma **voix** à Nomerfide
30	229	Nomerfide	Hircan	achevons nostre Journée, à laquelle Hircan mectra la fin
31	237	Hircan	Geburon	il donnoit sa **voix** . . . je luy eusse donné ma **voix** . . . je la bailleray au plus saige
32	241	Geburon	Oisille	à qui donnerez-vous vostre **voix**. —A vous, Madame
33	246	Oisille	Simontault	à qui madame Oisille donnera sa **voix**. —Je la donne à Symontault
34	250	Simontault	Nomerfide	sçachons à qui Symontault donne sa **voix**. —Je la donne à Nomerfide
35	254	Nomerfide	Hircan	sçachons de Nomerfide, à qui elle donne sa **voix**. —Je la donne à Hircan
36	261	Hircan	Ennasuite	sçachons à qui Hircan donnera sa **voix**. —Je la donne à Ennasuitte
37	265	Ennasuite	Dagoucin	escouter à qui Ennasuitte donnera sa **voix**. —Je la donne à Dagoucin
38	269	Dagoucin	Longarine	sçachons à qui Dagoucin donne sa **voix**? —Je la donne à Longarine
39	272	Longarine	Saffredent	à qui donnera sa **voix** Longarine? —Je la donne à Saffredent
40	274	Saffredent	Parlamente	sçachons à qui Saffredent donnera sa **voix** . . . luy donnerays tousjours ma **voix**
41	282	Parlamente	Saffredent	à qui elle donnoit sa **voix**
42	286	Saffredent	Parlamente	à qui donnera Saffredent sa **voix**? . . . ce sera à vous-mesmes
43	295	Parlamente	Geburon	je vous donne ma **voix**
44	301	Geburon	Nomerfide	je vous prie, Nomerfide, que je vous donne ma **voix**
45	304	Nomerfide	Simontault	parquoy, je vous donne ma **voix** pour la dire
46	308	Simontault	Oisille	je vous prye que vous nous le dictes
47	311	Oisille	Dagoucin	je vous donne ma **voix** pour la dire
48	315	Dagoucin	Ennasuite	je vous donne ma **voix** pour la dire
49	317	Ennasuite	Hircan	je vous en racompteray ung d'une grande dame
50	323	Hircan	Longarine	je vous donne ma **voix**
51	328	Longarine	Oisille	je donne ma **voix** à Madame Oisille
52	333	Oisille	Simontault	je vous donne ma **voix** pour la dire
53	336	Geburon	Ennasuite	je vous donne ma **voix**
54	342	Ennasuite	Saffredent	je vous donne ma *place*
55	344	Saffredent	Nomerfide	et vous donne ma **voix**
56	347	Nomerfide	Hircan	je vous prie . . . que vous nous le veuilliez dire
57	353	Hircan	Parlamente	je vous donne ma **voix**
58	356	Parlamente	Dagoucin	je vous donne ma *place* pour le racompter
59	360	Simontault [b]	Longarine	je vous donne ma *place* pour en dire vostre opinion
60	365	Longarine	Geburon	je vous prie . . . que vous ne nous le veillez celler
61	369	Oisille	Saffredent	vous nous en veullez dire ce que vous en sçavez
62	377	Saffredent	Longarine	je vous donne ma *place*, et que nous la dictes
63	379	Longarine	Dagoucin	je vous prie . . . que vous prenez ma *place* pour le nous racompter
64	383	Dagoucin	Parlamente	prenez ma *place* et le nous dictes
65	387	Parlamente	Geburon	prenez ma *place* et le nous racomptez
66	389	Geburon	Ennasuite	parquoy, vous tiendrez mon *lieu*, s'il vous plaist

Tale	Page	Giver	Receiver	Text
67	392	Ennasuite	Simontault	je vous donne ma ***place***
68	395	Simontault	Nomerfide	je vous donne ma ***place*** pour le dire
69	397	Nomerfide^c	Hircan	si vous me voulez donner le ***rang***
70	400	Simontault	Oisille	je vous requiers . . . la nous vouloir compter
71	422	Nomerfide	Parlamente	j'eusse donné la myenne [ma ***place***] à Parlamente
72	424	Parlamente	Dagoucin	je vous donne ma ***place*** pour la dire
73	428	Dagoucin	Nomerfide	je donne ma **voix** à Nomerfide

^aThis is the first use of "place."
^bSimontault may have told tale 58.
^cHircan does not wait to be asked.

Genealogy of *Ursule Mirouët*

[father] JEAN-MASSIN-LEVRAULT

Madame Jean-Massin CRÉMIÈRE-LEVRAULT-DIONIS
& Monsieur CRÉMIÈRE-LEVRAULT-DIONIS

Madame CRÉMIÈRE-LEVRAULT-DIONIS
& Monsieur LEVRAULT-MINORET (died 1814)

Madame Levrault-Minoret MASSIN-LEVRAULT
(born 1793)
& Monsieur MASSIN-LEVRAULT Jr.

LES MASSIN

Paméla MASSIN-LEVRAULT

Madame Jean-Massin-Levrault MINORET & Monsieur MINORET

[sailor] MINORET

[captain] MINORET

Madame Minoret MASSIN-MASSIN & Monsieur MASSIN-MASSIN

Madame Massin-Massin CRÉMIÈRE-CRÉMIÈRE
& Monsieur CRÉMIÈRE-CRÉMIÈRE
mar. 1813

LES CRÉMIÈRE

[daughter] CRÉMIÈRE-CRÉMIÈRE

Angéline CRÉMIÈRE-CRÉMIÈRE

[oldest brother] MINORET & Madame MINORET

François MINORET-LEVRAULT (born about 1769)
& Zélie MINORET-LEVRAULT

LES MINORET

Désiré MINORET-LEVRAULT

Denis MINORET (born 1746)
& Ursule Mirouët MINORET (died 1793)
mar. 1778

[many deceased children] MINORET

Notes

One Introduction

1. Denis Diderot, *Œuvres complètes,* ed. Jean Macary, Aram Vartanian, and Jean-Louis Leutrat (Paris: Hermann, 1978), 3: 317.

2. See Ann Jefferson, *Reading Realism in Stendhal* (Cambridge, England: Cambridge Univ. Press, 1988), 15–16. Jefferson quotes an article from the *Mercure français du XIXe siècle* of 1826 in which the word *réalisme* was first used: "This literary doctrine, which is gaining ground every day and which would lead to a faithful imitation not of the masterpieces of art but of the originals that nature offers us, could very well be called *realism:* it would be, according to appearances, the dominant literature of the nineteenth century, the literature of the true."

3. Wolfgang Iser, "Representation: A Performative Act," in *The Aims of Representation: Subject/Text/History,* ed. Murray Krieger (New York: Columbia Univ. Press, 1987), 227.

4. Brian T. Fitch similarly notes the role of connotations—secondary meanings—that bring about the impression of a certain reality, the presentification of the signified. See *Reflections in the Mind's Eye* (Toronto: Univ. of Toronto Press, 1991), 9.

5. Sandy Petrey, "The Realist Speech Act, Mimesis, Performance and the Facts in Fiction," *Neohelicon* 15, no. 2 (1988): 17–18.

6. Albert Béguin, *Balzac. Le Livre du centenaire,* collected in Martin Kanes, ed., *Critical Essays on Honoré de Balzac* (Boston: G. K. Hall, 1990), 123.

7. Alexis Tadié, "La Fiction et ses usages: Analyse pragmatique du concept de fiction," *Poétique,* no. 113 (1998): 120.

8. Roland Barthes, *Leçon,* in *Œuvres complètes,* ed. Eric Marty (Paris: Seuil, 1995), 3: 806.

9. Stendhal, *Le Rouge et le noir* (Paris: GF-Flammarion, 1964), 398.

10. Krzysztof Jarosz, "De la mythologie du réel à la mythologisation de l'écriture critique," in *Mythologies de l'écriture et roman,* ed. Jean Bessière (Paris: Lettres Modernes, 1995), 67.

11. Michael Riffaterre, "L'Illusion référentielle," in *Littérature et réalité,* by Roland Barthes, Leo Bersani, Philippe Hamon, Michael Riffaterre, and Ian Watt (Paris: Seuil, 1982), 93.

12. Gérard Genette, "Frontières du récit," in *Figures II* (Paris: Seuil, 1969), 56.

13. Maurice Ménard, " '. . . la belle et large vallée du Couesnon . . .': Thème géographique et motif romanesque dans *Les Chouans* de Balzac," in *Vendée, Chouannerie, Littérature* (Angers: Presses de l'Université d'Angers, 1986), 251.

14. *Prétexte: Roland Barthes,* ed. Antoine Compagnon (Paris: UGE, 1978), 415.

15. Paul de Man, *Blindness and Insight: Essays in the Rhetoric of Contemporary Criticism* (Minneapolis: Univ. of Minnesota Press, 1983), 12.

16. Roland Barthes, "Réponses," *Tel Quel*, no. 47 (1971): 103.

17. Roland Barthes, "Tables rondes," in *Œuvres complètes*, ed. Eric Marty (Paris: Seuil, 1993), 1: 802–4.

18. Paul de Man, *Allegories of Reading* (New Haven: Yale Univ. Press, 1979), 109.

19. Christopher Norris, *Derrida* (Cambridge, Mass.: Harvard Univ. Press, 1987), 54.

20. Bernard Comment, *Roland Barthes, vers le neutre* (Paris: Christian Bourgois, 1991), 247.

21. Michael Riffaterre, Glossary, *Fictional Truth* (Baltimore: Johns Hopkins Univ. Press, 1990), 130.

22. Roland Barthes, *Sade, Fourier, Loyola* (Paris: Seuil, 1971), 41.

23. Shlomith Rimmon-Kenan, *Narrative Fiction: Contemporary Poetics* (New York: Methuen, 1983), 33.

24. Benveniste writes: "Reference is an integral part of the enunciation." *Problèmes de linguistique générale* (Paris: Gallimard, 1974), 2: 82.

25. Louis Hjelmslev, *Prolégomènes à une théorie du langage* (Paris: Minuit, 1968–71), 70–71, 73, 77.

26. Oswald Ducrot and Tzvetan Todorov, *Dictionnaire encyclopédique des sciences du langage* (Paris: Seuil, 1972), 335.

27. Edwin Duval, "'Et puis, quelles nouvelles?': The Project of Marguerite's Unfinished Decameron," in *Critical Tales. New Studies of the* Heptameron *and Early Modern Culture,* ed. John D. Lyons and Mary B. McKinley (Philadelphia: Univ. of Pennsylvania Press, 1993), 241.

28. The editor of Philippe de Vigneulles's tales gave the title *Cent nouvelles nouvelles* to the sole manuscript, in defiance of indications strongly suggesting that the title Philippe had in mind was *Les Cent nouvelles ou contes joyeux.* See my article, "Le Titre des nouvelles de Philippe de Vigneulles: Un éclaircissement," *Bibliothèque d'Humanisme et Renaissance* 39 (1977): 91–95.

29. Laurent Versini, Notes, in Laclos, *Œuvres complètes* (Paris: Gallimard [Pléiade], 1979), 1177.

30. Lucette Pérol, "Les Avatars du lecteur dans la genèse d'un roman: Diderot, *La Religieuse* et le 'charmant marquis,'" in *Le Lecteur et la lecture dans l'œuvre,* ed. Alain Montandon (Clermont-Ferrand: Université de Clermont-Ferrand, 1982), 101–14.

31. Carol Sherman, "Changing Spaces," in *Diderot: Digression and Dispersion,* ed. Jack Undank and Herbert Josephs (Lexington, Ky.: French Forum, 1984), 228.

32. Lucien Dällenbach, *La Canne de Balzac* (Paris: Corti, 1996), 12. *Readable* refers to Barthes's *S/Z.*

𝒯ᴡᴏ   Fiction and the Supplement in the *Heptaméron*

1. All quotations from the *Heptaméron* are from the edition by Michel François (Paris: Classiques Garnier, 1967); the twenty-fourth tale is on pp. 193–202.

2. See the edition of the de Thou manuscript by Yves Le Hir, under the title *Nouvelles* (Paris: Presses Universitaires de France, 1967).

3. M.-M. de La Garanderie, *Le Dialogue des romanciers: Une nouvelle lecture de L'Heptaméron de Marguerite de Navarre* (Paris: Minard, 1977), 11.

4. Gisèle Mathieu-Castellani, *La Conversation conteuse: Les Nouvelles de Marguerite de Navarre* (Paris: Presses Universitaires de France, 1992), 38–39.

5. Yves Delègue has rightly insisted on the extent to which dissimulation character-izes the tales, in "La Présence et ses doubles dans l'*Heptaméron*," *Bibliothèque d'Humanisme et Renaissance* 52 (1990): 278–80. Colette H. Winn summarizes the multiple ambiguities of "le parler," or speaking, in her article, "'La Loi du non-parler' dans l'*Heptaméron* de Marguerite de Navarre," *Romance Quarterly* 33, no. 2 (1986): 165. John D. Lyons demonstrates the association between dissimulation and the heart in "The 'Cueur' in the *Heptaméron*: the Ideology of Concealment," in *Les Visages et les voix de Marguerite de Navarre,* ed. Marcel Tetel (Paris: Klincksieck, 1995), 107–21, especially 112.

6. As Martha C. Perrigaud has reminded us, speech is on the side of pleasure, silence aligned with discipline and wisdom. See "Oisille's Tale of the Duchesse de Bourgogne: The Power of the Word," *Degré Second* 6 (July 1982): 26–27. Strong evidence can be found in the forty-seventh tale, told also by Dagoucin, in which the word *parler* suggests sexuality.

7. Roland Barthes, *Le Plaisir du texte* (Paris: Seuil, 1973), 31.

8. Philippe de Lajarte speaks of *consonance* when the voice of the narrator ap-proaches that of the character and *dissonance* when the narrator's voice distances itself from the character's, on the lexical, semantic, syntactic, symbolic, and axiological levels. See "La Structure vocale des psychorécits dans les nouvelles de l'*Heptaméron*," in *Les Visages et les voix de Marguerite de Navarre*, 81.

9. Patricia Cholakian interestingly suggests that a man's silence stems from male deferral to female lack of desire in *Rape and Writing in the* Heptaméron *of Marguerite de Navarre* (Carbondale: Southern Illinois Univ. Press, 1991), 37.

10. That is, the price of buying these territories is cheaper than the cost of winning them in battle. From Seyssel, *Histoire de Louis XII*. The antonym *bon marchand* means *gaillard, joyeux compagnon*, quite the opposite of the respectful courtly lover. *Marchand* in this sense is delightfully glossed by Dagoucin's commentary on the seventieth tale: if women did not love, men might as well as be merchants, "et, en lieu d'acquerir honneur, ne penser que à amasser du bien" [and, instead of acquiring honor, think only of amassing property] (419).

11. Marcel Tetel has given a concise rhetorical analysis of Elisor's poem, particularly of the role of time, in "The Rhetoric of Lyricism in the *Heptameron*," in *Critical Tales. New Studies of the* Heptameron *and Early Modern Culture*, ed. John D. Lyons and Mary B. McKinley (Philadelphia: Univ. of Pennsylvania Press, 1993), 47.

12. André Tournon describes this phrase as Parlamente's "tacit approval" of Dagou-cin, in his "Rules of the Game," in *Critical Tales,* 191.

13. Françoise Charpentier, "Désir et parole dans les devis de l'*Heptaméron*," in *Les Visages et les voix de Marguerite de Navarre,* 44.

14. Robert D. Cottrell, "Inmost Cravings: The Logic of Desire in the *Heptameron*," in *Critical Tales,* 10.

15. François's edition gives: "Retournez là d'où vous êtes partie, ô mon âme, les épreuves de ma vie sont si pénibles" [Return whence you came, o my soul, the trials of my life are so painful]—a distant translation at best.

16. Michel François believes the "Madame Marguerite" named here, in this description of the French court, is the author herself, but Simone de Reyff, in her edition, identifies her as the sister of Henri and daughter of François I. See editorial material in *Heptaméron,* ed. Simone de Reyff (Paris: Flammarion, 1982), 501: "As for Madame Marguerite, it is likely she refers to Marguerite de France, daughter of François I."

17. The "true" story of the proto-narrative contributes to what Kazimierz Kupisz interestingly calls "a veritable psychic autobiography" in "Autour de la technique de l' 'Heptaméron,' " in *La Nouvelle française à la Renaissance,* ed. Lionello Sozzi (Geneva: Slatkine, 1981), 394. In his article in the same volume, "Le Prologue de l' 'Heptaméron' et le processus de production de l'œuvre," Philippe de Lajarte minutely examines what he calls "a mask placed quite uselessly, it seems, on the beginning of the discourse" (404).

18. Delègue (274) suggests the gift may be oral. However, the analogy with images and paternosters and the reference to the eyes of the French court, plus the description of its original intent to do "the same [as Boccaccio]" and to "*write* no tale that is not a true story" (9), are sufficient indication of a written gift. And would the *devisants* have sat down to replay their oh-so-spontaneous conversations at the French court? Or, as John D. Lyons and Mary B. McKinley wrote in the epilogue to *Critical Tales,* "How do the storytellers reproduce verbatim—or improvise to perfection—texts of more than 150 decasyllabic verses (tale 13) or a complex polymetric translation from the Italian (tale 19) while telling the story orally under circumstances that do not lend themselves to extensive preparation?" (273).

19. *Voice* and *place* are given and taken, the two terms of the exchange. *Voice* predominates by far: forty-six times in tales 1 to 57, none in tales 58 to 72; but *place* and *lieu* (stead) occur twelve times in the last fifteen tales, after six times in tales 1 to 57. This change marks a progressive recognition of voice giving as place holding.

20. Antoine Compagnon, ed., *Prétexte: Roland Barthes* (Paris: UGE, 1978), 240–41.

21. Gisèle Mathieu-Castellani, "L'*Heptaméron:* l'Ère du soupçon," in *Les Visages et les voix de Marguerite de Navarre,* 134.

22. Claude-Gilbert Dubois, "Fonds mythique et jeu des sens dans le 'Prologue' de L'*Heptaméron,*" in *Études Seiziémistes offertes à Monsieur le Professeur V.-L. Saulnier* (Geneva: Droz, 1980), 160.

23. The thirteenth tale contains a self-reflexive letter about the alternative between speaking and dying. Addressing an allegorical figure called "le Parler," the writer has him speak his love to the woman. This speech, a replacement for the man's own speaking, is doubly mediated: by the letter writing and by the prosopopeia of the Parler—in all, a brilliant case of rhetorical supplementarity.

24. Colette H. Winn, "An Instance of Narrative Seduction: The *Heptaméron* of

Marguerite de Navarre," *Symposium* 39 (1985): 217–26; Philippe de Lajarte, " 'L'Hep-taméron' et la naissance du récit moderne: Essai de lecture épistémologique d'un discours narratif," *Littérature* 17 (1975): 31–42.

Three   Listen, Hear

1. Denis Diderot, *Jacques le fataliste et son maître,* ed. Simone Lecointre and Jean Le Galliot (Geneva: Droz, 1976), 26.

2. "What on earth! You who are of Diderot's sect and mine, don't you read the blank spaces in books? Read the blanks, read what I didn't write and which is neverthe-less there." So said l'abbé Galiani to Suard, on September 8, 1770—sage advice for any reader of Diderot. The abbé is quoted by Eric Walter in *Colloque International Diderot (1713–1784),* ed. Anne-Marie Chouillet (Paris: Aux Amateurs de Livres, 1985), 208.

3. Roland Barthes, *S/Z* (Paris: Seuil, 1970), 138. Charles Batson, in unpublished materials, has proposed *oyeur.* A stimulating reading of this episode, and of listening in relation to *jouissance,* or rapture, can be found in Jean Starobinski's contribution to the 1984 colloquium on Diderot, "Du pied de la favorite au genou de Jacques," in *Colloque International Diderot (1713–1784),* 359–80.

4. Denis Diderot, *Lettre sur les sourds et muets, Diderot Studies* 7 (1965): 45.

5. Roland Barthes, *Le Plaisir du texte* (Paris: Seuil, 1973), 41–42.

6. See Armine Kotin Mortimer, *The Gentlest Law: Roland Barthes's* The Pleasure of the Text (New York: Lang, 1989), 110–11.

7. Roland Barthes, "De l'œuvre au texte," in *Le Bruissement de la langue* (Paris: Seuil, 1984), 73.

8. Choderlos de Laclos, *Les Liaisons dangereuses* (Paris: Garnier-Flammarion, 1964). Note that all quotations from the novel include the page number and the number of the letter.

9. Henri Coulet, "Les Lettres occultées des 'Liaisons dangereuses,' " *Revue d'His-toire Littéraire de la France* 82 (1982): 610.

10. Joyce Lowrie has demonstrated the importance of Prévan as a mirror of Val-mont and of the Prévan episode as a reflection on the novel in "Pretexts and Reflec-tions: A Reflection upon Pre-Texts in *Les Liaisons dangereuses,*" *Modern Language Stud-ies* 18 (1988): 150–64.

11. Judith Spencer, "Spécularité scripturale et contrefaçon littéraire: Pour une lec-ture iconoclaste des *Liaisons dangereuses,*" in *L'Épreuve du lecteur: Livres et lectures dans le roman d'Ancien Régime,* ed. Jan Herman and Paul Pelckmans (Louvain: Éditions Peeters, 1995), 459.

12. Jean-Jacques Rousseau, *Les Confessions,* ed. Jacques Voisine (Paris: Garnier, 1964), 165–66.

13. Denis Diderot, *Encyclopédie* (Paris: Bordas, 1985), 138.

14. See, for instance, Jean-Baptiste Louis Gresset's play *Le Méchant* (1747); Mme de Merteuil quotes an alexandrine from this play in letter 63.

15. I am borrowing the term "ingérence" from Ross Chambers, who uses the

French word. Like Chambers, I think that it leads necessarily to death. See "Reading and the Voice of Death: Balzac's 'Le Message,'" *Nineteenth-Century French Studies* 18 (1990): 410.

16. Jean Rousset, "Les Lecteurs indiscrets," in *Laclos et le libertinage. 1782–1982. Actes du Colloque du bicentenaire des* Liaisons dangereuses (Paris: Presses Universitaires de France, 1983), 94.

17. Roland Barthes, "Sur la lecture," in *Le Bruissement de la langue*, 44–45.

18. Paul de Man, "The Rhetoric of Blindness: Jacques Derrida's Reading of Rousseau," in *Blindness and Insight: Essays in the Rhetoric of Contemporary Criticism* (Minneapolis: Univ. of Minnesota Press, 1983), 103, 106.

19. Choderlos de Laclos, *Œuvres complètes*, ed. Laurent Versini (Paris: Gallimard [Pléiade], 1979), 1411; Joan DeJean, *Literary Fortifications: Rousseau, Laclos, Sade* (Princeton: Princeton Univ. Press, 1984), 255.

20. Peter V. Conroy, Jr., *Intimate, Intrusive and Triumphant: Readers in the* Liaisons Dangereuses (Amsterdam: John Benjamins, 1987), 49–50.

21. Jacques Derrida, "Du tout," in *La Carte postale* (Paris: Aubier-Flammarion, 1980), 543. See also "Le facteur de la vérité," 441–524.

22. I do not wish to engage in the fruitful debate about Mme de La Pommeraye's morals, and the multiple possibilities of interpretation Diderot conscientiously included in his text; for my purposes, it is enough that some consider these two protagonists deceitful.

23. Marguerite de Navarre, *L'Heptaméron,* ed. Michel François (Paris: Classiques Garnier, 1967), 176–86.

24. Jean Catrysse, *Diderot et la mystification* (Paris: Nizet, 1970), 73.

25. Carol Sherman writes, "*La Religieuse* may be the most complex example of postponement, that is, of both proleptic and analeptic narrative spaces." See her "Changing Spaces," in *Diderot: Digression and Dispersion: A Bicentennial Tribute,* ed. Jack Undank and Herbert Josephs (Lexington, Ky.: French Forum, 1984), 227. Sherman summarizes brilliantly, in a page and a half (227–28), the dizzying effects of breaking the frame—which raises the question of the limits between fictive and nonfictive spaces and the subversion of this opposition itself.

26. Found on the last page in those editions that publish the preface after the rest of the novel, it is in any case last in the preface.

27. Quotations from Diderot's *La Religieuse* (Paris: Garnier-Flammarion, 1968) are referenced in the text.

28. Rosalina de la Carrera, *Success in Circuit Lies* (Stanford: Stanford Univ. Press, 1991), 18.

29. He is described, in the preface, inundated with tears as he writes the nun's story, explaining: "Je me désole d'un conte que je me fais" [I am disconsolate because of a tale I'm telling myself] (211).

30. Vivienne Mylne, *Diderot: La Religieuse* (London: Grant & Cutler, 1981), 43. Other readers have rightly stressed the role of seeing and being seen, interpretations

that I largely accept (see Jay Caplan, *Framed Narratives: Diderot's Genealogy of the Beholder* [Minneapolis: Univ. of Minnesota Press, 1985]; Denise Bourassa Knight, "Diderot's *La Religieuse*: Suzanne Simonin and the 'Youthful' Men Who See Her," *Nottingham French Studies* 24, no. 1 [1985]: 15–25; and n. 31); I am primarily interested in the auditory channel. See also M. Simonton's, "Suzanne's 'cri animal': Aural and Musical Imagery in Diderot's *La Religieuse*," *University of Toronto Quarterly* 55 (1986): 328–41.

31. Corinna Gepner, "L'Autoportrait de la narratrice dans *La Religieuse*: Les Ruses du regard," *Recherches sur Diderot et sur* l'Encyclopédie 17 (October 1994): 55–67.

32. P. W. Byrne, "The Form of Paradox: A Critical Study of Diderot's *La Religieuse*," *Studies on Voltaire and the Eighteenth Century* 319 (1994): 219.

33. Jean-Claude Bonnet, "Revoir *La Religieuse*," in *Interpréter Diderot Aujourd'hui*, Colloque de Cerisy, ed. E. de Fontenay and J. Proust (n.p.: Le Sycomore, 1984), 68.

34. Roland Barthes, "Écoute," in *L'Obvie et l'obtus* (Paris: Seuil, 1982), 221.

35. Such is also the reader's experience with Balzac's *Une Ténébreuse affaire*, the cause of which was moved, in proofs, to the final chapter.

36. Gisèle Mathieu-Castellani, "L'*Heptaméron*: l'Ère du soupçon," in *Les Visages et les voix de Marguerite de Navarre,* ed. Marcel Tetel (Paris: Klincksieck, 1995), 129.

Four   Semiotic Structures and the Unity of Composition

1. Oscar Wilde, "The Decay of Lying," in *Critical Theory Since Plato,* ed. Hazard Adams (New York: Harcourt, Brace, Jovanovich, 1971), 681. The context is an argument in support of the principle that life imitates art.

2. Martin Kanes, *Balzac's Comedy of Words* (Princeton: Princeton Univ. Press, 1975), 191.

3. In *Balzacian Montage* (Toronto: Univ. of Toronto Press, 1994), Allan H. Pasco has forcefully shown how Balzac created at least the parts that would construct a whole conceptual world.

4. Julia Kristeva, *Revolution in Poetic Language* (New York: Columbia Univ. Press, 1984), 86–89.

5. Roland Barthes, *Roland Barthes* (Paris: Seuil, 1975), 95.

6. See my article "*La Maison Nucingen,* ou le récit financier," *Romanic Review* 69 (1978): 60–71. See also three short discussions in my "Mimetic Figures of Semiosis," in *Repression and Expression: Social Codes and Literary Visions in Nineteenth-Century France,* ed. Carrol Coates (New York: Lang, 1996), 47–54. Ross Chambers, in *Story and Situation* (Minneapolis: Univ. of Minnesota Press, 1984), 33, writes of figural embeddings, which are representative in some sense of art or the production and reception of narrative.

7. The reference is to Nietzsche. See Paul de Man's *Allegories of Reading* (New Haven: Yale Univ. Press, 1979), 106.

8. Jean Ricardou, *Problèmes du nouveau roman* (Paris: Seuil, 1967), 55.

9. Honoré de Balzac, *Mémoires de deux jeunes mariées,* ed. Arlette Michel (Paris: Garnier-Flammarion, 1979), 306, 308. George Sand is quoted in editorial material in this pocket edition of the novel.

10. Arlette Michel, "Balzac juge du féminisme. Des *Mémoires de deux jeunes mariées* à *Honorine,*" *L'Année Balzacienne* (1973): 187.

11. Honoré de Balzac, *Mémoires de deux jeunes mariées, La Comédie humaine,* ed. Roger Pierrot (Paris: Gallimard [Pléiade], 1976), 1: 196. Note that parenthetical references to Balzac's novels omit the volume number.

12. I use the Sartrian word *tourniquet* to refer to a situation in which meaning reverses itself radically, just as one finds oneself suddenly on another side of the gate upon going through a turnstile, and just as suddenly returns to the first side on continuing around. In this context we can say: one spin puts us into fiction; spin again: it's reality; but yet another spin, it's fiction again; but let the spiral climb, and a higher reality emerges.

13. Honoré de Balzac, *Modeste Mignon, La Comédie humaine,* ed. Maurice Regard (Paris: Gallimard [Pléiade], 1976), 1: 553. Further references are in the text.

14. Roland Barthes, "Sur la lecture," in *Le Bruissement de la langue* (Paris: Seuil, 1984), 37.

15. Roland Barthes, *Le Plaisir du texte* (Paris: Seuil, 1973), 89.

16. *Este* signals nobility and power, wealth and lineage, with an added flavor of slightly exotic southern warmth: the Italian Este family. A major intertext of the second part, Goethe's *Torquato Tasso,* concerns Léonore d'Este, the princess loved by Tasso and his rival Antonio.

17. The other three are Constance Birotteau's, Ursule Mirouët's, and Eve Séchard's, according to Arlette Michel, *Le Mariage et l'amour dans l'œuvre romanesque d'Honoré de Balzac* (Paris: Champion, 1976), 3: 1528. Michel also concludes that it is impossible to reconcile the ideal and the positive (3: 1531); but one can join them by ruses, traps, and surprises. In my reading, ruses are those of writing.

18. Arlette Michel, "Balzac et la rhétorique: Modernité et tradition," *L'Année Balzacienne* (1988): 266.

19. Anne-Marie Meininger, "Préface," in *Modeste Mignon* (Paris: Gallimard [Folio], 1982), 29.

20. André Vandegans, "Fascinations et nostalgies balzaciennes dans *Modeste Mignon*: du propos à l'effet," *Bulletin de l'Académie Royale de Langue et de Littérature Françaises* 58 (1980): 20–55.

21. Honoré de Balzac, *Ursule Mirouët, La Comédie humaine,* ed. Madeleine Ambrière-Fargeaud (Paris: Gallimard [Pléiade], 1976), 3: 976. References are in the text.

22. *Le Petit Robert* (Paris: Société du Nouveau Littré, 1972), article "héritier."

23. Georges Poulet, "Balzac," in *Les Métamorphoses du cercle* (Paris: Plon, 1961), 209.

24. Thierry Bodin, "Généalogie de la médiocratie dans *Les Paysans*," *L'Année Bal-zacienne* (1978): 91–101.

25. Nicole Mozet, *Balzac au pluriel* (Paris: Presses Universitaires de France, 1990), 53.

26. Honoré de Balzac, *Ursule Mirouët*, ed. Madeleine Ambrière-Fargeaud (Paris: Gallimard [Folio], 1981), 389.

27. Nicole Mozet, "*Ursule Mirouët* ou le test du bâtard," in *Balzac, Œuvres com-plètes: Le Moment de* La Comédie humaine, ed. Claude Duchet and Isabelle Tournier (Saint-Denis: Presses Universitaires de Vincennes, 1993), 217.

28. Nicole Mozet, *La Ville de province dans l'œuvre de Balzac: L'Espace romanesque: Fantasmes et idéologie* (Paris: Société d'Édition d'Enseignement Supérieur, 1982), 219.

29. Allan H. Pasco, "Ursule through the Glass Lightly," *French Review* 65 (1991): 36–45.

30. Françoise Gaillard, "La Science: Modèle ou vérité. Réflexions sur l'*avant-propos* à *La Comédie humaine*," in *Balzac: L'Invention du roman*, ed. Claude Duchet and Jacques Neefs (Paris: Belfond, 1982), 71.

31. Arguing for a new form of nobility against his mother's prejudices, Savinien de Portenduère uses the telling metaphor "une chimère" (885) to designate the old system. The monstrous, composite chimera figures another contrast to the harmonious unity of Ursule.

32. Honoré de Balzac, *La Peau de chagrin, La Comédie humaine*, ed. Pierre Citron (Paris: Gallimard [Pléiade], 1979), 10: 75.

33. S. de Sacy quotes the *Conversations de Goethe pendant les dernières années de sa vie, 1822–1832*, collected by Eckermann, trans. Emile Délerot (Paris: Charpentier, 1883), vol. 2. See S. de Sacy, "Balzac, Geoffroy Saint-Hilaire et l'unité de composition," *Mercure de France*, 303, no. 1018 (1948): 303.

Five   Breaking the Book

1. For a comprehensive discussion of features of self-conscious fiction, see chapter 2 of Brian Stonehill, *The Self-Conscious Novel: Artifice in Fiction from Joyce to Pynchon* (Philadelphia: Univ. of Pennsylvania Press, 1988), 19–31.

2. Roland Barthes, "Écrire, verbe intransitif?" in *Le Bruissement de la langue* (Paris: Seuil, 1984), 27.

3. Philippe Sollers, *La Guerre du goût* (Paris: Gallimard, 1994), 11–12.

4. Roland Champagne, *Philippe Sollers* (Amsterdam: Rodopi, 1996), 23. Here is the translation of the French quoted: "*The novel is the way this society talks to itself,* the way the individual *has to live his life* to be accepted in it."

5. Philippe Forest, *Philippe Sollers* (Paris: Seuil, 1992), 256.

6. *Le Bulletin Gallimard*, no. 417 (1997): 13.

7. Philippe Sollers, *Carnet de nuit* (Paris: Plon, 1989), 64.

8. Philippe Sollers, *Femmes* (Paris: Gallimard [Folio], 1983), 11.

9. Philippe Forest, *Histoire de Tel Quel, 1960–1982* (Paris: Seuil, 1995), 590.

10. Sollers is the author of a study called *De Kooning, vite* (Paris: Éditions de la Différence, 1988).

11. A note on realism, at least in a popular sense: Two messages posted on Balzac-Liste in October 1996 about Jean-Edern Hallier's continuing *frasques,* his self-promotions and his distortions of fact, give an image of Hallier that so closely resembles the Boris of *Femmes* that they could have supplied a paragraph or two of the novel. Hallier died in 1997.

12. Katherine C. Kurk, "Philippe Sollers," in *The Contemporary Novel in France,* ed. William Thompson (Gainesville: Univ. Press of Florida, 1995), 133.

13. Jean Louis Houdebine points out that "the libertine, satanic inversion of the evangelical group (the speaker's twelve women) mentioned in *Femmes* . . . is found in *Paradis,* p. 243!" in "Le Souffle hyperbolique de Philippe Sollers," in *Excès de langages (Hölderlin, Joyce, Duns Scot, Hopkins, Cantor, Sollers)* (Paris: Denoël, 1984), 347.

14. Philippe Sollers, *Le Rire de Rome: Entretiens avec Frans De Haes* (Paris: Gallimard, 1992), 71–73.

15. Philippe Sollers, *Carnet de nuit,* 126: "Le narrateur de *Femmes* n'est pas celui de *Portrait du Joueur.* Lequel n'est pas celui du *Cœur Absolu.* Lequel n'est pas non plus celui des *Folies Françaises.* Ce dernier n'est pas le narrateur du *Lys d'Or.* On travaille dans les IRM, identités rapprochées multiples." [The narrator of *Femmes* is not the one in *Portrait du Joueur.* Who is not the one in *Le Cœur Absolu.* Who is also not the one in *Les Folies Françaises.* This last is not the narrator of *Le Lys d'Or.* I'm working in MRIs, multiple related identities].

16. "L'Étrangère" was the title of Roland Barthes's excellent analysis of Julia Kristeva, now published in *Le Bruissement de la langue,* 197–200.

17. Sollers may be alluding to an essay by Leo Strauss, "Persecution and the Art of Writing," *Persecution and the Art of Writing* (Glencoe, Ill.: Free Press, 1952), 25. The following observations are particularly pertinent to Sollers's project: "Persecution, then, gives rise to a peculiar technique of writing, and therewith to a peculiar type of literature, in which the truth about all crucial things is presented exclusively between the lines. That literature is addressed, not to all readers, but to trustworthy and intelligent readers only. [. . .] The fact which makes this literature possible can be expressed in the axiom that thoughtless men are careless readers, and only thoughtful men are careful readers."

18. Jean Ricardou, *Problèmes du nouveau roman* (Paris: Seuil, 1967), 111; Roland Barthes, "Introduction à l'analyse structurale des récits," in *Œuvres complètes* (Paris: Seuil, 1994), 2: 103.

19. Serge Doubrovsky, "Autobiographie/Vérité/Psychanalyse," *L'Esprit Créateur* 20, no. 3 (1980): 90. Doubrovsky credits neither Ricardou nor Barthes.

20. Serge Doubrovsky, "Sartre: Autobiographie/autofiction," *Revue des Sciences Humaines,* no. 224 (1991): 17.

21. "Les Prix littéraires," *Le Monde* (28 November 1989): 17.

22. Ross Chambers, "Reading and the Voice of Death: Balzac's 'Le Message,'" *Nineteenth-Century French Studies* 18 (1990): 408–9.

23. Serge Doubrovsky, "Textes en main," in *Autofictions & Cie,* ed. Serge Doubrovsky, Jacques Lecarme, and Philippe Lejeune (Paris: Université Paris X, 1993), 214.

24. Jeanine Parisier Plottel, "The Poetics of Autobiography in Paul Valéry," *L'Esprit Créateur* 20, no. 3 (1980): 38.

25. Renée Kingcaid, "Review of *Le Livre brisé,*" *Review of Contemporary Fiction* 12, no. 2 (1992): 239.

26. Marie Miguet-Ollagnier, "'La Saveur Sartre' du *Livre brisé,*" in *Autobiographie et avant-garde,* ed. Alfred Hornung and Ernstpeter Ruhe (Tübingen, Germany: Gunter Narr Verlag, 1992), 155.

27. Serge Doubrovsky, *Le Livre brisé* (Paris: Grasset, 1989), 220.

28. Hélène Jaccomard, *Lecteur et lecture dans l'autobiographie française contemporaine. Violette Leduc, Françoise d'Eaubonne, Serge Doubrovsky, Marguerite Yourcenar* (Geneva: Droz, 1993), 88.

29. Serge Doubrovsky, *L'Après-vivre* (Paris: Grasset, 1994), 24–25.

30. Alain Buisine, "Serge Doubrovsky ou l'autobiographie postmoderne," in *Autobiographie et avant-garde,* 163–64.

31. Stéphane Mallarmé, *Quant au livre,* in *Œuvres complètes* (Paris: Gallimard [Pléiade], 1945), 378.

32. Serge Doubrovsky, *La Vie l'instant* (Paris: Balland, 1985), 11.

33. Serge Doubrovsky, "L'Initiative aux maux: Écrire sa psychanalyse," in *Parcours critique* (Paris: Galilée, 1980), 190.

34. See Diderot's *Discours sur la poésie dramatique,* cited in Vivian Mylne, *Diderot: La Religieuse* (London: Grant & Cutler, 1981), 24.

35. Buisine (passim) stresses the formative role of Serge's Sartrian reading; there is no novelistic writing that is not also critical writing.

36. Marie Laurier, "Doubrovsky tel qu'en lui-même," *Le Devoir* (3 March 1990): sect. D, p. 1.

37. See Renée Kingcaid, "Romancing the Tome: The Seduction of Intertext in Doubrovsky's *Un Amour de soi,*" *Sub-Stance* 70 (1993): 31–32.

38. Michael Riffaterre, *Fictional Truth* (Baltimore: Johns Hopkins Univ. Press, 1990), 130.

39. Roland Barthes, *Le Grain de la voix* (Paris: Seuil, 1981), 225.

40. Ross Chambers has made the notion of a narrative's *point* central to his study of the social fact that the narrative mediates human relationships and derives its meaning from them, in *Story and Situation* (Minneapolis: Univ. of Minnesota Press, 1984).

41. My use of these terms stems from my reading of Paul de Man's "Excuses (*Confessions*)," in *Allegories of Reading* (New Haven: Yale Univ. Press, 1979), 278–301.

42. Martine Chard-Hutchinson writes: "Ilse's death breaks up the man as much as the writer because it makes fiction and autobiography coincide, forever destroying the

distance between the fantasy of death and its reality." "Mémoire, réticences et élans: *Le Livre brisé,* Serge Doubrovsky," in *Études romanesques 2. Modernité, Fiction, Déconstruction,* ed. Jean Bessière (Paris: Lettres Modernes, 1994), 170.

43. I am indebted to my colleague and friend Mireille Rosello for showing me this ironic parallel.

44. Philippe Lejeune, "Le Cas Doubrovsky," in *Moi aussi* (Paris: Seuil, 1986), 64, 68.

45. See Roland Barthes, "Theory of the Text," in *Untying the Text: A Post-Structuralist Reader,* ed. Robert Young (London: Routledge & Kegan Paul, 1981), 36.

46. Steven Ungar, "Rules of the Game: First-Person Singular in des Forêt's *Le Bavard,*" *L'Esprit Créateur* 20, no. 3 (1980): 67.

47. Aliette Armel, "La Tragédie du torero," *Le Magazine Littéraire,* no. 267 (1990): 80.

48. Ludovic Leonelli, "Entretien avec Serge Doubrovsky," *NRV* 3 (Autumn 1997) ⟨http://www.chapitre.com/plus/revues/nrventre.htm⟩ (5 August 1998).

49. Roland Barthes, *Roland Barthes* (Paris: Seuil, 1975), 60.

50. Serge Doubrovsky and John Ireland, "'The Fact Is That Writing Is a Profoundly Immoral Act': An Interview with Serge Doubrovsky," *Genre* 26 (1993): 49.

51. Drunk, Serge hallucinates a figure whom he addresses: "Je balbutie *mais j'ai écrit* m'interrompt *je ne te demande pas ce que tu as écrit mais ce que tu as fait* me redresse réplique *il y a des écrits qui sont des actes* ricanement guttural me percute le tympan *les miens peut-être pas les tiens* NOM DE DIEU SARTRE" [I stammer *but I wrote* interrupts *I'm not asking you what you wrote but what you did* sit up retort *there are writings that are acts* guttural snicker hammers at my eardrum *mine maybe not yours* GOOD GOD SARTRE] (216). Serge's writing obliterates Sartre's contemptuous decree.

52. Christian Charrière, writing in the *Figaro,* makes so many wrong-headed statements about the book and writes such a ludicrous imitation of Doubrovsky's style that his review condemns itself; yet how many share his view that Doubrovsky should have thrown his malediction of a book into the fire, after his wife died? See Christian Charrière, "Le Brise-femme," *Le Figaro Littéraire* (7 September 1989): 15.

53. Compare this brutal real to the "système des contraintes externes brutes" [system of raw external constraints], a kind of Lacanian Real, mentioned in *Fils* (Paris: Galilée, 1977), 420.

54. Radu Turcanu, "Le Désir d'être auteur: Doubrovsky et Sartre en intertexte," *Dalhousie French Studies* 35 (Summer 1996): 80.

55. Jacqueline Piatier, "Le Livre monstre de Serge Doubrovsky," *Le Monde* (8 September 1989): 18.

56. See in particular the volume of essays called *Autofictions & Cie,* for the revised definitions of autofiction.

57. Interview with Philippe Sollers, 23 November 1999.

58. Umberto Eco, *Postscript to The Name of the Rose,* trans. William Weaver (New York: Harcourt, Brace, Jovanovich, 1983), 67.

59. Roland Barthes, *Sollers écrivain* (Paris: Seuil, 1979), 7.

𝒮·ᵥ   The Magic of Realism

1. Julia Kristeva, *Le Langage, cet inconnu. Une Initiation à la linguistique* (Paris: Seuil [Points], 1981), 290.

2. Judith Spencer, "Spécularité scripturale et contrefaçon littéraire: Pour une lecture iconoclaste des *Liaisons dangereuses*," in *L'Épreuve du lecteur: livres et lectures dans le roman d'Ancien Régime,* ed. Jan Herman and Paul Pelckmans (Louvain: Éditions Peeters, 1995), 452.

3. Cf. this psychoanalytically oriented premise articulated by Peter Brooks, in *Psychoanalysis and Storytelling* (Cambridge, England: Blackwell, 1994), 50: "It is my premise that most narratives speak of their transferential condition—of their anxiety concerning their transmissibility, of their need to be heard, of their desire to become the story of the listener as much as of the teller."

4. Michel Butor, "Le Roman comme recherche," in *Répertoire I* (Paris: Minuit, 1960), 8.

5. Jacques Derrida, "Le Facteur de la vérité," in *La Carte postale de Socrate à Freud et au-delà* (Paris: Aubier-Flammarion, 1980), 492.

6. Stéphane Sarkany, "La Réalité en jeu de la critique sociologique," in *Roman, Réalités, Réalismes,* ed. Jean Bessière (Paris: Presses Universitaires de France, 1989), 26.

7. Kendall L. Walton, *Mimesis as Make-Believe: On the Foundations of the Representational Arts* (Cambridge, Mass.: Harvard Univ. Press, 1990), 51.

8. Philippe Hamon, "L'Architecture/le sens/le réel/la représentation," in *Roman, Réalités, Réalismes,* 38.

9. Clément Rosset, *Le Réel, traité de l'idiotie* (Paris: Minuit, 1977), 123.

10. Philippe Sollers, *La Guerre du goût* (Paris: Gallimard, 1994), 238.

11. Philippe Sollers, "Montaigne, le mutant," in *Théorie des exceptions* (Paris: Gallimard, 1986), 19.

12. Ludovic Leonelli, "Entretien avec Serge Doubrovsky," *NRV* 3 (Autumn 1997) (http://www.chapitre.com/plus/revues/nrventre.htm) (5 August 1998).

13. "Doubrovsky actualizes the theme of silence which enervates all autobiographies since Rousseau: there is a dialogue of the deaf between the different instances of the self, and between the hero and the characters of life." Hélène Jaccomard, *Lecteur et lecture dans l'autobiographie française contemporaine. Violette Leduc, Françoise d'Eaubonne, Serge Doubrovsky, Marguerite Yourcenar* (Geneva: Droz, 1993), 440.

14. Of course, the point I make by quoting this passage considerably distorts the views of the Platonist Jesuit, who shows his true classical colors when he writes: "The verisimilar is everything that conforms to public opinion." René Rapin, *Les Réflexions sur la poétique de ce temps et sur les ouvrages des poètes anciens et modernes.* 1674; revised 2nd ed. 1675, ed. E. T. Dubois (Geneva: Droz, 1970), 39, 41.

15. Boileau's precept is found in *L'Art poétique.* Balzac's is in the first preface to *Le Cabinet des Antiques, La Comédie humaine* (Paris: Gallimard [Pléiade], 1976), 4: 961.

16. Philippe Sollers, *Femmes* (Paris: Gallimard [Folio], 1983), 324.

17. Marie-Laure Ryan, "Allegories of Immersion: Virtual Narration in Postmodern Fiction," *Style* 29 (1995): 283.

18. Ross Chambers, "The Etcetera Principle: Narrative and the Paradigmatic," *French Literature Series* 21 (1994): 10.

19. James H. Reid, *Narration and Description in the French Realist Novel. The Temporality of Lying and Forgetting* (Cambridge, England: Cambridge Univ. Press, 1993), 16.

20. Michael Riffaterre, *Fictional Truth* (Baltimore: Johns Hopkins Univ. Press, 1990), 111.

21. Paul de Man, *Allegories of Reading* (New Haven: Yale Univ. Press, 1979), 10.

Bibliography

Armel, Aliette. "La Tragédie du torero." *Le Magazine Littéraire,* no. 267 (1990): 80.

Balzac, Honoré de. *La Comédie humaine.* Ed. Pierre-Georges Castex et al., 12 vols. Paris: Gallimard [Pléiade], 1976–81.

———. *Mémoires de deux jeunes mariées.* Ed. Arlette Michel. Paris: Garnier-Flammarion, 1979.

———. *Ursule Mirouët.* Ed. Madeleine Ambrière-Fargeaud. Paris: Gallimard [Folio], 1981.

Barthes, Roland. *Le Bruissement de la langue.* Paris: Seuil, 1984.

———. *Le Grain de la voix. Entretiens 1962–1980.* Paris: Seuil, 1981.

———. "Introduction à l'analyse structurale des récits." In *Œuvres complètes.* Ed. Eric Marty. Paris: Seuil, 1994. 2: 74–103.

———. *Leçon,* in *Œuvres complètes.* Ed. Eric Marty. Paris: Seuil, 1995. 3: 801–14.

———. *L'Obvie et l'obtus.* Paris: Seuil, 1982.

———. *Le Plaisir du texte.* Paris: Seuil, 1973.

———. "Réponses." *Tel Quel,* no. 47 (1971): 89–107.

———. *Roland Barthes.* Paris: Seuil, 1975.

———. *Sade, Fourier, Loyola.* Paris: Seuil, 1971.

———. *Sollers écrivain.* Paris: Seuil, 1979.

———. *S/Z.* Paris: Seuil, 1970.

———. "Tables rondes," in *Œuvres complètes.* Ed. Eric Marty. Paris: Seuil, 1993. 1: 802–4.

———. "Theory of the Text," in *Untying the Text: A Post-Structuralist Reader.* Ed. Robert Young. London: Routledge & Kegan Paul, 1981. 31–47.

Béguin, Albert. *Balzac. Le Livre du centenaire.* Paris: Flammarion, 1952. Quoted in Martin Kanes, ed. *Critical Essays on Honoré de Balzac.* Boston: G. K. Hall, 1990. 120–25.

Benveniste, Émile. *Problèmes de linguistique générale.* 2 vols. Paris: Gallimard, 1966, 1974.

Bodin, Thierry. "Généalogie de la médiocratie dans *Les Paysans.*" *L'Année Balzacienne* (1978): 91–101.

Bonnet, Jean-Claude. "Revoir *La Religieuse,*" in *Interpréter Diderot Aujourd'hui.* Ed. E. de Fontenay and J. Proust. Le Sycomore, 1984. 59–79.

Brooks, Peter. *Psychoanalysis and Storytelling.* Cambridge, England: Blackwell, 1994.

Buisine, Alain. "Serge Doubrovsky ou l'autobiographie postmoderne," in *Autobiographie et avant-garde.* Ed. Alfred Hornung and Ernstpeter Ruhe. Tübingen, Germany: Gunter Narr Verlag, 1992. 159–68.

Le Bulletin Gallimard, no. 417, 1997.

Butor, Michel. "Le Roman comme recherche," in *Répertoire I.* Paris: Minuit, 1960. 7–11.

Byrne, P. W. "The Form of Paradox: A Critical Study of Diderot's *La Religieuse.*" *Studies on Voltaire and the Eighteenth Century* 319 (1994): 169–293.

Caplan, Jay. *Framed Narratives: Diderot's Genealogy of the Beholder.* Minneapolis: Univ. of Minnesota Press, 1985.

Catrysse, Jean. *Diderot et la mystification.* Paris: Nizet, 1970.

Chambers, Ross. "The Etcetera Principle: Narrative and the Paradigmatic." *French Literature Series* 21 (1994): 1–24.

———. "Reading and the Voice of Death: Balzac's 'Le Message.'" *Nineteenth-Century French Studies* 18 (1990): 408–23.

———. *Story and Situation. Narrative Seduction and the Power of Fiction.* Minneapolis: Univ. of Minnesota Press, 1984.

Champagne, Roland A. *Philippe Sollers.* Amsterdam: Rodopi, 1996.

Chard-Hutchinson, Martine. "Mémoire, réticences et élans: *Le Livre brisé,* Serge Doubrovsky," in *Études romanesques 2. Modernité, Fiction, Déconstruction.* Ed. Jean Bessière. Paris: Lettres Modernes, 1994. 159–73.

Charpentier, Françoise. "Désir et parole dans les devis de l'*Heptaméron,*" in *Les Visages et les voix de Marguerite de Navarre.* Ed. Marcel Tetel. Paris: Klincksieck, 1995. 41–49.

Charrière, Christian. "Le Brise-femme." *Le Figaro Littéraire,* 7 September 1989, 15.

Cholakian, Patricia. *Rape and Writing in the* Heptaméron *of Marguerite de Navarre.* Carbondale: Southern Illinois Univ. Press, 1991.

Chouillet, Anne-Marie, ed. *Colloque International Diderot (1713–1784).* Paris: Aux Amateurs de Livres, 1985.

Comment, Bernard. *Roland Barthes, vers le neutre.* Paris: Christian Bourgois, 1991.

Compagnon, Antoine, ed. *Prétexte: Roland Barthes.* Paris: UGE, 1978.

Conroy, Peter V. *Intimate, Intrusive and Triumphant: Readers in the* Liaisons Dangereuses. Amsterdam: John Benjamins, 1987.

Cottrell, Robert D. "Inmost Cravings: The Logic of Desire in the *Heptameron,*" in *Critical Tales: New Studies of the* Heptameron *and Early Modern Culture.* Ed. John D. Lyons and Mary B. McKinley. Philadelphia: Univ. of Pennsylvania Press, 1993. 3–24.

Coulet, Henri. "Les Lettres occultées des 'Liaisons dangereuses.'" *Revue d'Histoire Littéraire de la France* 82 (1982): 600–14.

Dällenbach, Lucien. *La Canne de Balzac.* Paris: Corti, 1996.

———. *Le Récit spéculaire.* Paris: Seuil, 1977.

DeJean, Joan. *Literary Fortifications: Rousseau, Laclos, Sade.* Princeton: Princeton Univ. Press, 1984.

de la Carrera, Rosalina. *Success in Circuit Lies: Diderot's Communicational Practice.* Stanford: Stanford Univ. Press, 1991.

de Lajarte, Philippe. "'L'Heptaméron' et la naissance du récit moderne: Essai de lecture épistémologique d'un discours narratif." *Littérature* 17 (1975): 31–42.

——. "Le Prologue de l' 'Heptaméron' et le processus de production de l'œuvre," in *La Nouvelle française à la Renaissance*. Ed. Lionello Sozzi. Geneva: Slatkine, 1981. 397–423.

——. "La Structure vocale des psychorécits dans les nouvelles de l'*Heptaméron*," in *Les Visages et les voix de Marguerite de Navarre*. Ed. Marcel Tetel. Paris: Klincksieck, 1995. 79–96.

Delègue, Yves. "La Présence et ses doubles dans l'*Heptaméron*." *Bibliothèque d'Humanisme et Renaissance* 52 (1990): 269–91.

de Man, Paul. *Allegories of Reading: Figural Language in Rousseau, Nietzsche, Rilke, and Proust*. New Haven: Yale Univ. Press, 1979.

——. *Blindness and Insight: Essays in the Rhetoric of Contemporary Criticism*. Minneapolis: Univ. of Minnesota Press, 1983.

Derrida, Jacques. *La Carte postale de Socrate à Freud et au-delà*. Paris: Aubier-Flammarion, 1980.

Diderot, Denis. *Encyclopédie*. Ed. J. Charpentier and M. Charpentier. Paris: Bordas, 1985.

——. *Jacques le fataliste et son maître*. Ed. Simone Lecointre and Jean Le Galliot. Geneva: Droz, 1976.

——. *Lettre sur les sourds et muets*. *Diderot Studies* 7 (1965): 1–232.

——. "L'Oiseau blanc, conte bleu," in *Œuvres complètes*. Ed. Jean Macary, Aram Vartanian, and Jean-Louis Leutrat. Paris: Hermann, 1978. 3: 291–365.

——. *La Religieuse*. Paris: Garnier-Flammarion, 1968.

Doubrovsky, Serge. *L'Après-vivre*. Paris: Grasset, 1994.

——. "Autobiographie/Vérité/Psychanalyse." *L'Esprit Créateur* 20, no. 3 (1980): 87–97.

——. *Fils*. Paris: Galilée, 1977.

——. "L'Initiative aux maux: Écrire sa psychanalyse," in *Parcours critique*. Paris: Galilée, 1980. 165–201.

——. *Le Livre brisé*. Paris: Grasset, 1989.

——. "Sartre: Autobiographie/autofiction." *Revue des Sciences Humaines*, no. 224 (1991): 17–26.

——. "Textes en main," in *Autofictions & Cie*. Ed. Serge Doubrovsky, Jacques Lecarme, and Philippe Lejeune. Paris: Université Paris X, 1993. 207–17.

——. *La Vie l'instant*. Paris: Balland, 1985.

Doubrovsky, Serge, and John Ireland. "'The Fact Is That Writing Is a Profoundly Immoral Act': An Interview with Serge Doubrovsky." *Genre* 26 (1993): 43–49.

Dubois, Claude. "Fonds mythique et jeu des sens dans le 'Prologue' de L'*Heptaméron*," in *Études Seiziémistes offertes à Monsieur le Professeur V.-L. Saulnier*. Geneva: Droz, 1980. 151–68.

Ducrot, Oswald, and Tzvetan Todorov. *Dictionnaire encyclopédique des sciences du langage*. Paris: Seuil, 1972.

Duval, Edwin. " 'Et puis, quelles nouvelles?': The Project of Marguerite's Unfinished Decameron," in *Critical Tales. New Studies of the* Heptameron *and Early Modern Culture.* Ed. John D. Lyons and Mary B. McKinley. Philadelphia: Univ. of Pennsylvania Press, 1993. 241–62.

Eco, Umberto. *Postscript to The Name of the Rose.* Trans. William Weaver. New York: Harcourt, Brace, Jovanovich, 1983.

Fitch, Brian T. *Reflections in the Mind's Eye. Reference and Its Problematization in Twentieth-Century French Fiction.* Toronto: Univ. of Toronto Press, 1991.

Forest, Philippe. *Histoire de Tel Quel, 1960–1982.* Paris: Seuil, 1995.

——. *Philippe Sollers.* Paris: Seuil, 1992.

Gaillard, Françoise. "La Science: Modèle ou vérité. Réflexions sur l'*avant-propos* à *La Comédie humaine,*" in *Balzac: L'Invention du roman.* Ed. Claude Duchet and Jacques Neefs. Paris: Belfond, 1982. 57–83.

Genette, Gérard. "Frontières du récit," in *Figures II.* Paris: Seuil, 1969. 49–69.

Gepner, Corinna. "L'Autoportrait de la narratrice dans *La Religieuse:* Les Ruses du regard." *Recherches sur Diderot et sur* l'Encyclopédie 17 (October 1994): 55–67.

Hamon, Philippe. "L'Architecture/le sens/le réel/la représentation," in *Roman, Réalités, Réalismes.* Ed. Jean Bessière. Paris: Presses Universitaires de France, 1989. 31–39.

Hjelmslev, Louis. *Prolégomènes à une théorie du langage.* Paris: Minuit, 1968–71.

Houdebine, Jean-Louis. "Le Souffle hyperbolique de Philippe Sollers," in *Excès de langages (Hölderlin, Joyce, Duns Scot, Hopkins, Cantor, Sollers).* Paris: Denoël, 1984. 319–49.

Iser, Wolfgang. "Representation: A Performative Act," in *The Aims of Representation: Subject/Text/History.* Ed. Murray Krieger. New York: Columbia Univ. Press, 1987. 217–32.

Jaccomard, Hélène. *Lecteur et lecture dans l'autobiographie française contemporaine. Violette Leduc, Françoise d'Eaubonne, Serge Doubrovsky, Marguerite Yourcenar.* Geneva: Droz, 1993.

Jarosz, Krzysztof. "De la mythologie du réel à la mythologisation de l'écriture critique," in *Mythologies de l'écriture et roman.* Ed. Jean Bessière. Paris: Lettres Modernes, 1995. 65–76.

Jefferson, Ann. *Reading Realism in Stendhal.* Cambridge, England: Cambridge Univ. Press, 1988.

Kanes, Martin. *Balzac's Comedy of Words.* Princeton: Princeton Univ. Press, 1975.

Kingcaid, Renée. "Review of *Le Livre brisé.*" *Review of Contemporary Fiction* 12, no. 2 (1992): 239.

——. "Romancing the Tome: The Seduction of Intertext in Doubrovsky's *Un Amour de soi.*" *Sub-Stance* 70 (1993): 25–40.

Knight, Denise Bourassa. "Diderot's *La Religieuse:* Suzanne Simonin and the 'Youthful' Men Who See Her." *Nottingham French Studies* 24, no. 1 (1985): 15–25.

Kristeva, Julia. *Le Langage, cet inconnu. Une Initiation à la linguistique*. Paris: Seuil [Points], 1981.

———. *Revolution in Poetic Language*. Trans. Margaret Waller. New York: Columbia Univ. Press, 1984.

Kupisz, Kazimierz. "Autour de la technique de 'l'Heptaméron,'" in *La Nouvelle française à la Renaissance*. Ed. Lionello Sozzi. Geneva: Slatkine, 1981. 379–95.

Kurk, Katherine C. "Philippe Sollers," in *The Contemporary Novel in France*. Ed. William Thompson. Gainesville: Univ. Press of Florida, 1995. 127–44.

Laclos, Choderlos de. *Les Liaisons dangereuses*. Paris: Garnier-Flammarion, 1964.

———. *Œuvres complètes*. Ed. Laurent Versini. Paris: Gallimard [Pléiade], 1979.

La Garanderie, M.-M. de. *Le Dialogue des romanciers: Une Nouvelle lecture de L'Heptaméron de Marguerite de Navarre*. Paris: Minard, 1977.

Laurier, Marie. "Doubrovsky tel qu'en lui-même." *Le Devoir* (Montréal), 3 March 1990, sect. D: 1.

Lejeune, Philippe. "Le Cas Doubrovsky," in *Moi aussi*. Paris: Seuil, 1986. 62–70.

Leonelli, Ludovic. "Entretien avec Serge Doubrovsky." *NRV* 3 (Autumn 1997) (http://www.chapitre.com/plus/revues/nrventre.htm) (5 August 1998).

Lowrie, Joyce O. "Pretexts and Reflections: A Reflection upon Pre-Texts in *Les Liaisons dangereuses*." *Modern Language Studies* 18 (1988): 150–64.

Lyons, John D. "The 'Cueur' in the *Heptaméron*: the Ideology of Concealment," in *Les Visages et les voix de Marguerite de Navarre*. Ed. Marcel Tetel. Paris: Klincksieck, 1995. 107–21.

Lyons, John D., and Mary B. McKinley, eds. "Epilogue," in *Critical Tales: New Studies of the* Heptameron *and Early Modern Culture*. Philadelphia: Univ. of Pennsylvania Press, 1993. 263–80.

Mallarmé, Stéphane. *Quant au livre*, in *Œuvres complètes*. Paris: Gallimard [Pléiade], 1945. 369–87.

Marguerite de Navarre. *L'Heptaméron*. Ed. Michel François. Paris: Garnier, 1967.

———. *Heptaméron*. Ed. Simone de Reyff. Paris: Flammarion, 1982.

———. *Nouvelles*. Ed. Yves Le Hir. Paris: Presses Universitaires de France, 1967.

Mathieu-Castellani, Gisèle. *La Conversation conteuse: Les Nouvelles de Marguerite de Navarre*. Paris: Presses Universitaires de France, 1992.

———. "L'*Heptaméron*: l'Ère du soupçon," in *Les Visages et les voix de Marguerite de Navarre*. Ed. Marcel Tetel. Paris: Klincksieck, 1995. 123–34.

Meininger, Anne-Marie. "Préface," in Balzac, *Modeste Mignon*. Paris: Gallimard [Folio], 1982. 7–35.

Ménard, Maurice. " '. . . la belle et large vallée du Couesnon . . .': Thème géographique et motif romanesque dans *Les Chouans* de Balzac," in *Vendée, Chouannerie, Littérature*. Angers: Presses de l'Université d'Angers, 1986. 245–52.

Michel, Arlette. "Balzac et la rhétorique: Modernité et tradition." *L'Année Balzacienne* (1988): 245–69.

——. "Balzac juge du féminisme. Des *Mémoires de deux jeunes mariées* à *Honorine*." *L'Année Balzacienne* (1973): 183–200.

——. *Le Mariage et l'amour dans l'œuvre romanesque d'Honoré de Balzac.* 4 vols. Paris: Champion, 1976.

Miguet, Marie. "Critique/autocritique/autofiction." *Les Lettres Romanes* 43 (1989): 195–208.

Miguet-Ollagnier, Marie. "'La Saveur Sartre' du *Livre brisé*," in *Autobiographie et avant-garde*. Ed. Alfred Hornung and Ernstpeter Ruhe. Tübingen, Germany: Gunter Narr Verlag, 1992. 141–57.

[Mortimer], Armine Kotin. "*La Maison Nucingen*, ou le récit financier." *Romanic Review* 69 (1978): 60–71.

——. "Le Titre des nouvelles de Philippe de Vigneulles: Un Éclaircissement." *Bibliothèque d'Humanisme et Renaissance* 39 (1977): 91–95.

Mortimer, Armine Kotin. *The Gentlest Law: Roland Barthes's* The Pleasure of the Text. New York: Lang, 1989.

——. "Mimetic Figures of Semiosis in Balzac," in *Repression and Expression: Social Codes and Literary Visions in Nineteenth-Century France*. Ed. Carrol Coates. New York: Lang, 1996. 47–54.

Mozet, Nicole. *Balzac au pluriel.* Paris: Presses Universitaires de France, 1990.

——. "*Ursule Mirouët* ou le test du bâtard," in *Balzac, Œuvres complètes: Le Moment de La Comédie humaine*. Ed. Claude Duchet and Isabelle Tournier. Saint-Denis: Presses Universitaires de Vincennes, 1993. 217–28.

——. *La Ville de province dans l'œuvre de Balzac: L'Espace romanesque: Fantasmes et idéologie.* Paris: Société d'Édition d'Enseignement Supérieur, 1982.

Mylne, Vivienne. *Diderot: La Religieuse.* London: Grant & Cutler, 1981.

Norris, Christopher. *Derrida.* Cambridge, Mass.: Harvard Univ. Press, 1987.

Paris, Jean. *Balzac.* Paris: Balland, 1986.

Pasco, Allan H. *Balzacian Montage.* Toronto: Univ. of Toronto Press, 1994.

——. "Ursule through the Glass Lightly." *French Review* 65 (1991): 36–45.

Pérol, Lucette. "Les Avatars du lecteur dans la genèse d'un roman: Diderot, *La Religieuse* et le 'charmant marquis,'" in *Le Lecteur et la lecture dans l'œuvre*. Ed. Alain Montandon. Clermont-Ferrand: Université de Clermont-Ferrand, 1982. 101–14.

Perrigaud, Martha C. "Oisille's Tale of the Duchesse de Bourgogne: The Power of the Word." *Degré Second* 6 (July 1982): 25–40.

Le Petit Robert. Paris: Société du Nouveau Littré, 1972.

Petrey, Sandy. "The Realist Speech Act, Mimesis, Performance and the Facts in Fiction." *Neohelicon* 15, no.2 (1988): 9–29.

Piatier, Jacqueline. "Le Livre monstre de Serge Doubrovsky." *Le Monde,* 8 September 1989: 15, 18.

Plottel, Jeanine Parisier. "The Poetics of Autobiography in Paul Valéry." *L'Esprit Créateur* 20, no. 3 (1980): 38–45.

Poulet, Georges. "Balzac," in *Les Métamorphoses du cercle*. Paris: Plon, 1961. 203–30.

"Les Prix littéraires." *Le Monde,* 28 November 1989: 17.

Rapin, René. *Les Réflexions sur la poétique de ce temps et sur les ouvrages des poètes anciens et modernes.* 1674; 2nd revised edition 1675. Ed. E. T. Dubois. Geneva: Droz, 1970.

Reid, James H. *Narration and Description in the French Realist Novel. The Temporality of Lying and Forgetting.* Cambridge, England: Cambridge Univ. Press, 1993.

Ricardou, Jean. *Problèmes du nouveau roman.* Paris: Seuil, 1967.

Riffaterre, Michael. *Fictional Truth.* Baltimore: Johns Hopkins Univ. Press, 1990.

———. "L'Illusion référentielle," in *Littérature et réalité,* by Roland Barthes, Leo Bersani, Philippe Hamon, Michael Riffaterre, and Ian Watt. Paris: Seuil, 1982. 91–118.

Rimmon-Kenan, Shlomith. *Narrative Fiction: Contemporary Poetics.* New York: Methuen, 1983.

Rosset, Clément. *Le Réel, traité de l'idiotie.* Paris: Minuit, 1977.

Rousseau, Jean-Jacques. *Les Confessions.* Ed. Jacques Voisine. Paris: Garnier, 1964.

Rousset, Jean. "Les Lecteurs indiscrets," in *Laclos et le libertinage. 1782–1982. Actes du Colloque du bicentenaire des* Liaisons dangereuses. Paris: Presses Universitaires de France, 1983. 89–96.

Ryan, Marie-Laure. "Allegories of Immersion: Virtual Narration in Postmodern Fiction." *Style* 29 (1995): 262–86.

Sacy, S. de. "Balzac, Geoffroy Saint-Hilaire et l'unité de composition." *Mercure de France* 303 [May–August 1948], no. 1018, 1 June 1948: 292–305; no. 1019, 1 July 1948: 469–80.

Sarkany, Stéphane. "La Réalité en jeu de la critique sociologique," in *Roman, Réalités, Réalismes.* Ed. Jean Bessière. Paris: Presses Universitaires de France, 1989. 25–29.

Sherman, Carol. "Changing Spaces," in *Diderot: Digression and Dispersion: A Bicentennial Tribute.* Ed. Jack Undank and Herbert Josephs. Lexington, Ky.: French Forum, 1984. 219–30.

Simonton, M. "Suzanne's 'cri animal': Aural and Musical Imagery in Diderot's *La Religieuse.*" *University of Toronto Quarterly* 55 (1986): 328–41.

Sollers, Philippe. *Carnet de nuit.* Paris: Plon, 1989.

———. *Femmes.* Paris: Gallimard [Folio], 1983.

———. *La Guerre du goût.* Paris: Gallimard, 1994.

———. *Le Rire de Rome: Entretiens avec Frans De Haes.* Paris: Gallimard, 1992.

———. *Théorie des exceptions.* Paris: Gallimard [Folio], 1986.

Spencer, Judith. "Spécularité scripturale et contrefaçon littéraire: Pour une lecture iconoclaste des *Liaisons dangereuses,*" in *L'Épreuve du lecteur: Livres et lectures dans le roman d'Ancien Régime.* Ed. Jan Herman and Paul Pelckmans. Louvain: Éditions Peeters, 1995. 449–60.

Starobinski, Jean. "Du pied de la favorite au genou de Jacques," in *Colloque International Diderot (1713–1784).* Ed. Anne-Marie Chouillet. Paris: Aux Amateurs de Livres, 1985. 359–80.

Stendhal. *Le Rouge et le noir.* Paris: GF-Flammarion, 1964.

Stonehill, Brian. *The Self-Conscious Novel: Artifice in Fiction from Joyce to Pynchon.* Philadelphia: Univ. of Pennsylvania Press, 1988.

Strauss, Leo. *Persecution and the Art of Writing.* Glencoe, Ill.: Free Press, 1952.

Tadié, Alexis. "La Fiction et ses usages: Analyse pragmatique du concept de fiction." *Poétique,* no. 113 (1998): 111–25.

Tetel, Marcel. "The Rhetoric of Lyricism in the *Heptameron,*" in *Critical Tales: New Studies of the* Heptameron *and Early Modern Culture.* Ed. John D. Lyons and Mary B. McKinley. Philadelphia: Univ. of Pennsylvania Press, 1993. 41–52.

Tournon, André. "Rules of the Game," in *Critical Tales: New Studies of the* Heptameron *and Early Modern Culture.* Ed. John D. Lyons and Mary B. McKinley. Philadelphia: Univ. of Pennsylvania Press, 1993. 188–99.

Turcanu, Radu. "Le Désir d'être auteur: Doubrovsky et Sartre en intertexte." *Dalhousie French Studies* 35 (Summer 1996): 79–94.

Ungar, Steven. "Rules of the Game: First-Person Singular in des Forêt's *Le Bavard.*" *L'Esprit Créateur* 20, no. 3 (1980): 66–77.

Vandegans, André. "Fascinations et nostalgies balzaciennes dans *Modeste Mignon*: du propos à l'effet." *Bulletin de l'Académie Royale de Langue et de Littérature Françaises* 58 (1980): 20–55.

Walton, Kendall L. *Mimesis as Make-Believe: On the Foundations of the Representational Arts.* Cambridge, Mass.: Harvard Univ. Press, 1990.

Wilde, Oscar. "The Decay of Lying," in *Critical Theory Since Plato.* Ed. Hazard Adams. New York: Harcourt, Brace, Jovanovich, 1971. 673–86.

Winn, Colette H. "An Instance of Narrative Seduction: The *Heptaméron* of Marguerite de Navarre." *Symposium* 39 (1985): 217–26.

——. " 'La Loi du non-parler' dans l'*Heptaméron* de Marguerite de Navarre." *Romance Quarterly* 33, no. 2 (1986): 157–68.

Library of Congress Cataloging-in-Publication Data

Mortimer, Armine Kotin, 1943–

Writing realism : representations in French fiction /
Armine Kotin Mortimer.

p.   cm.

Includes bibliographical references and index.

ISBN 0-8018-6478-X (alk. paper)

1. French fiction—History and criticism.   2. Realism in literature.
3. Reality in literature.   I. Title.

PQ637.R4 M67 2000

843′.009′12—dc21   00-008409

DATE DUE

JAN 21 '03 X		
JAN 16 2003		